The Making of an Opera

The Making

Don Giovanni

WITH SPECIAL PHOTOGRAPHY BY ROGER WOOD
AND
WITH THE LIBRETTO BY LORENZO DA PONTE
AND AN ENGLISH TRANSLATION BY ELLEN H. BLEILER

JOHN HIGGINS
of an Opera
at Glyndebourne

ATHENEUM
New York *1978*

The publishers and author wish to thank Roger Wood for the photographs which he took specially for this book. They also acknowledge gratefully the permission of the Glyndebourne Festival Opera to reproduce other illustrations (details on p. ix) and the permission of Dover Publications, Inc of New York and Constable & Co Ltd of London to reproduce Ellen H. Bleiler's translation of Lorenzo Da Ponte's libretto of *Don Giovanni*.

Acknowledgment is also due to the following for permission to quote: Mr Peter Shaffer and *The Times*; *Proceedings of the Leeds Philosophical and Literary Society*, publishers of John S. Andrews' paper in which he quoted Sabilla Novello's translation of Hoffmann's *Don Juan*; Curtis Brown Ltd, London, agents for *Glyndebourne, A History of the Festival Opera* by Spike Hughes; Hamish Hamilton Ltd, London, and Doubleday & Co, Inc, New York, publishers of *5,000 Nights at the Opera, The Memoirs of Sir Rudolf Bing*; Oxford University Press, Oxford and New York, publishers of *Mozart's Operas* by E. J. Dent; Faber & Faber Ltd, London, and Harcourt Brace Jovanovich, Inc, New York, publishers of *Mozart the Dramatist* by Brigid Brophy; John Calder Ltd, London, publisher of *Mozart on the Stage* by Christopher Benn; Cassell & Co Ltd, London, and Oxford University Press, Inc, New York, publishers of *The Operas of Mozart* by William Mann.

To L.C.,

    mio tesoro

Contents

List of Illustrations

The illustrations are taken from the Glyndebourne Festival Opera archives, except for those photographs by Roger Wood which were specially commissioned for this book

xi

Acknowledgments

It would not have been possible to start tracking the course of Glyndebourne's *Don Giovanni* without the cooperation of those at the helm. Sir Peter Hall, the producer, John Pritchard, Glyndebourne's Musical Director at the time, George Christie and Moran Caplat all promised this. Those promises were kept, in triplicate. To each I say thank you and also to Glyndebourne's Press Officer, Helen O'Neill.

But this account of *Don Giovanni* would not have been possible either without the support and friendship of the cast of the opera and the staff at the Sussex opera house. No one pressed his or her opinion; everyone was profligate with his, or her, time when asked. Again thank you.

My further gratitude goes to Linda Christmas for encouragement when it was most needed; to the Editor of *The Times* for allowing me leave of absence; to my colleagues on that paper, Ion Trewin and Jennie Newton, for ensuring that the absence was completely undisturbed. Finally, I am indebted to Marcia and Tony Melville-Ross for a temporary home in West Sussex where opera was strictly taboo.

Chelsea, December 1977

PART ONE

Conception

1 *The Glyndebourne Style*

The operas with which Captain John Christie intended to open the theatre he had built on to his Sussex home in Glyndebourne were Mozart's *Don Giovanni* and Wagner's *Die Walküre*. There had been no shortage of music in the house previously. The Captain, inspired by visits to Bayreuth and Munich and the more recent Salzburg Festival, had put on semi-professional concerts in the Glyndebourne Organ Room for friends, tenants and staff. On at least one occasion he himself sang, as the crabbed and censorious Beckmesser in the third act of *Die Meistersinger* in 1928. Few appear to have judged his performance as carefully as he assessed those whom he engaged, although it was always said to be somewhat eccentric dramatically. For some time Christie had taught mathematics at Eton and he was rather fairer at marking than Beckmesser.

The inspiration for the theatre came when he married a young soprano from the Carl Rosa Opera Company called Audrey Mildmay in 1931. The financial climate was little more favourable then than it is now in 1978 for building a new opera house but Christie went ahead quietly. There was hardly any speculation in the British press about what was happening under the South Downs until a few months before the theatre was ready to open.

Eventually Christie was persuaded to talk and to write. He wanted to begin with *Don Giovanni* and he wanted to improve the dismal operatic situation in Britain where the true enthusiasts, Christie included, moved off in the summer to Europe for the

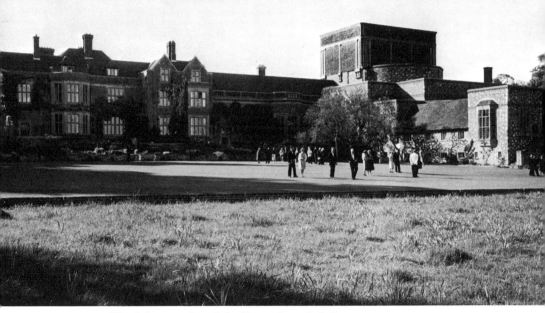

Glyndebourne: the original house is on the left, the theatre John Christie added is to the right

simple reason that they found the diet abroad so much better than what they were given at home.

Spike Hughes, whose history of Glyndebourne* from its beginnings to the 1964 season is kept at the right elbow of practically every member of the administrative staff, recalls that even in the final months of building Christie was undecided about the type of house he wanted. There were two possibilities:

1. To offer superb performances to people who will regard them as the chief thing in the day or week to be looked forward to, and who will not try to sandwich them between business interviews and a society party.

2. To give educational performances for the ordinary public, with the best possible stage setting and only English orchestras and lesser known singers.

I incline towards the superb performance, assisted by a marvellous holiday 'Festspiel' atmosphere . . .

---

* *Glyndebourne, A History of the Festival Opera,* Spike Hughes (Methuen, London and Crescendo Publishing, Boston).

Christie went on to follow his inclinations and opted for the first choice. Over forty years later the aims of Glyndebourne are very close to those he formulated in a single sentence. But he had much more of a social conscience than his opponents ever gave him credit for and he went on to say that it would be 'desirable' to give local performances after the Festival was over. Just before

**Advice, undoubtedly written by John Christie,
from the first programme**

WHERE TO LIVE

◆

Why not come and live within reach of this Festival Opera House? The Opera House needs your support so that its Festivals can be extended, so that there can be more Festivals, so that there can be Concerts, so that there can be Shakespearean Festivals, so that there can be Lectures. If you come to this district you can help this scheme. You will have Downs, Sea-air, Woods and "Kultur." If you scatter yourselves over England you are too far away to support this enterprise. If you are near at hand you can enjoy superb intellectual food which you cannot get elsewhere. Make this an artistic and creative centre. You will then enjoy this marvellous country all the more.

There is an excellent service of comfortable express trains to London and there are good roads for motoring. The country contains many famous schools for those who bring a family to the district.

Christie's death in 1962 Glyndebourne made the first of its annual appearances at the Promenade Concerts in London's Royal Albert Hall, a move inspired by Moran Caplat, the General Administrator. The next step was the formation of the Glyndebourne Touring Opera which has an autumn season after the Sussex stage has been cleared and closed for the winter. Christie might have been indecisive for a moment but in the end both his aims were achieved if that condescending adjective 'educational' can be deleted.

He was, though, forced to change his plans for the opening of the theatre on 29 May 1934. The main pressure came from his wife and from Hamish Wilson, who was to design all the operas for Glyndebourne's first four seasons, including *Don Giovanni* when it was eventually staged. The choice fell on Mozart's *Le nozze di Figaro* and *Così fan tutte*; both operas were produced by Carl Ebert and conducted by Fritz Busch. Christie hankered for his German opera and hoped for a Christmas season of Humperdinck with *Hansel und Gretel* and *Königskinder*. He was

Moran Caplat, Fritz Busch, Audrey Mildmay, Carl Ebert and John Christie in the Christies' drawing-room: the books remain, the dog is different

The triumvirate: Rudolf Bing, Fritz Busch and
Carl Ebert

looking forward to adding *Walküre*, *Siegfried* and *Der Rosen-
kavalier* the following summer. Yet, probably far more than
Christie realised, the style of Glyndebourne had already been set
and that style was Mozart.

He went to Germany almost by chance for his artistic directors
Busch and Ebert, from the Dresden and Berlin State Operas
respectively. They were soon joined by the Austrian Rudolf
Bing, subsequently Director of the Edinburgh Festival and
General Administrator of New York's Met. The Busch–
Ebert–Bing triumvirate immediately caused complaints of a
Central European bias, particularly in matters of casting.
Glyndebourne from its very beginnings quickly got used to
criticism and became reasonably adept at deflecting it, parti-
cularly when the telegrams and letters were dictated by Bing,
who more than earned his first season's fee of £100 and within a
year became General Manager of the Opera. Glyndebourne's
archives, which live beneath a trapdoor in the office of the
General Administrator, show that Bing lost no time at all in
mastering the nuances of English and worsting some of the
artists who tried to put out-of-hours pressure on John Christie.
Heddle Nash, who thought he should have first choice of all the
Mozart tenor rôles at substantial fees, was one of the victims,
although in this case Bing's victory was far from complete. Nash

was well connected in British musical society and believed in using his friends. Bing in his own account of his time at Glyndebourne* says nothing of the affair.

Bing in his autobiography looks back on Glyndebourne with a mixture of gratitude, romanticism and irony. Clearly for an Austrian Jew it was an ideal bolt hole from the oppression fast building up in Central Europe. Bing was constantly amazed at Christie's political naïveté and as late as 1939 was still having to argue against Audrey Mildmay taking engagements in German opera houses. But he was delighted to find a new home in what he extravagantly describes as 'that beautiful house in that most beautiful of peaceful countrysides,'† even though he was first driven there in 'an incredibly dirty old Lancia'.

He relished British eccentricity and Glyndebourne provided it in abundance. One morning Childs, the Christies' butler, came in at breakfast to announce that the cook had died. To Bing's intense amusement, the ensuing silence was broken by one of the house-guests, a general, saying, 'Under the circumstances, do you think I could have another sausage?' Bing admired John Christie's style and tells the story of a walk across the South Downs during the early days of the War with Bimperl, the pug which the Christies had named after Mozart's dog. Christie stopped and talked to some soldiers who were stationed in the area:

' "*That*," he said, pointing to his manor house and theatre, "is Mozart's house."

' "Ah, yes, sir," said one of the soldiers.

'Then Christie pointed to the pug playing at my feet. "And that," he added grandly, "is Mozart's dog." '

To Glyndebourne Rudi Bing brought the professionalism it needed in order to succeed. He was adept at dealing with the contracts that the existing staff knew so little about and he had the spirit of competition which marks out the best general managers. Bing almost got Gigli to sing Don Ottavio at

---

* *5,000 Nights at the Opera, The Memoirs of Sir Rudolf Bing* (Hamish Hamilton, London and Doubleday, New York).

† *Op. cit.*

Glyndebourne, following a tip from a lady friend of the Italian tenor, and noted with glee that Tauber was engaged for the same rôle at Covent Garden at just about the same time. It was no surprise that Christie quickly began to recognise Bing's skills. Within a few years he was negotiating for Glyndebourne to visit the Lucerne Festival and New York and for the Company to cooperate with Covent Garden. Sir Thomas Beecham at the Royal Opera had already made an attempt to lure Bing away from Sussex.

Perhaps that highly skilled trio of Bing, Busch and Ebert was occasionally guilty of favouring its own countrymen, partly because of sympathy for those suffering Nazi oppression and partly because managements naturally favour known quantities over unknown ones. No one though could level accusations of foisting an Austro-German repertory outside Mozart on the Sussex public. *Entführung* and *Zauberflöte* soon joined the small list of Glyndebourne operas and there the German language stopped. The only other excursions beyond Mozart before the War came to close the house were to Italy for Verdi's *Macbeth* and Donizetti's *Don Pasquale*.

The quality of those pre-War performances can be judged partly from records: *Figaro* (1934), *Così* (1935) and *Giovanni* (1936). Does constant playing and love of the sets, which have gone through regular re-pressings, give our opinions a rosier glow than they should have? Almost certainly so. Jani Strasser, who was Audrey Mildmay's singing teacher in Vienna and who was brought to Glyndebourne by the Christies before the theatre was even ready, is wary of the praise still heaped on the pre-War seasons at a distance of forty years:

'We look back from an historical viewpoint and that clouds everything. Undoubtedly some of the singers were not on a high level and some of the casting would not have been acceptable today. We put musical standards above dramatic ones, for instance, and did not mind too much about clumsy acting. Take that first 1936 *Don Giovanni*. Ina Souez, the Donna Anna, had a fine voice but she did not cut much of a figure on stage. Even John Brownlee, our first Giovanni, had shortcomings. The production in a way was built around his faults. He was cold and did not have a very flexible voice, so there was no alternative to a proud, autocratic, almost hefty interpretation. Brownlee was admired for his dash and swagger and some of those admirers had not the ears to recognise that the voice was too heavy for the Serenade.

'Salvatore Baccaloni, the Leporello, on the other hand was very juicy, very human. Someone described him as reeking of garlic and olive oil. That's rather an exaggeration, but he did bring out every facet of Leporello as a small, suburban man and if the singing was not very Mozartian—the voice was round but not all that well controlled—then he made up for those deficiencies with total spontaneity. Audrey Mildmay was the best Zerlina I saw until Mirella Freni came to the house in 1960; both artists understood instinctively that Zerlina is *contadina astuta*, a girl who is constantly thinking about herself and the best ruses to employ to get her own way.

'Yes, there were certainly high qualities in those pre-War performances even though the levels were inconsistent. I think we achieved what we did by establishing a team and keeping it together.'

Strasser, who until recently was Glyndebourne's chief répétiteur, is also one of its sharpest critics. Even in his retirement he paces the rehearsal rooms tutting, shaking his head and then suddenly producing a couple of sentences of approval with a Viennese endearment thrown in. Strasser though confirms that Glyndebourne in the shape of Christie and his artistic directors could only be successful if it established a nucleus of people living, working, arguing, planning and debating very closely together. Achievement and ideas were often born through disagreement. In those first seasons two styles were set: a theatre devoted to staging Mozart above all other composers, and an opera company run by a tiny and very tightly-knit group of people. Over the past forty years both styles have remained constant.

*   *   *

George Christie, Chairman of Glyndebourne since 1959, works from his library. The windows face away from the theatre

Kenneth Green's 1937 portraits of John Brownlee as
Don Giovanni and Salvatore Baccaloni as Leporello

and look past the terraces of the gardens to the fields of Sussex
sheep. There is a speaker to relay what is happening on stage but
it is hidden and little used; an obvious loudspeaker would be out
of place in this sombre, well-worn room which bears the marks
of Captain Christie from the morocco-bound Wagner scores,
which so far have remained unplayed, to the pug dog, latest in
line of the breed with which the older Christie was inevitably
photographed, sketched and painted. The son has expanded
rather than altered the father's basic rules. About a third of his
time is spent in fund-raising: nowadays those who call the tune
can no longer pay the pipers alone. The major supporter of the
1977 season, thanks to Christie's powers of persuasion, which
have matured greatly over the past few years, is the Imperial
Tobacco Company. It has supplied about three-quarters of the
production cost of *Don Giovanni*. W. D. and H. O. Wills, a
separate arm of the same organisation, has provided a tent to

keep picnickers in the supper interval from the lash of the rain or the rays of the sun, as well as a further sum for the upkeep of the buildings and gardens. Cynics have pointed out that until recently Christie was a non-smoker, although he rarely discouraged others from the habit, and indeed Peter Stuyvesant was Glyndebourne's first major industrial sponsor.

In the summer one wing of the house is given over to a limited number of producers and conductors as well as to the junior music staff, who find that even the rents charged by Sussex landladies make too large a hole in their Glyndebourne salaries. I have often heard opera visitors speculate, as they hurry to catch the last coach to Lewes station, that life is one long party after curtain fall. On first nights, when the Lily Davis studio, the latest of the rehearsal rooms, is turned into a discothèque, it may be and celebrations tend to lengthen with the summer. But during the late spring rehearsal period the Glyndebourne house has more than a touch of the monastery, although the talk usually revolves around music rather than God, and most of the lights have been switched off by 11.30 p.m.

George Christie makes no pretence of remembering those pre-War performances. He was taken into the back of the stalls to rehearsals, as he and his wife Mary take in their own children now. In those days each seat had a small cushion footrest rather in the style of a hassock. They could be piled up, according to Christie, into castles or pyramids and tumble down without making a sound to disturb the singers. A hassock collapse was the only critical comment he made.

Moran Caplat, who came to Glyndebourne in 1945 as Assistant to Rudolf Bing and took over as General Manager four years later when Bing moved to Edinburgh, lives in total contrast to Christie. His office within the theatre is almost completely clear of books, files and papers. His home, far enough away from Glyndebourne to prevent aggrieved artists placing their worries on the doorstep except when invited to do so, is full of programme covers, both used and unused, and set designs, including some of those by John Piper for the 1951 *Don Giovanni* which is reckoned to be one of the most handsome productions seen in the house.

Moran Caplat, George Christie and Jani
Strasser

**Mario Petri as Don Giovanni and Geraint
Evans as Masetto on one of John Piper's much
acclaimed sets for Glyndebourne's 1951 production at the Edinburgh Festival**

Christie solves his problems by talking to people, Caplat by
taking to the English Channel or the wider seas in a yacht.
Together the two men have made sure there have been no rash
moves away from the principles established before the War:
Mozart is the composer best suited to Glyndebourne, his major
operas depend on the quality of ensemble, which in turn
demands ample time to prepare, so Glyndebourne's duty is to
provide that time. As soon as the house surfaced from the War
via the première of Benjamin Britten's *The Rape of Lucretia* and
performances at the Edinburgh Festival, it realised that ideal
preparation conditions formed the best bait for attracting the
leading singers. Erich Kunz, George London and Sena Jurinac
were among the first to be persuaded. They were followed by
Birgit Nilsson, Joan Sutherland, Mirella Freni and Montserrat
Caballé among others.

Mirella Freni as Zerlina with Leonardo Monreale as Masetto, two Glyndebourne débuts in 1960

Glyndebourne may be parsimonious about some matters, but time is not one of them. The cast is expected a full month before the first night of a new production and for the 1977 *Don Giovanni*, which opened on 31 May, the first rehearsals were called for 26 April. Once the singers have arrived at Glyndebourne, leave of absence is given as grudgingly as it would be to a recruit during his first weeks in the army. 'Glyndebourne allows fewer NAs [not available for rehearsal] than any house I know,' grumbled one of the *Don Giovanni* cast. So Glyndebourne still sets its face against current operatic fashion which in the major theatres, and in some of the smaller ones as well, too often dictates that rehearsals are dovetailed with recording sessions, broadcasts, concert work and frequent dashes to the Continent to take up guest engagements.

The Sussex view is that artists should commit themselves totally or not come at all. Travel leads to fatigue, and changes from one rôle to another destroy the concentration. There is relief within the house that Heathrow is none too accessible except by car, and regret that Gatwick is only a couple of stations up the line. It all comes down to creating the ensemble and team work which Jani Strasser noted back in the late Thirties. This is best achieved by running a five-and-half-day rehearsal week including Saturdays and Sundays, a practice which would bring a queue of complaints in most German houses. Seven-day working weeks have also been known.

The Glyndebourne system brings results (usually) and incurs penalties. It probably worked best in the Fifties when access to and from Europe was a good deal less easy than it is now and when the word got around that Sussex was a decent place for a holiday. The singers themselves did not exactly get a rest, but they had time to prepare a new rôle or rethink an old one and their families could idle in pleasant surroundings. Those days of leisurely singing are past, aggressive agents have seen to that. In recent years Glyndebourne in common with other British opera houses has been embarrassed by the decline in the value of sterling. George Christie argues that his fees have 'in general kept pace with inflation', helped notably by a sharp increase in 1975, but they are still very modest by European standards. One

of the *Don Giovanni* cast was appearing for 25 per cent of his regular German salary. So many singers are unwilling to commit themselves to the Sussex pastures for more than two out of the four summer months.

Glyndebourne's reasonable response to a reasonable objection has been to double-cast major new productions which have a long performance run, in addition to having the regular understudies, or 'covers'. The two teams are entirely separate and the performances are talked about in terms of 'Series I' and 'Series II' so that audiences are steered away from the impression that they will be seeing the Second Eleven take the field if they go late in the season. Suspicion in this area is warranted as it is regular practice in some European houses to begin with star singers and a famous conductor and then withdraw one by one the names that sell the tickets as the run continues. On the whole Glyndebourne cannot be faulted on this count, although generally only the Series I singers are coached by the original producer. In the case of *Don Giovanni* all the singers but two (Masetto and the Commendatore) left the production at the beginning of July as did Glyndebourne's musical director, John Pritchard. Their replacements were directed by Hall's assistant, Stewart Trotter, and conductor Bernard Haitink, after they had had an opportunity to see their predecessors once or twice. Trotter was also in charge of the Touring Company's *Don Giovanni*, cast mainly from the understudies, when it went out on the road in the autumn.

Any future economies are unlikely to affect rehearsal time, despite the fact that there are those who claim that a month's preparation of a single opera gives singers a chance to get bored. The reply here is that the wrong producer, the wrong conductor or indifferent répétiteurs and coaches will induce boredom within days, not weeks. If the music staff is inspiring enough, then the preparation period cannot be too long. And fees are a matter for the individual singers. There is nothing new about being asked to choose between a large sum for an engagement which might yield little or no personal satisfaction and a smaller one for an opportunity to display rather more artistry.

Perhaps some of these answers are a shade pat. Perhaps

Glyndebourne will be forced to raise its payments or persuade someone to fund artists as well as productions. The one surety is that it will continue for as long as possible to give its singers time to evolve a new conception of a rôle or rid themselves of old misconceptions. The shadows of Busch and Ebert stretch long.

The cast list of Glyndebourne's first *Don Giovanni*

GLYNDEBOURNE FESTIVAL OPERA HOUSE

Lessees : JOHN CHRISTIE LTD.   General Manager : RUDOLF BING.

FRIDAY, JUNE 12th, 1936, at 6.45 p.m.

(In the original Italian)

IL DISSOLUTO PUNITO

O SIA IL

DON GIOVANNI

Dramma giocoso in due atti

Poesia di Lorenzo da Ponte

Musica di

W. A. MOZART

Conductor :	Producer :
FRITZ BUSCH	CARL EBERT
Scenery designed by	Costumes designed by
HAMISH WILSON (English)	HEIN HECKROTH (German)
	(Dartington Hall)

Don Giovanni - - - - -	JOHN BROWNLEE (Australian)
a young and extremely licentious nobleman	
The Commendatore - - - -	DAVID FRANKLIN (English)
Donna Anna - - - - -	INA SOUEZ (British)
his daughter, betrothed to	
Don Ottavio - - - - -	KOLOMAN V. PATAKY (Hungarian)
Donna Elvira - - - - -	LUISE HELLETSGRUBER (Austrian)
a lady from Burgos, abandoned by Don Giovanni	
Leporello - - - - -	SALVATORE BACCALONI (Italian)
servant to Don Giovanni	
Masetto - - - - -	ROY HENDERSON (Scottish)
lover of	
Zerlina - - - - -	AUDREY MILDMAY (English)
a peasant girl	

The SCENE is laid in a City in Spain

THE GLYNDEBOURNE FESTIVAL ORCHESTRA
(Leader : GEORGE STRATTON)

THE GLYNDEBOURNE FESTIVAL CHORUS

Dinner and cold supper will be served during the interval after Act I.

2 *The Opera of All Operas*

'*Die Oper allen Opern*', the opera of all operas, was E. T. A. Hoffmann's description of *Don Giovanni*. Hoffmann wrote his short story *Don Juan** when he was director of the Bamberg theatre. In it the narrator, half-asleep after supper in an inn, hears the sounds of an orchestra tuning up and, after summoning a waiter, is told that the corridor outside his room leads directly into a private box of the local theatre reserved for hotel guests. The opera to be given is '*Don Giovanni* by the celebrated Mr Mozart of Vienna' and the price of the ticket can easily be added to the account.

The invitation is irresistible and the traveller takes his place in the box. He becomes much involved with the performance of an opera he clearly knows well and takes no notice when towards the end of the first act he hears a rustle of clothes in the box behind him. When the interval lights go up he finds that it is Donna Anna who is sitting beside him. She talks to him, in Tuscan dialect, of Mozart, his opera and her own part and then returns to the stage. The traveller is moved to particular ecstasy by Elvira's Act II aria '*Mi tradì*': 'I was overwhelmed by a soft, warm rush of beatitude and voluptuously closed my eyes, uttering a sigh of endless yearning.' At the end of the performance the narrator, irritated by the trite comments of the audience, returns to his room. He finds it oppressive and decides to go back to the box with a bowl of punch and jot down his thoughts on the opera,

---

* *Don Juan*, E. T. A. Hoffmann (Berlin, 1812).

speculating on Anna and Giovanni as beings superior to the rest of humanity. 'What if Anna had been originally ordained by Heaven to disclose to Don Juan, by means of love, the innate superiority of his soul and to release him from the despair of his fruitless longings?'

At two in the morning, still brooding on the plea contained in Anna's '*Non mi dir*', he feels a wind blowing through the theatre, scents the perfume he first noticed in the box the previous evening, and thinks that he hears Anna's voice in the distance. At lunch later three men at a neighbouring table mention casually that they will not be hearing the Italian woman who sang Donna Anna again as she died at precisely two that morning after being in hysterics during the second act of the opera.

Hoffmann's story has not interested British critics very much, although Dent gives it a few paragraphs in his study of Mozart's operas.* One explanation perhaps is that it has been consistently ignored by Hoffmann's many translators for reasons quite unfathomable. Jacques Barzun included it in his anthology *The Pleasures of Music*, and there has been an American translation, but the only one I have come across in this country is that by Sabilla Novello, daughter of Vincent Novello who founded the music publishing house. It was presented in 1956 by John S. Andrews to the Leeds Philosophical and Literary Society and the quotations above are taken from it.†

The British disregard for Hoffmann—perhaps we are content with Offenbach's version of him—is also a disregard for the influence he had on nineteenth-century attitudes to *Don Giovanni*, particularly in Germany. The power of the story comes in part from a romanticised version of what might well have been a personal experience. It has been established that Hoffmann was in love with one of the sopranos at Bamberg and that the Gasthaus Zur Rose did join on to his theatre there. But far more important is Hoffmann's view of Don Giovanni as a man torn

---

* *Mozart's Operas*, E. J. Dent (Oxford University Press, Oxford and New York).

† 'Mozart's and Hoffmann's "Don Giovanni" ', John S. Andrews, *Proceedings of the Leeds Philosophical and Literary Society*, vol. VIII.

Audrey Mildmay, John Brownlee and Salvatore Baccaloni as Zerlina, Don Giovanni and Leporello in the first Glyndebourne production

between heaven and hell and Anna as a woman who arrived too late to save him.

Hoffmann's view of *Don Giovanni* is one-sided. He takes the comic or *giocoso* part away from the *dramma giocoso* of Mozart and Da Ponte in order to emphasise the supernatural and the struggle between heaven and hell. Giovanni himself is very much a figure of the Romantic movement, a man incapable of doing good like Karl Moor in Schiller's first play *Die Räuber* (which Verdi turned into *I masnadieri*). He is also a superman out to challenge both the power of God and the conventions of society. In other words, Hoffmann, writing some twenty-five years after the first performance of *Don Giovanni*, saw him very much as a man of his own time and his views were to have considerable influence until Søren Kierkegaard came along a century later with a different judgment. He judged Don Giovanni's actions with a belief in 'the demoniac power with which music may lay hold upon an individual', that seduction is uniquely expressed by music, the immediate medium, which words, the meditative medium, cannot apprehend. Shaw followed soon after with *Man and Superman* where in the central act, too often omitted in performance alas, Juan/Giovanni finds himself in a hell where he is hunted by women and becomes the prey, not the predator. But then Shaw had a thesis to prove about women being the stronger sex.

The discovery in Hoffmann's *Don Juan* is that Mozart's opera is wide open to interpretation. It is a work which feeds off both the Classical style and the Romantic movement then just beginning. It straddles a period when the Western world was changing, when the rule of the aristocracy was being challenged and when accepted standards were being questioned. It is the lack of commitment in *Don Giovanni* which accounts for part of its fascination. Mozart and Da Ponte pass no judgment on their hero or anti-hero, according to one's viewpoint. When at the end of the opera Leporello, Masetto and Zerlina come forward to sing their old refrain (*'l'antichissima canzon'*) to a jolly tune about the evildoer who has gone down to hell, they are totally untouched by the brush with death. That's the way evil men finish, runs the very brief moral.

This epilogue, a classical device if ever there was one, scarcely suited the taste of the moral nineteenth century. It was regularly lopped off so that the audience could go home with the sight of hellfire and demons enveloping Giovanni in their retinas and the sound of Mozart's apocalyptic trombones in their ears. Süssmayr started the practice in 1798 and others were only too happy to continue. In doing so they totally destroyed the balance of the work which ends on a note of pleasure and not penance. Mozart and Da Ponte were entertainers, not preachers.

Was it the interpretative challenge set by *Don Giovanni* to every generation since it was composed that made John Christie choose it as the work with which he wanted to open Glyndebourne? Or did he go along with Hoffmann in believing it was the opera of all operas? There is now no answering such questions, but it was certainly much safer to begin with *Figaro* and *Così* which pose considerably fewer difficulties in both casting and staging. *Don Giovanni* is one of opera's Everests: the summit is alluring but the rockface is slippery, particularly to baritones and producers; so much so that it is almost a platitude for regular opera-goers to claim that they have never seen a perfect performance. Superb *Figaros* are recalled, the most rewarding of *Ring* cycles, outstanding *Otellos*, yet when it comes to *Don Giovanni* there is generally a pause and an admission that there was something wrong with even the most cherished evening.

The elusive quality of the opera, the apparent impossibility of illuminating all its facets in the right proportion, the search for the definitive performance which is almost as unattainable as the definitive *Hamlet*, are all part of its seductive nature. And Glyndebourne, for over forty years Britain's leading Mozart house, has on its own admission had more failures than successes with the work.

Three weeks before the first night of Peter Hall's *Don Giovanni* production, Moran Caplat rather gloomily confessed that he had never seen a totally satisfactory staging of the opera anywhere. It was not merely the influence of the rain cascading on the terrace outside his office window. A review of post-War *Giovannis* at Edinburgh, where Glyndebourne was once a regular Festival visitor, and in Sussex had failed to throw up a top-class interpretation and in most cases that was primarily because the baritone (or bass) had failed to measure up to the title rôle. That impression was cruelly reflected by Glyndebourne's photographic archives (rather more accessible than the correspondence files) where I had spent most of the afternoon. The pictures of Leporello (Geraint Evans in his early days) bristled with life; so did those of Anna (Welitsch and later Jurinac). Ilva Ligabue's Elvira was full of strength—no one could have turned *her* into the half-crazed crosspatch favoured by some producers; Anny Schlemm and Mirella Freni caught both the charm and artfulness of Zerlina; Leopold Simoneau never for once suggested that Ottavio was the 'biggest milksop in all opera' as Brigid Brophy once described him.* But the Giovannis, John Brownlee's

* *Mozart the Dramatist*, Brigid Brophy (Faber & Faber, London and Harcourt Brace Jovanovich, New York).

Ruggero Raimondi, the 1969 Don Giovanni

striking profile apart, were an oddly negative lot among the stacks of glossy prints.

Moran Caplat agreed. 'I've never heard or seen a really good Giovanni yet. It's an impossible character. It's like trying to play God on stage—or should it be the Devil?—you simply can't do it. What is he? Great seducer . . . playboy hero . . . charmer . . . rebel . . .? He remains to me a complete enigma. It is a young man's part which needs an older singer's maturity and it requires an artist who can stand completely outside himself and regard his actions dispassionately. Some actors have this ability, but very few baritones. Ruggero Raimondi who came to us in 1969 was the most successful of the Giovannis during my time at Glyndebourne, even though he was inexperienced when he sang for us and gave only a sketch of the performance that was to come later elsewhere.

'No, as you say, it is the interpretations of the other rôles which stick in the mind. Welitsch's Donna Anna made a great impression, perhaps because I was so young. Would it now? I'm not sure, but the answer is probably yes. Simoneau was an almost perfect Ottavio vocally and Richard Lewis in the same part had wonderful breath control, superb clarity of tone and made a most handsome figure on stage.'

Caplat left no doubts that *Don Giovanni* was an opera which Glyndebourne, despite its dedication to Mozart, tackles with considerable trepidation. Before Peter Hall's arrival it had only had four productions since the War. The first two were by Carl Ebert and his son Peter, using the same John Piper sets. Then came Günther Rennert's staging with the much criticised Ita Maximowna designs. That lasted only two seasons, 1960 and 1961. Six years later the regular producer–designer team of the time, Franco Enriquez and Emmanuele Luzzati, were little more successful. They tried to apply the dazzling greens and yellows, which had brought their Glyndebourne *Zauberflöte* such acclaim, to *Don Giovanni* but the result was not to everyone's liking. Not even Da Ponte's Seville looked anything like the Enriquez–Luzzati toytown with blocks of scenery propelled by the humans within. That production also lasted for only a couple of seasons while the *Figaros*, *Così*s and *Flutes* stood any number of revivals.

In the present decade Glyndebourne patrons had to do without
Don Giovanni altogether until 31 May 1977.

George Christie is as critical as his General Administrator
Moran Caplat. 'You could say that we have had a chequered and
not altogether satisfactory line of *Don Giovannis* since the War—I
can pass no comment on those Thirties seasons. The first man in
the title rôle I remember is Mario Petri here in 1951, who to my
still adolescent eyes looked like a giant Italian goalkeeper,
although I must have been taken to hear Paolo Silveri in
Edinburgh three years earlier. Petri, I'm glad to say, is still alive
and still singing. The John Piper sets I still recall with gratitude,

'Meta di voi': Paolo Silveri as Don Giovanni
and Ian Wallace (with a blunderbuss) as
Masetto in Glyndebourne's 1948 *Don Giovanni*
at Edinburgh

Mario Petri, the 1951 Don Giovanni

particularly the baroque street scene for Act I, used again for the opening of the second act, with its brilliant ochre church and the houses and arches of Seville flecked with red. The design for the garden in Giovanni's house was horrid, but Piper and Ebert solved the problem of the descent to hell by having an almost *Götterdämmerung*-like holocaust for the end of the opera so that the epilogue is sung by Anna, Zerlina and the rest staring at the charred remains of Giovanni's home.

'I have a feeling that Piper despite his success was not altogether happy with Glyndebourne. Perhaps it was because of his strong ties with the English Opera Group at a time when relations between Aldeburgh and Glyndebourne were not as warm as they might have been. I think too there was a certain chill between him and Carl Ebert. Whatever the reason *Don Giovanni* was the sole opera he designed for us.

'In 1954 we had high hopes of getting it right. We had a strong cast particularly among the women, led by Jurinac as Elvira and Anny Schlemm as Zerlina, and Georg Solti, who had been acquiring a substantial reputation in Germany, was making his first appearance in England as an opera conductor. Despite all these advantages it was curiously unsuccessful. The ingredients just did not come together properly.

'Among the Giovannis I didn't much care for Kim Borg, and Kostas Paskalis was disappointing after the quality of his Macbeth for us. Possibly his lack of height told against him. No, our last Giovanni, Ruggero Raimondi, was the best I have heard here. He came with a great number of natural assets: he was a person of good taste and background, the aristocratic bearing was there, the voice was young and fresh. He had a degree of cynicism, which is essential to the part. Probably his weakness at that time was a lack of daemonic quality. His characterisation was almost certainly quite a long way from what Peter Hall is trying to achieve at the moment, but it had life and unity. Moran Caplat and Jani Strasser signed him after hearing one of his first Giovannis at La Fenice and their choice was more than justified.

'Sena Jurinac was by far and away the best Donna Anna we have had here so far. Her Elvira disappointed because of the overall lack of success of that 1954 series I've mentioned. Geraint

Evans' early Leporellos were a delight and so was the timing of Sesto Bruscantini in the part later. I agree with you that the Enriquez–Luzzati production was not a success mainly because the idea of having moving blocks of scenery for swift changes of set did not work out. The concept of having part of the final supper scene set in the cemetery, so that the invitation and the Statue's acceptance and arrival were all in Giovanni's mind, had possibilities which were not fully explored.'

Glyndebourne's *Don Giovannis* have usually foundered on the casting of the title rôle and the set designs. Jani Strasser, who has coached every *Don Giovanni* at Glyndebourne up to the present one, is rather more severe on Raimondi than Christie or Caplat. 'The raw material was excellent, but when he was here often he was too frivolous. Encouraged by Wieslaw Ochman, in many ways an admirable Ottavio, he was constantly making jokes on stage; this diminished the fury which must be at the heart of every Giovanni. When that man is crossed he is dangerous and the anger must be transmitted to the audience.

'The best two Giovannis in my experience are Cesare Siepi and Ezio Pinza. Siepi had a beautiful, smooth, warm voice with all the honeyed sensuousness for that duet with Zerlina, "*Là ci darem*". Sometimes he was a bit lazy and he laughed at himself. I remember reprimanding him once in Geneva for using the same tricks and he replied, "Okay, Jani, if you think that my Giovanni should be taken to the cleaners then I will let you do the sponging and pressing." Pinza was much heavier and stressed the dark side of the character. You never thought his laughter was genuine and he never attempted the suave gentleman that Siepi portrayed.'

I agree with Strasser that for many years Siepi was the world's leading Don Giovanni. He liked a large stage, a Covent Garden or a Met; he liked to show off vocally in the misnamed Champagne Aria and physically in a series of glittering costumes. But the animal attraction was there as well as the touch of class. Above all he was dangerous. So too is Raimondi in the right production—to judge him on the Glyndebourne showing alone is to underrate him. At Munich a couple of years later, under Günther Rennert's direction, he produced a sexual marauder

Günther Rennert, Glyndebourne's producer in
1960–1

slavering after the first woman to come in sight. *La caccia di
ragazze*, girl-hunting, was at the core of this performance where
the relish for life was not diminished until the Statue's final
handshake. Stafford Dean, Glyndebourne's 1977 Leporello, was
in that production and showed how foolish Britain had been to
let him go to Germany to pursue his Mozart career.

Strasser admired Rennert's Glyndebourne production in the 1960 and 1961 seasons with two reservations. He did not care for either of the Giovannis, although Moran Caplat reckons that the second of them, the Hungarian Georgy Melis, was rather better than he was given credit for. The other is that Rennert turned Leporello (Geraint Evans) into a robber-cum-highwayman and so took away the humanity and petit-bourgeois protectiveness which characterised Evans' early appearances. He regrets that Kostas Paskalis and his Leporello, Paolo Montarsolo, never achieved on stage the rapport established in rehearsal. 'Off stage it was marvellous, and then every evening when the curtains rose somehow it all managed to crumble.'

When Glyndebourne decided to put on *Don Giovanni* again for the 1977 Festival they knew well just how difficult it was. There were no model productions to admire, *Don Giovanni* has collected far more criticism than the other Mozart operas staged in the house. If the worries were there they were not allowed to show and on 29 January 1974 Moran Caplat wrote to Peter Hall about *Figaro* and added, 'We further assume with equal confidence that you will produce *Don Giovanni*, to be conducted by John Pritchard in the 1977 Festival, with rehearsals from mid-April and the first performance about 22 May.'

In the event the dates were just over a week out, but the confidence was not misplaced.

3 Chopping and Changing

Most major opera houses feel an obligation to balance their repertory and are reluctant to duck this duty. The musical director and general administrator may not care for Puccini, but *Bohème*, *Butterfly* and *Tosca* take the stage because the public likes to hear them. The house resources may not appear strong enough to mount a *Ring* cycle, but the *Ring* goes on all the same because the theatre which ignores it appears to lose face, although Rudolf Bing during his time at the Met waged a long and successful war against Wagner. *Faust* and *Carmen* are brought in when French opera is thought to be having a rough deal, *Boris Godunov* and *Eugene Onegin* when the Russophiles start to complain of short measure. Commissions go out to living composers so that criticisms of neglecting contemporary opera can be answered.

Glyndebourne is under no such pressures. In part it stems from the nature of festival opera, which tries to develop its own character rather than running an educational service. In part it looks back to John Christie's original precepts. Although he wanted Wagner and Humperdinck heard in Sussex he was happy to begin with all-Mozart seasons. Opera-lovers who did not love Mozart, if such creatures existed, could keep away. Mozart stays at the very centre of the Glyndebourne canon. Sometimes he is represented by only a single opera, as in 1977 with *Don Giovanni*; sometimes he claims three of the season's normal five productions as in 1978 when *Giovanni* is joined by *Così* and *Zauberflöte*. When the bicentenary of his death arrives in 1991

LE NOZZE DI FIGARO

Susanna - - -	**AUDREY MILDMAY** (English)	
Countess - -	**AULIKKI RAUTAWAARA** (Finnish)	
	(Staatsopern: Helsingfors and Berlin)	
Cherubino - -	**LUISE HELLETSGRUBER** (Austrian)	
	(Staatsopern: Vienna and Berlin; Salzburg Festival)	
Marcellina - -	**HERTHA CSONKA GLATZ** (Austrian)	
Barberina - - -	**WINIFRED RADFORD** (English)	
Figaro - -	**WILLI DOMGRAF-FASSBAENDER** (German)	
	(Staatsopern: Berlin and Vienna)	
Count - - -	**ROY HENDERSON** (Scotch)	
	(Covent Garden)	
Bartolo - - - -	**NORMAN ALLIN** (English)	
	(Covent Garden)	
Basilio - - - -	**HEDDLE NASH** (English)	
	(Covent Garden)	
Antonio - - - -	**FERGUS DUNLOP** (English)	
Curzio - - - -	**MORGAN JONES** (Welsh)	

Conductor - **FRITZ BUSCH**

Producer - CARL EBERT *Scenery* - HAMISH WILSON

ACT I.   The Room allotted to Susanna and to Figaro (early morning)

ACT II.   The Countess's Bedroom (morning)

ACT III.   SCENE I.   Parlura Parva in the Palace

SCENE II.   The Portico and Garden Stairs (evening)

ACT IV.   The Garden (night)

MUSICAL STAFF

FRITZ BUSCH, formerly Head Conductor Staatsoper, Dresden.
Festivals: Bayreuth, Salzburg, Buenos Aires.

CARL EBERT, formerly Intendant Städtische Oper, Berlin.
Festivals: Salzburg, Buenos Aires.

HANS OPPENHEIM, formerly Head Conductor Deutsche Musikbühne, Berlin.
Head Conductor Städtische Oper, Breslau.

ALBERTO EREDE, formerly Conductor Augusteum, Rome, Italian Opera den Haag.

HANS STRASSER, Professor of Singing, Vienna, Budapest, and Glyndebourne.

The cast list of Glyndebourne's first production

there will doubtless be pressure for every other composer to be excluded from the house.

Mozart is the base around which Glyndebourne arranges its repertory. The plans as presented to the press and public year by year may seem to have no particular design behind them beyond a choice of works suitable for a theatre with well under a thousand seats. The administration has never been keen on playing its hand too openly. But it has quite consciously tried to set a style for a specified period and then abandon it when explorations in a certain area appear to have gone far enough.

In the Fifties and early Sixties nineteenth-century Italian comic opera was the inspiration. *La cenerentola* was followed by other Rossini works including, inevitably, *The Barber of Seville* and *Le Comte Ory*, Donizetti's *L'elisir d'amore* and finally back to Rossini with *La pietra del paragone*. Thereafter, it was thought, the direction should change. The inspiration for this series was the veteran conductor Vittorio Gui, who drew on his detailed knowledge of the Italian houses and their roster of artists to help with the casting. Glyndebourne has turned to those whom it trusts when pencilling in names against rôles: it was, for instance, Ljuba Welitsch who suggested looking at a young Yugoslav singer called Sena Jurinac when the first post-War *Così* was being discussed.

Glyndebourne's next move was towards baroque opera and Monteverdi's *L'incoronazione di Poppea*. Raymond Leppard arranged the score, as he did later for Cavalli's *La Calisto* and Monteverdi's *Il ritorno d'Ulisse in patria*, the two operas which started Peter Hall's association with Glyndebourne, as well as for *L'Ormindo*. Few people realised just what Leppard was beginning with *Poppea* at the time, but in retrospect Glyndebourne can take much of the credit for the baroque revival which has rolled across Western Europe and America.

Moran Caplat, George Christie and their Music Director, John Pritchard, then decided on two concurrent cycles for the mid-Seventies. Peter Hall, after his success with seventeenth-century opera, was to take over Mozart. His style would be totally opposed to the Enriquez–Luzzati team, whose productions would gradually be phased out of the repertory. He would confine himself to the quartet of masterpieces, with John Cox directing *Idomeneo*. For the time being, *Die Entführung* was to be left out of the reckoning because there was a strong feeling by some of those making the decisions that it was well below the level of the other works. Glyndebourne has always shied away from minor Mozart despite pleas from patrons and artists to tackle operas such as *La finta giardiniera* and *Il re pastore*.

The other cycle was to revolve around Richard Strauss. John Cox won plaudits all round when he directed *Ariadne auf Naxos*, which had been in and out of the repertory in Carl Ebert's days. The freshness and exactitude of Cox's staging, which led to his appointment as Glyndebourne's Director of Production, suggested other and lesser-known Strauss pieces could be put on. It was a policy of building from success in the same way that the Gui–Ebert *Cenerentola* started the burrowing into Rossini. *Ariadne* was followed by a re-thought *Capriccio* (1973), which banished all memories of its half-hearted reception when it was first heard in Sussex in 1960, and a superb *Intermezzo*. Doubts about the resistance of the Glyndebourne audience to twentieth-century scores and quantities of German text were erased by the skill with which Cox, John Pritchard and the Swedish soprano Elisabeth Söderström worked together. The Strauss series came to an end in 1977 with *Die schweigsame Frau*, conducted by Andrew Davis and again directed by Cox.

Around Mozart and Strauss the other composers were arranged, Verdi (*Falstaff*), Janáček (*The Cunning Little Vixen*) and Stravinsky (*The Rake's Progress*) among them. And well before the two cycles had run their allotted span there were arguments about which track the house should next follow. Under the influence of Bernard Haitink, who took over from John Pritchard at the end of the 1977 season, the choice fell on Haydn, whose operas are as little known on the British professional stage as those of Monteverdi were when Leppard first introduced him in 1962.

*   *   *

Most of the early casting at Glyndebourne is now done by Moran Caplat, George Christie and the Opera Manager, Brian

Elisabeth Söderström as Christine in John
Cox's production of *Intermezzo*

Dickie, who also runs the Touring Company. Their suggestions then go to the conductors and producers involved. Scouting is done mainly in the winter when the theatre is virtually closed apart from the workshops, busy preparing sets and costumes for the coming season or for other houses, and the transport department who make the three-mile journey into Lewes station to pick up the occasional visitor. Caplat and Dickie, who has built up close connections with one or two of the French opera companies, tend to scour Europe, moving their allegiances according to the state of the market. At one period Hungary, Romania and Bulgaria were producing a high proportion of the singers, too high in the view of some critics. Germany declined as a hunting-ground as the value of the Deutschmark rose and in the mid-Seventies was replaced by Scandinavia not least because of the ties Elisabeth Söderström and her colleague from the Stockholm Opera, Kerstin Meyer, formed with Sussex.

John Pritchard, as skilful an operatic huntsman as Vittorio Gui in his day, recommends and auditions in Australia and the West Coast of America, the two main places outside Britain where his conducting assignments take him. John Cox reports from whatever country he happens to be working in during the winter months.

The Glyndebourne archives are crammed with memos of recommendation and fearsome warnings to keep clear of Mr X or Mme Y. The feelings run strongly, but there is a reluctance to engage any new singer until he or she has been heard and approved by at least two members of the Selection Committee, either on stage or after auditions.

In August 1974, when the first tentative cast was being drawn up for *Don Giovanni*, Moran Caplat wrote to Peter Hall asking for his ideas on the type of personality he wanted for each rôle in the opera. A precise reply would have been expected from a regular opera producer with *Don Giovanni* well established in *his* repertory; Hall, who had never tackled the work before, had equally firm ideas. At that stage he saw Mozart's *dramma giocoso* as a work concerned with doubles and disguises. Giovanni and Leporello were two sides of the same man while Anna and Elvira were facets of the same woman. It was essential in the case of

Giovanni and his servant for the two singers to be of roughly the same build and shape so that the disguises and switching of clothes at the beginning of the second act could be made credible. Already Hall was working towards a realistic *Giovanni* which would pull the audience into the drama while making the minimum use of artificial theatrical effects.

In the same detailed letter Peter Hall moved from his theories on Anna/Elvira and Giovanni/Leporello as doubles, the two faces of the same coin, to the other characters. Don Ottavio he saw as middle-aged, a father figure, a friend rather than a lover of Donna Anna. The conventional foppish suitor, singing sweetly and ineffectually, was to be avoided at all costs. At the beginning of the opera Ottavio tries to comfort Anna after the death of the Commendatore and claims that she will find in him both a husband and father (*'Hai sposo e padre in me'*). The *padre* was to be emphasised at the expense of the *sposo*. The peasant pair, Masetto and Zerlina, should have an almost incestuous brother-and-sister relationship.

It was not going to be the easiest opera in the world to cast.

With Hall's dramatic preferences spelled out clearly, perhaps too clearly, and John Pritchard's musical demands well known, Glyndebourne drew up their short list of singers. It was as follows:

Don Giovanni: Michael Devlin, Benjamin Luxon, Richard Stilwell

Leporello: Gabriel Bacquier, Stafford Dean, Donald Gramm, Richard Van Allan

Donna Anna: Elisabeth Harwood, Kiri Te Kanawa, Teresa Kubiak

Donna Elvira: Helene Döse, Margaret Price, Julia Varady

Don Ottavio: Claes-Haaken Ahnsjö, Ryland Davies, Leo Goeke

Zerlina: Frederica von Stade

Commendatore: Matti Salminen, Pierre Thau

No worries were expressed about Masetto, an easy rôle to cast. Indeed there have only been five different singers in the complete run of *Don Giovannis* up to the 1977 season. During the rest of 1974 most of the discussions at Glyndebourne, in London over

Benjamin Luxon as Ulysses (with Anne
Howells as Minerva) in *Il ritorno d'Ulisse in
patria*

working breakfasts and via notes to Peter Hall at the National Theatre, centred on the choice of artists for Leporello and the title rôle.

Kiri Te Kanawa and Ryland Davies had both agreed to the parts suggested to them and in a world starved of Mozart sopranos and tenors this appeared a solid start. Hall was particularly concerned to find the right Giovanni. He had to have a baritone through whom he could 'discover' the opera. A good voice was a natural prerequisite but intelligence and the ability to think out the part in rehearsal were also needed. One or two Giovannis with 'good voices' were tried and did not measure up to Hall's demands. Moran Caplat was somewhat concerned that Glyndebourne, with its policy of twin series for new productions, had to find not one cast but two, and that was before the matter of physical resemblances was tackled.

By the end of 1974 the title rôle in the first performance appeared to be going to the American baritone Richard Stilwell. He had already cut a handsome figure on stage at Glyndebourne and the voice was rich. It was proposed that Benjamin Luxon should play Leporello to him; both were tall and bearded which would at least answer Hall's requirements on mistaken identities. On the first revival Ben Luxon, who had already worked with Hall in *Ulisse* and *Figaro*, could take over the title rôle.

In principle the plan was an attractive one, but Peter Hall immediately began to have doubts. He had little experience of Stilwell on stage and was not convinced that here was the singer for that pathfinding trip through *Don Giovanni*. Nor was he convinced about Luxon as Leporello, although he had no reservations about him being cast as the protagonist. What about considering Richard Van Allan? Moran Caplat vetoed this on the grounds that he was contracted to sing Don Giovanni in a production at the English National Opera which would appear a year and a half before Glyndebourne's. Once again old principles were being adhered to: Glyndebourne had always avoided assigning singers to parts in which they were already familiar to London audiences.

The hesitation between Stilwell and Luxon went on, but the needle of opinion was moving over towards the British singer.

Peter Hall was very much in favour of him and was not turned against his preference even by Stilwell's notable Pelléas at Covent Garden, although he was sufficiently impressed by Stilwell as Ford in the 1976 *Falstaff* at Glyndebourne. In that rôle he was succeeded by Ben Luxon; sometimes comparisons are laid on by accident. In the end Peter Hall's persuasiveness won the day and the part went to Ben Luxon with another British baritone, Thomas Allen, taking over for the second series at the instigation of John Pritchard. The judgment in favour of Luxon was probably helped by his lengthy association with the house which dated back to his appearance as Eugene Onegin with the Touring Company in 1970. Moran Caplat suggested him to Raymond Leppard for the title role of *Il ritorno d'Ulisse* and although Leppard had been thinking in terms of a tenor for the part, the suggestion was accepted and the score accordingly adjusted, but only to a minor extent. Then came the Count in the Hall-Pritchard *Figaro*. Storch in *Intermezzo* was proposed but Luxon was already committed elsewhere by the time the offer arrived.

What would have been the result had the die been cast in Stilwell's way? 'Fascinating,' according to one member of the

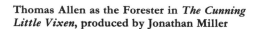

Thomas Allen as the Forester in *The Cunning Little Vixen*, produced by Jonathan Miller

Richard Van Allan as Selim in *Il Turco in Italia*
for Glyndebourne on tour

Selection Committee. 'He would have had the metal for the part, metal that was finely tempered steel. The weakness would have been difficulty in putting across the humour of the opera. Richard is a wonderful artist but he is at the same time a very serious one. Against this Glyndebourne would have gained in having a much greater contrast with Tom Allen who is very much a singer in the Luxon mould.' The point is a fair one as in 1977 Allen, before appearing in *Don Giovanni*, sang the Forester in a revival of Janáček's *The Cunning Little Vixen* and looked uncommonly like Luxon in the part a couple of years before.

Luxon as Giovanni forced a little rearrangement on Glyndebourne, but the troubles were minimal compared with what was to follow. He had been pencilled in for Falstaff, which was being revived in Jean-Pierre Ponnelle's production for the 1977 season. He was reluctant to do it because he thought, with a good deal of justification, that it was coming too early in his career, so the proposal of the first run of Giovannis and a few Fords at the end of the season came as an ideal alternative. Even so Luxon's first Falstaff cannot now be too far off.

Leporello provided little difficulty. Stafford Dean was the natural candidate. For the last decade he had made a speciality of Mozart's servants, Leporello and Figaro, but despite the fact that he was brought up within a few miles of London, practically all of his appearances had been in Europe, particularly in Germany, and in America. There were no worries about the Covent Garden audience being familiar with his performance because none of Dean's one hundred and fifty or so Leporellos had been sung at that house, although he had done Masetto there. Glyndebourne only needed an assurance that the state of affairs would continue. It was given, and Dean rejoined the house where once he had been in the chorus and had taken the small part of the Bailiff in Massenet's *Werther* in 1966 and 1969. Richard Van Allan agreed to do the second series Leporello to Tom Allen's Giovanni, which had been approved by Peter Hall and John Pritchard over one of their Waldorf breakfasts. Someone in the Glyndebourne accounts department must have noted that both pairs of master and servant were British and become greatly cheered that there would be no long-distance airfares to pay.

The rest of the male cast also looked fairly settled. Pierre Thau, a very experienced French bass who had sung the Commendatore at the Aix Festival, the Paris Opéra and in Hamburg among other places, was available and willing. Ryland Davies had eventually declined Ottavio, but scouting trips by Caplat and Cox to Sweden had uncovered Gosta Winbergh, who was fast establishing a reputation at the Stockholm Opera. The search ended there. Masetto could be chosen later.

The female side of the edifice though was crumbling. Kiri Te Kanawa, who had melted even the most diehard misogynists with her Countess in *Figaro*, had decided to give up Donna Elvira in favour of a very highly paid engagement on offer from the Paris Opéra to sing Pamina in their new *Zauberflöte* which was to open about a month before *Don Giovanni*. Margaret Price was not available for Anna. And Frederica von Stade, who as Cherubino in 1974 had almost filched that *Figaro* from Miss Te Kanawa, was having second thoughts about Zerlina. Those second thoughts were final ones and she ended by saying that the part was not for her.

At the beginning of 1976 Glyndebourne's cupboard looked virtually bare of Annas, Elviras and Zerlinas. Anna was going to be the most difficult rôle to cast and on 12 January Moran Caplat drew up a list of fourteen possible singers for the part of whom one, the Romanian Horiana Branisteanu described by Caplat in his private notes as 'first class . . . obviously going right to the top', was eventually engaged for the second series. John Pritchard was greatly in favour of Maria Ewing, von Stade's chief American rival, for Zerlina, but Miss Ewing after initial interest did a von Stade and preferred to make her British début in another part.

However Pritchard on a visit to Australia with Jani Strasser came up with the solution to the Elvira problem. Joan Carden, who had made a brief appearance once at Covent Garden as Gilda in which she did herself little justice, was singing Elvira admirably and was also available for Glyndebourne. She was signed at once. The Selection Committee then turned their ears and eyes to Zerlina and produced six possible candidates. Elizabeth Gale, who had been singing a number of soubrette

rôles for Glyndebourne in and out of the Festival, had the
support of Pritchard and Caplat and was chosen for Series I with
the Hungarian soprano Adrienne Csengery engaged for the July
dates.

Still there was no Anna. John Pritchard's proposal was Leona
Mitchell, considered by many of the most astute voice-fanciers as
the best of the new generation of negro singers. Peter Hall vetoed
this on the dramatic grounds that he could not have a black
soprano as an aristocratic Spanish lady in an otherwise all white
cast. He was in favour of coloured singers for many parts but not
for this one; it would ruin the realism and careful social structure
which were to form the very heart of the production. Hall was
adamant despite arguments that time was running out and that
the whole opera was in jeopardy.

On 26 November a suggestion was made that Joan Carden
might be persuaded to move from Elvira to Anna and that
another singer could be found for the lighter rôle. Moran Caplat
was against it but did not dismiss the idea. The name of Rosario
Andrade, a young Mexican who was singing Anna in Brussels,
was put forward. At the end of December John Pritchard went
over to hear her and wired back saying that he would prefer her
as Elvira. The next day a cable went off to Joan Carden in
Australia who eventually agreed on 9 February, after a number of
misgivings, to learn the new rôle of Anna in the ten weeks before
coming to England. So Elvira was cast as Anna and Anna as
Elvira.

Before the year ended one more hurdle had to be cleared. The
Ottavio, Gosta Winbergh, had run into difficulties with the
Stockholm Opera who were declining to release him for the
period Glyndebourne required and there were more problems
with some Hamburg engagements to which he had agreed. The
Selection Committee, who had only just finished juggling with
Don Giovanni's various ladies, felt that this particular skein was
too tangled to unravel and turned to Leo Goeke, one of the
tenors on the original 1974 short list who had also appeared with
distinction as Tom Rakewell in *The Rake's Progress*. Goeke
agreed on condition that he was absent for ten days of the May
rehearsal period so that he could carry out some of his North

American commitments. Peter Hall, who likes to keep the complete cast with him during the preparation time, was reluctant but in the end, possibly feeling that he had been obstinate over Leona Mitchell, he gave way.

At the end of January, four months before the first night, the *Don Giovanni* cast for the first series was complete:

Don Giovanni	Benjamin Luxon
Leporello	Stafford Dean
Donna Anna	Joan Carden
Donna Elvira	Rosario Andrade
Don Ottavio	Leo Goeke
Commendatore	Pierre Thau
Zerlina	Elizabeth Gale
Masetto	John Rawnsley

And that, to the relief of everyone, is the way the Series I cast stayed.

4 The Opera Producer

There is nothing particularly new about directors moving from the straight to the lyric theatre. When over thirty years ago David Webster was trying to put Covent Garden back on its very wobbly legs after the War, he began by preferring those who had proved themselves with actors rather than singers. He turned to Tyrone Guthrie, who had never staged an opera before, for *La traviata* and next took the risk of putting the young Peter Brook, then the darling of the avant-garde—is he not still?—in overall charge of productions. Brook dazzled with *Boris Godunov*, enraged with *Salome*, had a majestic row with the Music Director of the time, Karl Rankl, and left.

It was twenty years before the Royal Opera House decided to appoint another Director of Productions and the man they chose for the job was a one-time disciple of Brook, Peter Hall. It was a post he never took up.

The flow of producers from the spoken drama to opera is for the most part a one-way tide and its momentum has been increasing. It is easy enough to argue in generalities the case for going outside the band of men who have devoted their lives to putting singers, acting and non-acting, on the stage. Opera has to be kept up to date and open to the latest influences in the non-lyric theatre. The days of the roughly blocked-out productions with the star arriving at the last moment to give his or her regular interpretation are numbered. Opera is in danger of appealing to a small specialist audience and should go out and attempt to attract the theatre public . . . There is a grain of truth in all these reasons so regularly advanced, and more than a grain of falsehood.

Opera houses rub shoulders with so called avant-garde at their peril. The consternation in Paris in December 1976 when the Opéra turned to Peter Stein and his team from the Berlin Schaubühne for their new *Ring* was as great as that which greeted Peter Brook's *Salome*. The Opéra, like Covent Garden, took fright and cancelled the project. And every general administrator is well aware that he has a number of highly popular singers who would in no way respond to the disciplines of theatre producers, particularly if they have had no musical training.

No, the task of the administrator is to fit the right man to the right opera and give an occasional touch of the forelock to fashion, which at the moment is for plundering the talents of the straight theatre. The recent renaissance of Milan's La Scala has to a substantial extent been due to the annual production there by Giorgio Strehler. Florence's Maggio Musicale has turned to Luca Ronconi and La Scala followed suit in the 1977–8 season. The opera houses of Munich, Vienna and elsewhere regularly look to Otto Schenk, particularly for the German repertory. The New York Metropolitan Opera went even further when in the face of noisy opposition from sections of the public and the press they went ahead and appointed John Dexter to take charge of production. Their determination has been more than justified by the 1976–7 season when Dexter silenced his critics by the almost total reversal of his professional life. During his time in Britain he directed only the occasional opera in breaks from the theatre; in New York he now confines himself to a play a year on Broadway.

Peter Hall was almost tempted to Covent Garden by the type of offer that made Dexter hitch his star to the Met. When at the end of the Sixties Georg Solti decided that it was time to move on from the Royal Opera House, the Board agreed that he should be replaced by a British duo. It was suggested that Colin Davis would take over the musical side while Peter Hall would have responsibility for what happened on stage.

Hall's association with the house went back to the mid-Sixties when he staged *Moses und Aaron* to all-round acclaim. At that time most opera managements had considered Schoenberg's unfinished work far too big a risk to take on. Solti and Hall together proved that it was more than manageable and a good deal of publicity about the orgiastic dance round the Golden Calf and semi-nudity on stage, rather daring in those days, sold the seats. For once Schoenberg got rather more advance publicity in the popular press than in the quality papers. Those who had argued in favour of selecting a theatre rather than a regular opera director for this particular piece found themselves more than vindicated, although Hall's next production, *Die Zauberflöte*, by comparison was considerably flawed.

In Solti's last year at Covent Garden, 1970, Peter Hall produced Tchaikovsky's *Eugene Onegin* for him, but the real attention was focused on the partnership with Colin Davis which began with the première of Sir Michael Tippett's *The Knot Garden*. Hall later worked again with Solti on Wagner's *Tristan und Isolde*. There were reservations about both productions, centring mainly on Tippett's libretto for his own opera and some of the effects in *Tristan*, including the spilling out of the dying hero's guts in the last act, but clearly Hall got on easily with both conductors. With Davis in particular an excellent professional relationship looked probable: in age, background, education, taste, temperament, enthusiasm the two men were exceptionally close. It looked as though an ideal marriage had been arranged which was to take Covent Garden into a new theatrical era. A Mozart cycle was planned, a new *Ring* and a Verdi series. Then, just as Peter Hall was due to take up his new position, he announced that the Opera House was not for him. Colin Davis was as surprised as anyone and announced ruefully that he felt rather like the bride who was left standing at the altar. (The two men later had no difficulty in making up this rift.) The Board were perhaps less astonished. The long series of tussles with them was one of the reasons Hall gave for his decision.

The cynics claimed that the directorship of Britain's National Theatre, a post which Hall was later to take up, was already on the horizon and added that the salary on offer from Covent Garden was inadequate. The real reason probably for Peter Hall's 'defection' was that he realised that the demands of Covent Garden were large enough to leave little or no time to work elsewhere. Even with the maximum amount of delegation, three or four new productions a season, the supervision of revivals,

**Raymond Leppard, Janet Baker and Peter Hall
in the Organ Room at Glyndebourne after a
rehearsal for _La Calisto_**

planning and casting meetings and administration would eat up
virtually the whole of each year. Instinct too probably dictated
that it would be foolish to spend most of his early forties in one
opera house.

Glyndebourne too had been courting Hall. The wooing dated
back to 1967 when Hall left the Royal Shakespeare Company.
The following year for a number of reasons, all of which
appeared valid at the time, he opted to join forces with Covent
Garden rather than direct regularly at Glyndebourne. It was only
when he became disenchanted with the Royal Opera House that
he started to establish a bridgehead at Glyndebourne with his
1970 production of Cavalli's _La Calisto_. Three years earlier
Glyndebourne had suggested to Hall that he might take overall
charge of production, but he had declined. There was no reason

now though why he should not direct at Glyndebourne when the right opportunity and the right opera coincided.

Calisto, Hall's first excursion into baroque opera, provided a dazzling, magnetic evening. The musicologists, or some of them, had taken Raymond Leppard to task for tinkering with Cavalli, but there was little but praise for the way Hall had handled the anguish of love, human and divine, in Arcadia. He was quickly signed up for the next Leppard baroque opera, *Il ritorno d'Ulisse in patria* by Monteverdi for the 1972 season.

The Royal Opera House's loss was Glyndebourne's gain. Hall could work at the Sussex house without being shackled by any administrative chores or even being tied down to an opera a season. It was an arrangement which, as it turned out, fitted in admirably with the demands of the National Theatre. There was in the early Seventies an idea that, when the National was built, Glyndebourne should do a London season there each year, taking two existing operas from the Summer Festival and mounting a third, and new, production on the South Bank. But the 1973 economic recession killed off that particular embryo.

Nevertheless Glyndebourne were determined on a Hall Mozart series, which was to begin with *Le nozze di Figaro*. He was engaged to work on this for the 1973 season, following it as soon as possible with *Don Giovanni*, *Così* and *Zauberflöte*. It was accepted that there would be a major break in the cycle to allow him to move the National Theatre Company out of its home at the Old Vic up to the new buildings on the South Bank of the Thames. George Christie and Moran Caplat, having been in the arts administration business for some time, were well aware that opening dates for new theatres are subject to postponement, although they could hardly have foreseen the amount of effort, time and hassle that was eventually going to be needed for Hall and his colleagues to get into the Lyttelton, the Olivier and the Cottesloe.

In addition to Mozart, Glyndebourne persuaded Hall to direct another project which was to take place outside Festival time. For some years there had been unhappiness at the way contemporary opera had been tackled. Henze's *Elegy for Young Lovers* with the Auden–Kallman libretto had been reasonably successful, but most other attempts to put new works in the repertory had failed at the box-office. The public too often only bought tickets for them when nothing else was available. So it was suggested that the theatre would be opened for a few days in the autumn, with October as the preferred month, to put on commissioned work. The idea was to establish, with Arts Council aid, a regular output of new operas with the best and most successful of them going into the Summer Festival later. At that time of year there would be no question of picnics, but a new audience might be attracted to Glyndebourne, and there was a chance of the repertory being rejuvenated.

The first invitation went out to Harrison Birtwistle. The opera was called *Orpheus* and Peter Hall was to direct. At the time of writing, *Orpheus* has still not been performed at Glyndebourne or anywhere else, although it is planned for production by the English National Opera. The October season, like the proposed visits to the National Theatre, fell victim to the economic recession. Birtwistle is now Hall's Musical Director on the South Bank.

The 1973 *Figaro* was exceptionally well cast, particularly on the female side. Elisabeth Harwood was the Countess, giving way later in the season to Kiri Te Kanawa; Ileana Cotrubas broke a Glyndebourne precept in that she had previously been heard as Susanna at Covent Garden, but she was well established already at the Sussex house; Frederica von Stade, at the very beginning of her international career, was the most responsive Cherubino imaginable.

But the rehearsals were not easy. John Bury's sets were scarcely easy to move, although much admired by the audience, and Glyndebourne had not scheduled enough technical time to cope with them. In any case it is much more difficult to put on a new production in the middle of the season (the opening night of *Figaro* was 1 July) than it is to ring up the curtain at the end of May. There is a constant tug-of-war for the various rehearsal areas and particularly for the theatre stage itself. The technical staff are sometimes reluctant to strike day by day productions already in the repertoire. Both the costumes and the sets came late from the workshops and Benjamin Luxon, it was reckoned in

**Kiri Te Kanawa as the Countess in Peter Hall's
Glyndebourne production of *Le nozze di
Figaro***

some quarters, had not given himself sufficient time to prepare the rôle of the Count.

Figaro throughout its rehearsal period ran late and once or twice was in danger of postponement, a device which the late Walter Felsenstein used regularly at the Komische Oper in East Berlin when he was not happy with the way affairs were going. A rearranged date though would have caused Glyndebourne considerable anguish. The troubles were kept from the ears of the press who greeted the first night with a great deal of enthusiasm, although it was reckoned that the later performances, and the 1974 revival, were more cohesive than the early ones.

Practically no one recognised this production as the beginning of a new Mozart cycle mainly because Glyndebourne had kept its future plans to itself. It was noted though that there had not been a new *Figaro* since 1955 and that Peter Hall had substantially rethought the opera. All the conventional pieces of comic action had been stripped away so that the emotions provoked by the sexual bargaining which goes on during the *folle journée* of Mozart, Da Ponte and Beaumarchais could be brought to the surface. Cherubino in Frederica von Stade's interpretation was at the end of Figaro's catalogue of military delights in Act I, '*Non più andrai*', neither conventionally admiring nor even doubting but in tears. The peasants scattered their flowers before the wedding march in Act III almost contemptuously so that the Count had to wade through entangling bouquets. The line separating the aristocracy from the people was constantly shown as a very narrow divide which was always in danger of being crossed. In many ways this was a fierce *Figaro*, not least in its delineation of the drive of sexual desire. Some of the audience were sent home happy by the firework display which closed the opera in Count Almaviva's garden, a green-black, creeper-covered set by John Bury that in some way looked forward to his designs for *Don Giovanni*. Others saw the implication in Peter Hall's production that this moment of apparent friendship was a very temporary lull in the class and sex warfare.

Figaro showed those at Glyndebourne who did not know it already that Hall had a totally individual way of working, quite different from that of most opera producers. He set out to create this *Figaro*, as four years later he was to create the *Don Giovanni*, through the artists at his disposal. He arrives with a general view of the piece and a certain number of attitudes which he is anxious to put across to the audience. But he is as ready to discard as he is to invent.

The Hall trial-and-error method of production is anathema to the full-time opera director, who generally starts with each move precisely worked out and alters only when he finds his singers either unwilling or unable to follow them. Many artists prefer to be given neat instructions, provided of course that they have the right of reply; it saves on rehearsal time and gives them more opportunity to concentrate on their singing. But the danger with the man who comes in with everything cut, dried and neatly packaged, who is staging his tenth *Giovanni* or his twentieth *Figaro*, is monotony.

Economic pressures have forced certain producers, who claim that in comparison with singers they are poorly rewarded by opera houses, to repeat themselves. Their *Barber* in Amsterdam will look much the same as it did in Sydney; their *Bohème* in Bordeaux will be an almost identical twin of the one directed for Frankfurt, apart from cast and language. And why not? will come the reply. The producer who gave himself time to rethink every opera that he staged would fast find himself on the breadline and the fact that Frankfurt, for instance, wants what Bordeaux has already had is a good indication that Bordeaux is satisfied. The only requisite is that the productions should be decently spaced out geographically.

Yet the very fact that opera-goers are partly living in a travelling circus world where certain producers go on perpetuating their ideas, both inspired and erroneous, is a principal reason to add to those given at the beginning of the chapter for administrators to steal from the straight theatre. They may well stand a chance of getting something fresh and imaginative, especially if they provide the right working time and conditions.

Moran Caplat is well aware of the demands made by the Hall approach. 'We try to cast the Hall operas a little differently, I suppose, from the others. In particular we attempt to find

John Pritchard in the pit; above Peter Hall and
production assistants

intelligent singers for him because of his method of working. He
puts his ideas to the test during rehearsals and he has to have
response to them in exactly the same way he responds to the
suggestions of others. He has never arrived here overladen with
preconceived ideas and has always preferred to work through the
material we have provided for him. To some extent Carl Ebert
operated in the same way: he never came with a prepared score
marked with exact movements but instead used to devise each
day's work the evening before.

'Part of the skill is trying to fit the singers to the right
conductor and producer. It is important that they have trust in
what you tell them about someone. There has never been any
point in "selling" an artist. If you do then there is every chance
that he or she will end up as the whipping boy of the production,
the person from whom all the errors and ills stem.

'We try to accommodate Peter wherever possible, although we don't always pull it off. Take the original idea of Donna Anna and Donna Elvira being almost interchangeable. That one went by the board because of the constant switches of cast in those two rôles. In no way could you say that Rosario Andrade and Joan Carden are alike. Peter has the same idea for the sisters in our *Così* next year and perhaps we'll be able to do rather better for him.

'Late alterations have been with us from the beginning. I remember that we were well into *Calisto* rehearsals when he wanted to change two of the singers. After some discussion this was agreed. It might cause irritations but it often brings superb results. Look at Ileana Cotrubas' Susanna in *Figaro*: any number of singers have followed her in the part here but I still think I am seeing the interpretation worked out between Peter and her.

'We also respect his desire never to stage the same piece twice, although we came close to breaking that rule before next year's *Zauberflöte* was taken over by John Cox. We would never ask him to direct the second series as well as the first any more than we would insist that John Cox did, although John regularly handles revivals of his own work. Peter puts on the first set of colours and his assistant does the later shading in. The prospect of fitting new singers into existing productions was one of the reasons why Peter left Covent Garden, so it is scarcely in anyone's interest to try and make him do the same thing here.'

*   *   *

John Pritchard began his Glyndebourne conducting career when he was called from sunbathing on the beach at Eastbourne in the summer of 1952 to take over a performance of *Don Giovanni* from the ailing Fritz Busch. Twenty-five years later he ended his spell as the Musical Director of the theatre with the same opera and with *Falstaff*. After conducting *Giovannis* beyond number, Pritchard, bland, urbane and capable of silencing an orchestra with a single well-directed jibe, might be expected to sound a little cynical about 'discovering' an opera through the singers.

'I confess that when we began work on *Figaro* together I was a little sceptical of the straight stage "discovery" approach. I had been used to the expertise of the opera producers who knew the opera, and that includes the orchestral score, backwards. Rennert, for example, used to arrive with everything devised down to the last detail. He knew the mechanics of each scene. Peter works from precisely the reverse direction: he is interested in the end result. But I quickly came to admire his imagination and his persistence; he would never brush anything under the carpet. If there was a problem which other producers always avoided because they did not have a ready-made solution, then Peter would immediately assume it was his duty to wrestle with it until the right way out was found.

'Of course at moments during that *Figaro* it was touch and go whether it would get on stage or not. I remember delivering an ultimatum during one of the late rehearsals that if the carpenters did not produce the Act III set by the time we had finished the preparation of the first two acts then we should call the whole thing off.

'In *Giovanni* there have been no such problems and the pacing has been very easy. Glyndebourne has always been liberal with time. In what other house would the Commendatore be called for rehearsals four weeks before the orchestra arrive? The conditions here are almost ideal for Peter's method. There is a slight danger that all the hours at his disposal could allow him to push one or two singers a little further than their capabilities allow. His great strength is that the flow and counterflow of ideas never permit any boredom or that feeling dreaded in every opera house that the whole project is going off the boil.'

5 *First Thoughts*

Peter Hall spreads his preparation time wide on an opera. The simple desire to cast well in advance ensures that. The idea of the resemblance between Giovanni and Leporello, Anna and Elvira came at least two years before rehearsals started, when Hall was running through the score.

'I immerse myself in a work; I play it from beginning to end time and again on the piano. I write things down in a file; I forget them; I write them down again. I read as much as I can around the piece. There's Brigid Brophy's *Mozart the Dramatist*,* which manages to be stimulating and utterly infuriating at the same time . . . there's Moberly's *Three Mozart Operas*,† which too often states the obvious. I dip into the letters, although these are very scanty in their references to Mozart's visit to Prague and the period of *Don Giovanni*'s composition.

'Certain patterns begin to form. There is for instance the fascination both Mozart and Da Ponte had with disguise. It is there in the last act of *Figaro* in the Count's garden and it forms the very core of *Così fan tutte*. I'm not sure that the real implication of the change of identity by Ferrando and

---

* Miss Brophy's study of Mozart stresses the similarities between Don Giovanni and Hamlet. The arguments are forceful but Miss Brophy sometimes appears to be defending a perverse cause.
† R. B. Moberly's *Three Mozart Operas* (Victor Gollancz, London and Dodd, Mead, New York) dissects *Don Giovanni* in a highly personal way. But it draws too heavily on Dent's colloquial English translation and does not suggest wide experience of the opera on stage.

Guglielmo has been thoroughly explored yet; perhaps we shall have a go when *Così* comes on at Glyndebourne in 1978. And there it is again in *Don Giovanni* both in the arrival of the *tre maschere* at Giovanni's party in the first act and in the switch of clothes by Leporello and Giovanni in the second.

'When so much time is given over to disguise there is no point in treating the matter lightly. Don Giovanni and Leporello are divided by rank and clothes, and that's it. If you separate them physically by having the tall master and the squat servant favoured in some productions then you destroy at once some of the suggestions in the score and the libretto. Mozart and Da Ponte are saying that man is basically a forked animal and between the sheets there may not be too much difference between one example and another. Agreed, Leporello is much less successful than Giovanni, but that's primarily because he's craven, he's a coward and hasn't the *chutzpah* possessed by his master to take on the world.'

Hall's first thoughts were on similarities and the fact that practically all the action in *Don Giovanni* takes place at night. The time-scale in the opera has been the subject of countless essays. The classicists have argued that Da Ponte kept to the unities as he did in *Figaro*. Don Giovanni kills the Commendatore in the middle of the night and the following morning meets Elvira and immediately after Zerlina, Masetto and their fellow peasants. The party at Giovanni's *casinetto* occupies part of the afternoon and by evening, despite the adventures of the day, Giovanni is ready to lay siege to Elvira's chambermaid. Darkness has already fallen when Leporello is unmasked in the Act II sextet, but he is loyal enough to join his master in the graveyard a few hours later and invite the Statue, under duress, to what must have been a particularly late supper the very same day.

Those who like symmetry may be cheered by persuading themselves that the Commendatore comes back to take Don Giovanni off to heaven or to hell (*'Pentiti, cangia vita, è l'ultimo momento!'* — 'Repent, change your life, it is your last moment!') just twenty-four hours after he has been run through the heart. The realists find it easy enough to pick hole after hole in the theory. Even a twenty-three-year-old of exceptional stamina would have been pressed by the physical demands of this particular *folle journée*, although there would have been every sympathy with Leporello's pangs of hunger at the sight of Giovanni guzzling down his supper (*'Ah che barbaro appetito!'*). The equestrian statue of the Commendatore also raises its stone head. In no way could that have been produced in a few hours, although some directors have got around the problem by giving a sight of the stone horse early on in the opera with the suggestion that the Commendatore, like Chateaubriand, prepared his own monument before his death. It would have been a relatively simple matter for the inscription, which Leporello reads to his master, to be carved on:

> DELL'EMPIO, CHE MI TRASSE AL PASSO
> ESTREMO, QUI ATTENDO LA VENDETTA
>
> 'Here I await vengeance on the
> vile man who killed me'

Christopher Benn, whose thirty-year-old book *Mozart on the Stage** contains a most lucid and objective study of *Don Giovanni* considerably influenced by the pre-War Glyndebourne performances, gives everyone much more time to live and to breathe and argues in favour of a five-day span of action. Three of them go to the first act, with a day apiece to the murder of the Commendatore, the encounter with Elvira and the peasants, and the party at Giovanni's castle. The scenes up to the graveyard invitation take up the fourth day. The brief interlude for Donna Anna's *'Non mi dir'* and Don Giovanni's last supper occupy the fifth. The only stumbling block here, as Benn points out, is Giovanni's reference to the time, the only specific one throughout the opera, when he nips over the graveyard wall, *'Ancor non sono due della notte'* ('It's not yet two o'clock at night'). The supper invitation a few minutes later is for that evening (*'questa sera'*). Dent† has argued ingeniously that two hours

---

* *Mozart on the Stage*, Christopher Benn (re-issued by John Calder, London).
† *op. cit.*

John Bury with sketch pad

means two hours after sundown so that supper the same evening was perfectly in order. Benn prefers to stay with 2 a.m., the beginning of a new day during the course of which dinner would be served.

In the end the wrangling over the hours is more a matter for academics than for regular opera audiences. Christopher Benn blandly and accurately remarks, 'As in so many great works, the time factor does not appear to have been thought out very carefully by the authors.' He could have gone on to note that precisely the same problem applies to *Così fan tutte*, where the officers go off to 'war' and return within a few hours. But it is odd that Da Ponte, whose stage directions are so detailed and were to be followed almost line for line by Peter Hall when rehearsals started, was little concerned with the period dividing one incident from another.

Peter Hall at one point started to wrestle with the time-scale, endorsing John Pritchard's point that he was a director who delighted in bringing out the problems others liked to sweep under the carpet. He then decided that it was not particularly relevant. The important factor was to emphasise the power of darkness, both physical and metaphorical. The opera begins at night when Don Giovanni exits from Donna Anna's room and it ends after dinner with the confrontation between Giovanni and the Statue. The timing of the Epilogue, described as happening 'a few minutes later', is irrelevant; it is basically addressed to the audience and more than once has been put in the country setting where we first saw Zerlina and Masetto—Franco Zeffirelli's Covent Garden staging is an example. But the sun is rarely present. Lack of light clouds the whole of the second act from the moment when Giovanni and Leporello change dress and voice, through the courtyard scene where Giovanni is sought with the help of flaring torches, to the graveyard where evening and night seem almost interchangeable. Disguises and false identities are born out of the darkness.

How literally to enlighten the audience about what was going on in the dark was one of the first obstacles in the initial discussions on staging *Don Giovanni*. Peter Hall, apart from an early talk with Benjamin Luxon on the nature of the opera, had no communication with the cast until the start of rehearsals, but he was of course in regular contact with his designer, John Bury. There is not much chatter from Bury, who has provided the sets and costumes for all of Hall's operas so far as well as for a high proportion of his productions at the National Theatre. Bury, unobtrusive despite his plump figure and long bearded face, moves softly around the theatre, never passing a comment unless asked for one, never introducing himself unless forced to do so. Outwardly he gives the impression of being phlegmatic and unflappable, but this probably is no more than a guard against stage managers who want uncomplicated sets to move and singers who care desperately about their appearance on stage. The relationship between Hall and Bury is instinctive rather than vocal. Hall once said: 'We communicate almost in grunts. I outline what I have in mind, John listens, says nothing and then goes away to produce a sketch or a model which I too tend to greet in monosyllables.'

This perhaps is an exaggeration because at the beginning of 1976 Bury and Hall had a series of discussions over the set, a model of which was due to be delivered to Glyndebourne in October that year, usually rather a formal occasion. The first aim was that enlightenment of the audience, the trick by which they could be persuaded that it was pitch black while giving them total visibility of what was going on. Hall's first idea was to reverse the colours. 'We thought of having a bright, white set, but this would have killed Mozart's rococo realism. It would have been a bit like doing Ibsen without a room. We played with the idea of making darkness light, but rejected it as being too camp.' It might too have looked a little old-fashioned and been compared with Peter Shaffer's light-reversal farce, *Black Comedy*.

'Eventually we settled for a black set very brightly lit, rather along the lines of our first Glyndebourne collaboration, *La Calisto*. We would achieve that suggestion of darkness integral to the work by using the blackest of backgrounds and every foot of depth [Glyndebourne's stage is very cramped at the sides but stretches far back towards the gardens] while putting strong lights on the faces of the singers.'

So far no guidelines had been laid down about the period of the opera beyond the fact that it should not be too specific. Hall believes that historical accuracy in Mozart is generally limiting and was against anything that might suggest a fashion plate. Here he was at one with Da Ponte who does very little to emphasise the 'Spanish town' assumed to be Seville. Donna Elvira comes from Burgos and tells us so, but she was an invention of Molière who, in *Don Juan, ou le Festin de Pierre*, had Don Juan abduct her from her convent on the promise of marriage. The Juan–Elvira liaison according to Molière lasted three days, a long time by Giovanni's standards, and *Festin* opens with Elvira's equerry Gusman, running Juan's servant, Sganarelle (Leporello) to earth in a 'Mediterranean maritime town'. Da Ponte took over Elvira lock, stock and almost barrel, but he made no attempt to differentiate between a lady from northern Spain and one who lived in the south. She is merely a woman who has been abandoned by her

DON GIOVANNI

Emanuele Luzzati's costume sketch
for Don Giovanni, 1967

husband, assuming that Giovanni did find a moment during his
stay in Seville to take the marriage vows. Da Ponte is
unconcerned about local colour in his invention of the maskers at
Giovanni's ball, a Venetian concept if ever there was one, and in
the last wine to pass Giovanni's lips, Marzimino, a convenient
rhyme for the command '*Verso il vino!*' ('Pour the wine!'), but a
bottle which would never have been available in Seville.
Marzimino is a grape from the Veneto region of north-east Italy
which produces a thin and rather acid drink swallowed by the
locals and the occasional music critic anxious to go back to
original sources.

The period of the opera seemed far more important to Hall as he probed into the score than any identifiable geographical setting. 'I decided quite early on that I wanted nothing to do with the fashionable Spain of theatre convention. It's a profoundly cynical piece, but it's difficult to be cynical in an antique never never land of Spain. Yet if the audience is confined by a specific period—to Goya, say, or even to David—then you run the risk of limiting it in other directions. Historical accuracy always makes for non-involvement. We are looking at a "period"—and it has nothing to do with our own human behaviour. The more I stumbled through the opening bars on the piano the more I decided that this opera had to be set at the watershed of history, the point where the modern world met the old one. In other words at the very beginning of the nineteenth century.

'The production, like *Don Giovanni* itself, had to look forwards and backwards at the same time. Parts of it are baroque, summing up much of the mediaeval spirit, yet elsewhere it is part of the *Sturm und Drang* movement, foreshadowing Beethoven and Kleist. In that final scene when the Statue arrives the music looks on to Beethoven, and then to the religiosity of *Parsifal*. To Mahler even. And all that is at the start of the overture as well. Yet in the midst of this new Romanticism the orchestra is constantly chuckling at the fallibility and crudity of man in a thoroughly eighteenth-century way. Time and again I was struck by the way the real laughter of the piece was in the orchestra pit. In a way it sums up the paradox of Mozart himself: he is a religious atheist, a fanciful husband and a lecher, a man who mixes in his letters purity and the utmost vulgarity.

'Giovanni, his hero, is totally heartless and indifferent to human suffering. All Mozart's major operas are about sex and Giovanni uses his sexual appeal and appetite to challenge accepted standards of morality. Mozart was very careful not to give away his moral position. We incline to Giovanni in the way we tend to support individualism; he is a young man taking on the world. But then he goes to hell and the social confederacy which he has challenged comes to the front of the stage, shrugs its shoulders and tells the audience, "There you are, that's the way it ends."

'In many ways the opera is an intellectual testimony to cocksmanship. Giovanni waves his penis at the heavens to see if there is anyone up there taking notice of him. He is not particularly conducting a campaign against women; they just happen to be his chosen instrument for testing if God exists. It's worth remembering that in *Don Giovanni* the women generally come to him rather than vice versa. [This point rather escaped Shaw in his *Don Juan in Hell* parody.] But Giovanni does push himself and everyone around him to the absolute limit.'

The concept of Giovanni, which was to change little during rehearsals, formulated in Hall's mind early on. He was determined to flee as far as possible from the concept of the ageing roué who was doing as well as he could in Seville at the end of his sexual span. Giovanni was to be fairly close to Molière's twenty-three-year-old Don Juan, a man entering the adult world, testing it and then taking it on. This was one of the reasons why Hall stood out against casting Richard Stilwell in the part, against the advice of Moran Caplat and John Pritchard.

'I had watched Stilwell in *Ulisse* and greatly admired both the voice and the handsome stage presence, but I was put off by what I can only describe as the American virility style of acting. They push their manliness so much that you start doubting it. And I was afraid this would nullify the point I wanted to make of the women coming to Giovanni rather than the other way round. I didn't want any hint of male narcissism in the performance. Later I saw Stilwell as Ford, a stunning interpretation. I thought that I might have very badly misjudged him. By then it was too late to make any changes.

'At the same time I wanted Giovanni to be a very cool character *on stage*. We had to strip away the "doggy" personality associated with some baritones and at the same time remove anything that might be described as "seduction" acting. I was looking for someone of considerable personal warmth because I thought that it was only with this that I could risk the chill, cruel self-centredness of Giovanni. Only very sympathetic rich personalities can portray outrageous shits on the stage without apologising for them.'

The development of Giovanni himself led to the style of the

staging. The concept of the watershed opera, the time when the classical movement was giving way to the romantic one began to dominate. Hall wanted to suggest the period when the world was shifting under the influence of Giovannis on the one hand and the instigators of the French Revolution on the other.

'It was quite late on when I rang up John Bury and said that we had to set the opera at the point when the old and the new worlds collided. By chance I had just seen Erich Rohmer's film *Die Marquise von O*, based on Kleist's story of the same name. Kleist was part of the *Sturm und Drang* movement, which I had already decided must be represented in the Glyndebourne production and the film had an added element of classical beauty. The women looked particularly good with their high breasts and low-cut bodices. I asked John to go off and see it at once because I was convinced that the period of 1800–10 was right for our *Don Giovanni*. He telephoned back and complained that opera-singers were not usually the same shape as Rohmer's leading ladies and pointed out practically that by the start of the nineteenth century gentlemen, even in Spain, had given up wearing the swords demanded by Da Ponte.

'We compromised by giving Giovanni a sword-stick.'

At the beginning of October 1976 Glyndebourne was moderately surprised by John Bury's first costume designs and the discovery that *Don Giovanni* for the first time in Sussex was to be moved twenty years forward from the date of its première in Prague. The Empire flavour in these first sketches gave some of the characters a deceptively, and inaccurately, nautical look to the delight of Moran Caplat, Lt. Cdr. R.N.V.R. The *Sturm und Drang* movement was allowed its first influence, which six months later was to grow considerably.

6 *Approach Work*

John Bury began to sketch his ideas for the *Don Giovanni* towards the end of 1975. Certain basic principles were taken for granted, including the raked stage which he had devised for his first joint Glyndebourne project with Peter Hall, *La Calisto*. It would not be the kind of slope to send anyone reaching for bottom gear or to make singers more worried about their footing than their voice, but it would tilt the opera slightly towards the audience and give an illusion of a little extra height to those on stage.

It was agreed without discussion that there should be no break in the drama except between the acts. In many *Don Giovannis* arias are taken in front of the curtain while the scene-shifters go about their task, all too often ruining the music and driving the artists to rage as one prop bangs into another. Mozart allows virtually no time for sets to be raised, lowered or even adjusted; the music of one scene goes directly into the next with only a silent beat for breathing space. Even so John Bury accepted that the action had to be continuous. 'It's an unwritten rule for Peter and myself that whatever the obstacles the curtain must not come down until the end of each act. Perhaps it is pride; perhaps it is an element of showmanship; perhaps we just believe instinctively that no story should be interrupted.'

Glyndebourne itself has a time problem. The beginning and end of each opera is loosely controlled by the times of the trains which run from London's Victoria station to the South Coast. Opera visitors are delivered by coach from Glynde shortly after five o'clock each afternoon and they are despatched to the return train not later than five past ten. Thus the performance cannot begin much before half past five or end after five to ten, unless the gardens are to be scattered with those who, quite literally, have missed the last bus home. The dinner interval of seventy-five minutes is also considered sacrosanct and there were complaints during the early days of the Hall–Bury *Figaro* when it was clipped to allow for scene-changing intervals between both the first two and the last two acts. Glyndebourne has always been in favour of a fast-running show. *Figaro* is usually a tight fit and *Don Giovanni* could have gone the same way had it been designed along the lines of, say, Franco Zeffirelli's Covent Garden production of the Sixties with its opulent multiple sets.

Speed was accepted and so was darkness, although early on John Pritchard made the point that it was essential for the conductor at least to see the singers and vice versa. The first conversation between Hall and Bury concerned the nature of darkness. According to Bury, 'We quickly rejected all really radical solutions, such as Peter Brook devised for *A Midsummer Night's Dream*, although that production influenced me considerably. Nor did we want a fancy black and white show. The requirement was a set where the faces could be seen. The only way of getting what we wanted was by using dark textures, principally dark houses and dark trees, to suggest a moonlit night.

'I also believed that we should have the minimum number of scene changes. Too many *Giovannis* hop from place to place with little justification. In Act I, for example, it is only unwritten tradition that has made Giovanni and Leporello meet Donna Elvira in one part of Seville and then go off to the other side of town for the encounter with Zerlina, Masetto and the peasants on their way to church. And what is the reason for giving Giovanni a separate set in which to sing the so-called Champagne Aria? Nothing more than an excuse for a little visual variety.'

Throughout the talks on the appearance of *Don Giovanni*, Peter Hall insisted on the maximum realism. At one point he was in favour of the Commendatore making his supper arrival astride a real horse and experiments were made to see to what extent hooves could be muffled to deaden the sound they made. Moran

The supper interval

Caplat drily remarked that hooves were not the only part of a horse to make a noise and the idea was dropped. Hall did however stick out for professional musicians on stage during the finales to both acts. Three separate groups are called for in the Act I party to play the dance music for Giovanni's guests before and during his attempt on Zerlina; and another batch of wind players are required to play *Tafelmusik*, including the celebrated *Figaro* quotation, while he is at supper in Act II. Hall insisted that Mozart composed antiphonal music in these sections and that his wishes should be respected.

It is a fairly obvious economy to have the sound coming from the orchestra pit while extras mime on soundless instruments on stage. Moran Caplat complained that to pay and to costume the two separate sets of musicians for eighteen performances at Glyndebourne and a further six at the Lyttelton—by this time the August transfer of *Giovanni* to London had been agreed—would need close on £10,000. The solution used by John Christie for Glyndebourne's first *Don Giovanni* of hiring amateur musicians and students for the stage bands would scarcely be countenanced by the Musicians' Union now. Christie drew from the National Physical Laboratory and sometimes none too wisely as Spike Hughes has recalled:

> . . . there was a moment of panic one evening when, not long before the players were to appear, a professor from the National Physical Laboratory fainted from the heat. A lady in the orchestra went to his assistance and tried to loosen what she thought was his brightly patterned cretonne vest; she discovered he was not wearing a vest. The bright patterns were tattooed on his chest and she promptly fainted away as well.*

Peter Hall won the day on his demand for professional musicians and in Act I they were divided between the balconies on either side of the stage and on a raised dais in the centre.

John Bury completed his first model for *Don Giovanni* in March 1976. Those two balconies at the front of the stage, apart from supporting instrumentalists, represented Donna Anna's bedroom and Donna Elvira's lodgings and later, with virtually no alteration, were the galleries of Giovanni's ballroom. Glyndebourne's depth was emphasised by using movable layers of scenery: an iron gate and high wall for the entrance to the Commendatore's house; trees (all black with one green exception) constructed, as they were in *Calisto*, on plywood trellises with metal supports; a substantial wall for the graveyard; and an impression of nothingness at the end so that Giovanni could be pulled into the fiery void at the furthest possible remove from the audience. The Commendatore was given a solid equestrian statue closely modelled on that of George III at the corner of Pall Mall and Cockspur Street in

---

* *op. cit.*

London. The statue was to be quite conventional and there were to be no explanations of how the monument was erected so quickly—one production gave the audience a sight of a stonemason packing his bags after a long day's work as the curtain went up on the graveyard.

The one objection by Peter Hall to the model was that the scenery had to be struck into the wings for set changes. The quest for realism was at the root of the complaint. He wanted each movement to be as natural as possible and believed that the sight of trees and walls rising upwards and outwards would have given a false note of theatricality. Hall and Bury went away to work on the problem together and by August had come up with the idea of two small revolves on either side of the stage. They had to be small, Glyndebourne's width allowed for nothing else.

The proposal was presented to Glyndebourne and its technical heads and supported by the suggestion that the revolves could also be employed in the 1978 season for *Così fan tutte*. The idea

John Bury's 1977 set for the opening scene

John Bury's set for the Act I finale

was eventually turned down on grounds of cost, lack of time to construct the right machinery, and most of all because of the difficulty of dismantling revolves day after day. Glyndebourne never plays the same opera on successive nights and has to accommodate works in rehearsal on stage during the morning session. The revolves would have been a luxury and a mighty technical problem combined. Hall continued to insist that the movement of the scenery could under no circumstances be vertical, so a compromise was reached by having everything mounted on runners, designed to slide noiselessly across the stage and meet in the middle.

The aim was not fully achieved. The chandeliers and some of the trees had to be lowered. But Hall and Bury by and large got a 'lateral' *Giovanni* with no pauses between the scenes. Bury

presented his final model on 26 October to all-round approval
and the Glyndebourne workshops started to put their metal and
plywood together, to build Spanish grilles and black Seville
houses. For once they had plenty of time; in the past final designs
had sometimes been delivered in January and even February,
rather than mid-autumn.

The basic work was done in November and December in a
room which looked like a training ground for apprentice
witches: cauldrons bubbling, Bunsen burners glowing. Only
there were no familiars. Dogs ruled the construction unit, dogs
in baskets, dogs snuffling under the tables, dogs running about
with pieces of Seville trees in their mouths.

The second act gave John Bury such trouble as there was. The
courtyard scene, in which Leporello, disguised as Giovanni, tries
to ditch Elvira and is instead unmasked by the other avengers,
was re-designed three times. The twin themes of disguise and
darkness are here at their most intense and Da Ponte's directions
are far from specific: 'A dark courtyard *or garden* [my italics]
outside the house of Donna Anna.' A minimum of three doors
are needed, one for the arrival of Leporello and Elvira, another
for the entry of Anna and Ottavio, and a third for Masetto and
Zerlina, who forestall Leporello just as he is on the point of
sliding off. Bury ended with a pitchy black courtyard much in
accordance with Elvira's arietta ('*Sola, sola in buio loco*'—'Alone,
alone in a dark place') with windows giving on to a street in
which the torches of Giovanni's pursuers could be seen.

Inevitably, the graveyard sparked argument and experiment.
According to Bury the solutions of turning the set, moving it
slightly, setting it at an angle to the audience were tried and
rejected. It ended by being four-square on stage. 'We thought of
trundling statues on as monuments to flank the Commendatore,
but then decided to have extras as frozen stone bodies instead.'
Bury was dubious about this solution and was quite prepared to
have it altered in rehearsal.

He had no reservations though about Peter Hall's request for
Empire costumes. 'Before Peter came along with that idea I'd
sketched the dresses in a style slightly earlier than Empire. I was
determined not to use Mozart's own period, any more than we

did for *Figaro*, because it is dull in clothes terms. Not a great deal of adjustment had to be made, because I did not want to be too precise. The girls were kept firmly in Empire fashion, but Giovanni was pushed a little forward in time and Ottavio a little back.

'Slavishness is never a virtue. We probed around to find out how things probably looked and worked both at the première in the Tyl Theatre, Prague, and at the Theater an der Wien when *Don Giovanni* was staged for the Viennese. This piece of mental resurrection was not intended to lead to a reproduction, although in practice it could have done because both theatres are much the same size as Glyndebourne. It was simply an exercise that might have yielded an idea or two.

'We didn't want to go anywhere near bull-fighting Spain. A nod in that direction was quite sufficient, which was about all Da Ponte and Mozart ever gave. Some producers go for a lot of heavy wiggery and turn the whole opera into a Cook's Tour. We reckoned that there was no need to have a mantilla in sight.'

*   *   *

At the beginning of April 1977, three weeks before the first rehearsals, Peter Hall was becoming more and more obsessed with the cynicism of the piece. 'I'm captivated, intrigued, even astonished by the mocking comment of the orchestra which I don't find in any other Mozart opera. The *dramma giocoso* consists to a great extent in the orchestra taking the piss, with music which is very hard, very ballsy. The polarity is there in the overture. It begins by chilling us and then starts chuckling away as though it were telling the audience that it mustn't take all this very seriously. Mozart delights in wrong-footing his listeners, just as Webster and Marlowe and Jonson do.

'That's why it's so important to have the Epilogue, which our Victorian forefathers were so keen to omit. At one minute the devils are there in the score as Giovanni is tugged down to hell and the next moment all the survivors are shrugging it off as just one of life's incidents.

'It is curious that Mozart, the Mason who should have believed that only through accepting death could you live, was really afraid of dying. Did he have any credence in that hell to which he sent Giovanni? I rather doubt it. It was more a fear of the unknown. Hell was a total loss of identity and perhaps that is why he brushed it away with that urbane Epilogue. He took a look at the hereafter, as he might have done had he been writing for the mediaeval theatre and then suddenly ducked away and became enlightened eighteenth-century man again. Mozart's mercurial changes of mood in *Don Giovanni*, his refusal ever to commit himself to an absolute position, will be among the most difficult qualities to achieve in production.'

In April the National Theatre was looking forward to a Don Juan season. Glyndebourne, with the help of a further grant from Imperial Tobacco, was booked into the Lyttelton for six performances, which would allow those who could not afford the price of Sussex tickets and a Sussex train fare a chance to see the company on stage, although £10 for a stalls seat was little below Glyndebourne levels. It would also permit those who had applied too late for a run of performances sold out within hours of the opening of the booking a second bite at the box-office. The National were supporting their first opera season with a new translation by the novelist John Fowles of Molière's *Le Festin de Pierre*, the main source of Da Ponte's libretto apart from the Don Juan opera composed by Giuseppe Gazzaniga to a script by Giovanni Bertati, *Don Giovanni Tenorio, ossia il convitato di pietra* from which he drew most liberally.* A rather different view of the rake's progress, *Don Juan comes back from the War* by the Austro-Hungarian writer Odon von Horvath, was scheduled for the Cottesloe Theatre. There was to be an entertainment adapted from Byron's *Don Juan*. Max Frisch's *Don Juan* play was considered too cerebral; Bernard Shaw's *Man and Superman* was unavailable because the rights had been bought by the London impresario Eddie Kulukundis and leased to the Royal Shakespeare Company. Even so, *Don Juan at the N.T.*, as the season was called, looked as though it would provide substantial backing until an unofficial strike caused its wings to be clipped considerably.

---

* A most comprehensive account of *Don Giovanni*'s literary ancestors is given by E. J. Dent, *op. cit.*

Peter Hall prepared for his first days at Glyndebourne after a break of almost four years, feeling that he had an immense store of knowledge and yet no knowledge at all. 'A week before rehearsals begin there is a sudden moment of panic when you decide that you are not nearly familiar enough with the score and the libretto. That subsides and you begin to think how glorious it would be to rehearse for a month and then design the opera rather than moving into sets already existing, even though they have been made to your own specifications. Impossible dream.

'I go into a production with a set of points I want to put across rather than a total solution. Almost certainly some of them will be dropped in the same way that about thirty per cent of the scenery will be altered. [It was not.] I still have no idea at all how I will stage certain parts of the opera, including the Act I finale. But for the moment there is nothing more to be said until we all assemble on stage on the first day and share out responses. The cast with the exception of Ben Luxon is virtually unknown to me. It isn't like the theatre where the faces are all familiar and you usually begin by giving a little speech of welcome and then go on to suggest how you think the play will shape. On the first day at Glyndebourne we'll just take it from the top, ACT I SCENE I.'

PART TWO

The Rehearsals

1 Day One

Just before ten o'clock on Wednesday, 26 April 1977 Peter Hall got off the London–Eastbourne train at Lewes. His figure was as sombre as the John Bury sets already standing on the Glyndebourne stage, black leather coat, black trousers, black polo-neck sweater, two weighty black bags. The mood was of a totally different colour. Hall's new production of Ben Jonson's *Volpone* had opened the previous night at the National Theatre to prolonged applause. The notices in the morning papers, read on the way down, were almost uniformly favourable. Most directors would expect at least a day's break between the end of one assignment and the start of the next but sometimes praise is more effective than rest.

Glyndebourne's white minibus stopped on the way to pick up early season staff: secretaries, cooks, carpenters, gardeners. It was much like the school-bus collecting children for the start of a new term. For Hall the Sussex Downs, chilly but unruffled and already opulently green, made a break from the South Bank's theatre complex, already commonly known within the business as the Concrete Bunker. His first production away from the National in four years was not in any way going to be treated as a holiday, but at least it put fifty miles between him and the chores of administration. So Hall's thoughts were sunny, not least because at the time he had no idea how often he would be forced over the next six weeks to take the train back to London and the Bunker.

The theatre seemed scarcely to have stirred from its winter sleep. No names were written on the Message Board by the telephone exchange. The Courtyard Café concealed behind the stage ('STRICTLY ARTISTS AND STAFF ONLY') was empty and not even the first sandwich had been cut and wrapped. Singers who had not been to Glyndebourne before, which meant almost half the *Giovanni* cast, introduced themselves rather formally, new boys at the start of a new year.

Rehearsals at Glyndebourne begin and end punctually. Late arrivers are greeted with much the same hostility as members of the audience foolish enough to try to get into the auditorium once the curtain has gone up. The first *Giovanni* call was for 10.30 a.m., Act I Scene I. Miss Carden (Donna Anna), Mr Luxon (Don Giovanni), Mr Dean (Leporello) and M. Thau (Commendatore), please. At 10.25 the loudspeaker proved itself to be in working shape and the five-minute warning bells were rung. Within the theatre dust sheets covered all but the first two rows of the stalls and a space in the middle for the producer's desk. Water running through the radiators produced a continuous churning, visceral sound, but on that opening day no effect at all on the temperature. The house was as dank as the gardens outside and those who had been foolish enough to take off their coats quickly replaced them. At the first break scarves were fetched from travelling-bags and car-boots. Singers look after their throats inside and outside.

Peter Hall gathered his first quartet together in the front row of the stalls, joined by the two production assistants, Stewart Trotter who had worked with him at the National on *Volpone* and Timothy Tyrrel who was starting his second year at Glyndebourne as a staff producer. Jean Mallandaine, the chief répétiteur on *Don Giovanni*, listened from the pit and the stage managers, Geoffrey Gilbertson and Susan Usher, from in front of one of John Bury's black wooden balconies. Hall had claimed that he would not make a speech to his cast, but he broke his word. What was intended to be a personal introduction developed into a description of his method of working and a discussion of his basic views about *Don Giovanni*, a tutorial with the singers asking the questions.

In these opening minutes of conversation Hall showed his knack of producing a totally informal atmosphere. There was no suggestion of talking down in this particular tutorial.

'The trouble with a work like *Don Giovanni*,' he began, 'is that we all think we know it inside out. I'm far from convinced that this is so. What we are familiar with is an opera which has collected any number of accretions and traditions over the years, it is a picture which has been so covered with varnish that it is no longer possible to see the true lines and colours beneath. I think our first task is to take the varnish off and try to find out what is lying down there below.

'I'd hate to arrive with "my" production of *Giovanni* and in any case I hate staging things too early. In these opening days we'll simply take the opera scene by scene and see what emerges, this means working in the most relaxed way you can. I want the staging to come from you as much as from me. All I'd like to do at the moment is to put forward one or two basic ideas. I believe that disguise is an important theme in this opera. Mozart and Da Ponte were always interested in how little divides the servant from the master—and that most women are much the same in the dark. So, Stafford and Ben, please study one another as closely as possible. *Don Giovanni* is also about darkness, which was rather easier to suggest in an eighteenth-century theatre using candlelight than it is now. But that's a problem we'll have to wrestle with. The only other general point I would make now is that in this opera house it is possible to have a conversation with the audience. Most of Mozart's ensembles are constructed on this principle. Each character talks directly to the audience. It's almost impossible in a big house, but it's the life and blood of Mozart, and you can do it here. I want each of you to believe that you have a right to talk to the audience as you would to an individual. Pick a face, and then another, and try to buttonhole people.

'Now let's take it from the top, Scene I. What did happen up there in Anna's bedroom before the curtain rises? Did Giovanni have her or not? I don't know, but I'm suspicious. If an unexpected midnight marauder had come in through the window or made his way up the stairs and in by the door, then

Peter Hall on stage

Anna surely would have screamed a lot earlier than she did. I've an idea that Anna for the moment at least is besotted with this mysterious figure. Perhaps she even suspects it's Giovanni. After all *she* is trying to hold him back while he's trying to fight his way out.'

The conversation circled around the first of *Don Giovanni*'s ambiguities. The exact nature of the Anna–Giovanni encounter can never be defined with assurance, although one or two commentators on Mozart tend to give the impression that they were up there in the bedroom too. Hoffmann* tries to leave no doubt that Giovanni had his way with Anna who became yet another entry in Leporello's catalogue of conquests. Pierre Jean Jouve, in his scene-by-scene analysis of the opera, *Le Don Juan de Mozart*,† has no doubts either:

> *Donna Anna échevelée poursuit hors de sa maison un visiteur voilé.*
> *Elle veut l'atteindre; elle veut tout à la fois le chasser, le garder et le*
> *punir; surtout elle veut connaître le visage masqué, elle veut savoir qui*
> *est le Séducteur, qui a abusé d'elle.*
>
> Donna Anna, dishevelled, comes from her house in pursuit of a masked visitor. She wants to hold him back; she wants at the same time to chase him away, to keep him and to punish him; above all she wants to see the face behind the mask, to know the Seducer who has abused her.

Critics may be sure; Da Ponte is far from specific. Later in the act when Anna thinks she recognises Giovanni as the man who killed her father and raped (or tried to rape) her she is somewhat evasive in the story she tells Ottavio. (Recitative, '*Era già alquanto avanzata la notte*' — 'It was already quite late at night.') She tells of her struggles in the fierce grip of the figure who has come into her room, her cries for help, and even has the gall to tell Ottavio that in the first instance she took the intruder for him. It is an unconvincing narrative which gives the impression of being hastily tailored for Ottavio and it is far from precise about

---

* *op. cit.*
† *Le Don Juan de Mozart*, Pierre Jean Jouve (Librairie Universelle de France, Paris).

Giovanni's success or lack of it. There is not much difficulty in putting up an opposing case in which Giovanni's last days form a series of sexual disasters: he is rejected by Anna, pursued by Elvira who interests him no longer, foiled when he tries to have his way with Zerlina; he might not even have succeeded with Elvira's chambermaid.

In Tirso de Molina's play, *El Burlador de Sevilla*, which is generally reckoned to be the fountainhead of the Don Juan legend (although it is quite possible that someone else got there first), Donna Anna gets away unscathed. Don Juan's attempted rape of Donna Anna and the subsequent assassination of the Commendatore do not take place until the second act after he has had encounters with various other ladies. Just before he dies he goes to the trouble of saying that Donna Anna is still a virgin. Only the most cynical will believe that he is lying and having yet another joke at the expense of humanity.

Dent in his study of *Don Giovanni** follows Tirso's line and states quite categorically that Don Giovanni 'has no practical success with any of his so-called victims'. In part this might be a reaction against the Victorian view of Anna which turned her into a tragic figure after the fashion started by Hoffmann. Dent has little time for her and strips off the tragedy: '. . . it may be doubted whether she is really anything more than self-absorbed and aloof.'

Some critics, once possibly from a sense of decorum, brush aside the enigma of Anna's bedroom, but this is to evade the whole relationship between her and Giovanni. Ostensibly she is out to avenge the murder of her father, the Commendatore, just as in the graveyard the Statue promises to wait until his killer is brought to judgment. But she has her own conscience to square as well. If she in any way willingly submitted to Giovanni, then she was in part responsible for the death of her father. Elvira is frequently seen to be the nervous and neurotic woman in *Don Giovanni*; Anna, depending on the interpretation of the opening moments of the opera, may be the one whose mind is more torn by cares and guilt. The bitter memory, the *rimembranza amara* as

---

* *op. cit.*

Don Ottavio calls it, could bite far deeper than those around Donna Anna realise.

The discussion moved from what did or did not happen between the sheets to Don Giovanni's state of mind when he is pursued into the night by Anna. Ben Luxon thought that this was a situation Giovanni had dealt with a hundred times while he was providing new entries for Leporello's catalogue. Stafford Dean disagreed, stressing that Giovanni was in considerable personal danger. Consciously or unconsciously he was already taking on Leporello's colours, who at this moment fears for his own skin— '*Potessi almeno di quà partir*' ('If at least I could get away from here'). Peter Hall used this opening half-hour of discussion to sketch out a few views of Giovanni's character.

'Giovanni in these first moments is in danger, but in a way he likes it. He spends much of his adult life dicing with danger. He takes on fearlessly whatever fate happens to put before him. The killing of the Commendatore is the result of a dare. Giovanni does not stop to consider that he is an old man, that he is a fellow aristocrat and a fellow citizen of Seville. His only attitude is that if the Commendatore wants a fight then, fine, carry on. And may the stronger man win. He's daring God, or somebody, to manifest himself again. The fascinating side of Don Giovanni's character is that he has no conscience and no morality. We are all brought up to believe, and most of us like to believe, that if you behave as a shit then one day you will get your come-uppance. Giovanni is out to question all that.

'Don Giovanni mocks everything, sex, women, God. The reason why he invites all the peasants to the ball which concludes Act I—apart from his designs on Zerlina—is to deride a social occasion. When he calls for a toast and sings "*Viva la libertà*" he's really saying "Bugger the world". He forces the maskers into the same toast and delights in the fact that they sing it through their teeth.'

Perhaps Peter Hall thought he had gone too far into the opera at this moment and revealed too much of his hand rather than playing the cards singly during the rehearsals. A discussion was in danger of turning into a lecture and the singers were already too intent weighing and testing these concepts to produce any of their own for the moment. It was time to start singing. Ben Luxon, Stafford Dean and Joan Carden crossed the gangplank from the stalls across the orchestra pit to John Bury's raked stage, a dark blend of buff, brown and black linoleum diamonds.

The piano started to give out the opening bars of accompaniment to Leporello's lonely vigil outside Donna Anna's house, '*Notte e giorno faticar*', but Peter Hall stopped it at once and analysed with Stafford Dean those first words of the opera.

'The initial image we want is of a resentful servant who is locked outside while something good is probably going on upstairs. But that is only momentary. Basically I think that Leporello has a good deal of admiration for Don Giovanni and the closer we find master and man in these early days of rehearsal then the better it is likely to be, although that could well change later. [It did.] Da Ponte implies that one man stripped in bed is much the same as another. But we've got to remember that Leporello at heart is a coward. He is also very resentful—like a cowardly Figaro. He would like to be a gentleman.'

Ben Luxon took Peter Hall's point about the companionship of Giovanni and Leporello: 'I think they're very close and have a lot of fun together.' It was a theme he was to return to later when the balance of love and hate between master and servant had gone through multiple changes. Stafford Dean was more anxious to build the background of the character. How was it that a mere servant could both write and read, as both the catalogue and the inscription on the Commendatore's monument prove? Was the theory, put forward by some Mozartians, that Leporello had been brought up by priests and had subsequently taken against religion a tenable one? Dean added, accurately, that there was not much of the revolutionary in Leporello despite the remark in the opening recitative that he wanted to be a gentleman ('*Voglio far il gentiluomo*'); Leporello's main interest was in keeping his own position secure.

Peter Hall agreed. 'Leporello is no Figaro. He has no ambition to usurp his master's rôle in life and I certainly don't want to play it that way. But I do want to keep a certain amount of ambiguity for the moment. The whole opera has so many contradictory tones and there lies its difficulty and its fascination. If you play it as a straight comedy or a straight tragedy it does not work. That's why we've set it a little after 1800 so that the balance can be kept between the mockery and Enlightenment of the eighteenth century and the Romanticism of the nineteenth. I believe that the music often looks forward to Beethoven but also that much of it faces back the other way.' Another idea had slipped out of the Hall bag, so he quickly returned from theories to practicalities.

'Stafford, the theme of this opening monologue is the accepted irritation of being born on the wrong side of the tracks. You've got to put that across in a matter of minutes and the only way is to grab the audience in the almost confidential manner of a Frankie Howerd [the English comedian]. As I said earlier, choose someone to speak to and then someone else, and go on milking them the whole time.'

Hall strides to the front of the stage and puts on a very rough semblance of a Frankie Howerd face; Dean strips off his orange leather jacket for action; the central heating goes on gurgling; and the piano resumes after the intermission of speculation on the opening phrases of *Don Giovanni*.

The object of Leporello's jealousy, which turns to fear at the sound of a scuffle above, is the light in the window of one of John Bury's black-framed balconies. Leporello gives up grumbling about the life he has to lead in the middle of the night and makes himself scarce, which is easy enough on a darkened stage. The arrival of Giovanni and Anna, who is crying that she will not let him escape even if she dies in the attempt, is not so simple. The stage direction is merely that Giovanni, dressed in a long cloak and trying to hide his face from Anna, comes out of the Commendatore's house. This has been developed over the years so that certain libretti or synopses have Giovanni hurrying out of the palace or even running down the staircase. A wide-brimmed hat and a cloak are frequently used to conceal the face, although baritones reasonably enough complain that both hamper their crucial opening phrases. Peter Hall decided early on that a proper mask gave the minimum hindrance and the maximum cover. The real problem is how Anna and Giovanni move from bedroom to floor level in the very few minutes of music given them by Mozart.

The first suggestion, a romantic one, was that the couple should struggle briefly on the balcony watched by the apprehensive Leporello with Giovanni taking the quickest exit and leaping down on to the stage. Ben Luxon and Joan Carden duly sang and struggled, not too energetically. And Luxon leaped. There was a crash and a cry of anguish from Luxon, who had underestimated both the seven-foot drop and the rake of the stage and had landed on his right ankle rather than on the balls of both feet. Stafford Dean went to the front of the stage and asked the empty auditorium whether there was a Don Giovanni in the house. But the laughter died as it was realised that Ben Luxon was in some pain. He called for a pail of cold water, which was quickly brought.

It was now noon, time for Ottavio's first call. Leo Goeke, who had flown in from New York that morning, arrived on the dot and must have been a little surprised to find his Don Giovanni, trouser rolled up to the thigh, sitting in the middle of the stage with his right leg in a bucket. Peter Hall's productions have never had a reputation for being conventional, but this was something else. The props department exchanged the pail for a walking-stick, an appointment was made for Ben Luxon with a Lewes doctor after lunch so that the damage to the foot could be assessed, and the rehearsals went on.

The idea of the descent from the balcony to the stage was tacitly abandoned, although not before Luxon had remarked that if Giovanni really was going to make such an athletic arrival then he would like to see a demonstration leap or two by the production team. Thereafter Anna and Giovanni always came on stage at ground-level and just how they moved so rapidly from bedroom to garden was left to the imagination of the audience. The second series, though, took the risk and Giovanni reverted to the original idea of swinging over the balcony.

The very first minutes after the curtain rises presented problems and the ensuing duet between Anna and her assailant created more. In this instance there was too much rather than too little music before the Commendatore arrives in response to the shouts and scuffles. Peter Hall went back to Anna's possible obsession with her masked visitor:

'In some ways she probably does not want him to go. She is not even certain whether she wants help or not. Some of those cries in the score, *"Gente! Servi!"* ("Help! Servants!"), are marked *pianissimo*. It is quite clear though that she is desperate to find out who he is—Don Giovanni will have to have a mask which she tries to rip off. Giovanni's actions are ambiguous also. He could surely have overpowered Anna had he wanted to or merely called Leporello to help. But for a few moments he waits. I think he's enjoying the situation, taunting her with his disguise and enjoying her cries and her anguish. He's living dangerously, as we agreed at the very beginning, and we've got a chance here to establish him at once as a sadist, a man who revels in the distress of others, particularly if they are women. I've an idea too that Giovanni would give the Commendatore a sight of his face at the moment of death. The evil has got to be there from the word go.'

Ben Luxon scarcely looked the personification of evil as he hopped across the drizzle-dampened path to the staff restaurant with the walking-stick that was to be on loan from the props department for some time to come. The first session had lacked neither physical nor mental action. It had proved that taking an opera from the top might be the logical way of starting but it was not necessarily the easiest. Peter Hall seemed like a manager well satisfied with his team's performance despite the injury to his striker.

'At this juncture we're all asking where we go, what do we do. I don't think we should worry just now about either. Let's follow the music and see where it leads. I don't want our work to be settled yet awhile. That's for later.'

2 *Following On*

Ben Luxon's injury put a brake on rehearsals. The afternoon session was postponed so that a doctor's report could come from Lewes. It was that Luxon must put no weight on the ankle for about a week. He duly reappeared on crutches looking a little like a sea dog urging on his crew despite a blow from battle on the high seas. The blue fisherman's sweater, the blond beard and equally blond mane enforced the impression. There was a great deal of bonhomie—'How fast can you do the hundred yards, Stafford?' Luxon shouted at his Leporello as he hopped off homewards away from the Commendatore's corpse. This was on the surface. Below there were already worries. Most singers fret that their voice will not be at its peak for the moment when it really matters. Ben Luxon was already concerned that he might not be able to move round the stage as nimbly as needed on 31 May.

Timing was also going to be difficult. Giovanni is rarely off the stage during the opera and a man on two crutches moves at a different pace to a man on two legs. Peter Hall had intended to give over as much of the opening week as possible to Anna and Ottavio because of Leo Goeke's imminent departure for America, but there was a limit to the extent rehearsals could be rearranged. So he just went through the opera scene by scene, blocking out the first moves and sketching in the first ideas. He was careful though not to unleash again that flurry of theories which had emerged on the first morning. The aim was to experiment, to find the roughest of outlines rather than to seek the perfect solution to even the smallest scene.

'Try it again . . . let's have another go. We'll take it apart later.'
Hall was making full use of Glyndebourne's luxurious rehearsal
timetable by apparently squandering it in questions and
discussions. Part of the scheme was to knit the cast together by
giving them the impression that the first night was far, far away,
that there were neither worries nor pressures. This suggestion of
time rolling into the distance like the Sussex Downs may have
been a bit false but it was recuperative. Most opera-singers are
used to intensive rehearsals, sometimes only a matter of hours
before the curtain goes up. Glyndebourne needs and demands a
period of adjustment.

The style was familiar to Ben Luxon. Other singers found it
strange, including Stafford Dean who had been away for more
than ten years. He had changed his Leporello to fit in with the
requirements of different houses and rethought it from time to
time, notably for Günther Rennert's Munich production, but
had never been asked to strip the part right down to its skeleton.
Some basses with a hundred and fifty Leporellos beneath their
belt would have demurred at the Hall approach. Dean rarely
spoke against it.

The first days seemed even more baffling to the Donna Elvira,
Rosario Andrade, who spoke no English at all and was very
hesitant in French and Italian. Some of the barriers were broken
when Glyndebourne hired a Spanish interpreter from Brighton
to be on hand for all rehearsals. There was reluctance to do this
because a similar call some years earlier for an interpreter had
yielded a retired major who spoke fluent Portuguese and nothing
else. Even with the language problem partially solved, Madame
Andrade had clearly never come across a theatre which rehearsed
six hours a day, six days a week for a month before curtain up.

By the time Peter Hall was coming to the end of the first run-
through Glyndebourne itself had stirred into life. The chorus
had arrived, two dozen of them, mostly in their early twenties. The
house does not encourage long-term commitments in this area
and looks instead for singers who have just left music college and
need some stage experience before moving on to their first
comprimario rôles. Three years is advised as the maximum time at
Glyndebourne, although some like the atmosphere and the

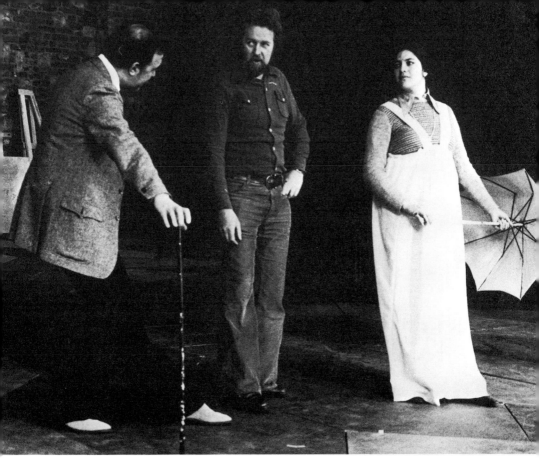

Peter Hall rehearses Benjamin Luxon (Don
Giovanni) and Rosario Andrade (Donna
Elvira)

Harvey's Ale—whose brewery can be sniffed by the River Ouse
when the wind is in the right direction—enough to linger on.
Richard Bradshaw, Glyndebourne's energetic Chorus Master,
had flown in from San Francisco, to which he was to return
before the season was a great deal older. Brian Dickie's twice-
weekly 10 a.m. meetings began, a kind of Citizens Advice Bureau
to which coaches, répétiteurs, assistant producers, stage
managers bring their problems. Dickie gives an almost house-
masterly impression of blandness as he deals with coughs
and colds, bad Italian pronunciation and singers late for
rehearsal. The blandness is deceptive: Dickie, whose job it is in
part to look after the singers, insisted on a day and a half off for

the *Giovanni* cast when the first run-through was complete on the very sensible grounds that some of the artists would be fatigued from a totally novel preparation method.

On the first Monday in May the box-office opened for the season. The usually empty foyer, still dank and cold, had a serpentine queue waiting on benches for the turn at the window. It was a cross between Gian Carlo Menotti's *The Consul* and the prelude to a rather wet village fête. Flasks of coffee were being shared and rugs were spread over the knees. Within an hour or so a notice went up to say that all *Don Giovanni* tickets were sold and before lunch another card announced that there were no more £5 seats for any of the operas that season. By mid-afternoon the queue had faded away; clearly it had comprised locals who knew just when to come for what they wanted.

Inside the theatre Peter Hall was making all he could of his last hours on the proper stage. In the first month the opening operas are split between the main auditorium, where as much as possible of the full set is erected, and the rehearsal stage overlooking the gardens where the working space of the theatre is reproduced without scenery that has to be flown. The stints in each are usually about five days. Individual coaching of both the principals and the understudies goes on behind the closed doors of studios scattered all over Glyndebourne. The only other rehearsal room, the Lily Davis, a large square gymnasium-type structure with glass doors that turn it into an oven when the sun shines, is generally reserved for the chorus. Practice is private, unlike Santa Fé for example where Mozart, Verdi, Cavalli and an obscure piece of Americana are likely to carry from open-air studios across the gardens, challenging each other for attention.

After five days of rehearsal and the testing with the piano of every note of the opera apart from the overture and the Leporello–Zerlina scene, which was to be omitted at Glynde-bourne as in every other stage performance I have seen,* Peter Hall was ready to assess what he had achieved.

'Let's begin with what is wrong, or rather what is missing. I confess that I have no idea how to end Act I, which is the only

---

* It is however included in Erich Leinsdorf's recording made for Decca.

area of the opera which worries me. When I first started to think about it, long before coming to Glyndebourne this time, I believed the answer might be to employ one or all of those stage bands and have Giovanni force his way through the crowd and out of trouble. Now I am turning against that particular solution. There is a great deal of music between the moment when Don Giovanni's number appears to be up, when the maskers as well as Masetto and Zerlina say that they know all about him ("*tutto, tutto già si sa*"), and the end of the act. And what about that pistol Ottavio flourishes in Giovanni's ear? If he fired it the opera would end then and there.

'Oddly enough, Da Ponte, whose directions we have been following almost to the letter so far, is very imprecise about the end of the act. He just lets it finish and it isn't even specified who is left on stage.'

Christopher Benn* noted that there is no music for the chorus during the final minutes. 'There is no point in the peasants singing with the soloists in the final ensemble, and after the turmoil aroused by Zerlina's screams they can conveniently fade out with the musicians, leaving the soloists alone for the final ensemble.' Benn is one of the few commentators to suggest that the stage could well be clear apart from the principal singers. Jouvet† in a lyrical passage has Giovanni winning the day by the bright steel of his sword and Dent merely castigates Da Ponte for writing a finale 'inferior to those of *Così* and *Figaro*', though he does not specify which act of the latter opera he is considering.

'The only definite thing at this moment is that there will be no swashbuckling finale. Swinging on chandeliers or fighting a way out with the help of a few servants is right against the spirit of the music. This is Giovanni's most vulnerable moment. He is cornered by his accusers on earth and has brought down the wrath of heaven, as we hear from that thunderclap which interrupts the finale. Perhaps we'll make something of that thunder.

'The Act II sextet in the courtyard is giving less trouble than I feared. I thought it might be the most difficult scene in the opera,

---

* *op. cit.*
† *op. cit.*

not least because everyone has to behave as though they really are in the dark. Elvira in particular is terrified of being left alone by the disguised Leporello. But we seem to be getting the right feeling there. I have still to work out the doors for the multiple arrivals and departures—I could do with an extra exit and perhaps we'll make one.

'The element which has given most satisfaction is the development of Don Giovanni's character. Ben has grasped the sadistic humour of the part and is transmitting that to everyone else. Everything that Giovanni does is savage, so there is no point for instance in playing Elvira as a fool—little satisfaction would come from savaging an idiot.

'There have been a few minor troubles in these opening days. Some of the cast are still not used to working with a director who says "I don't know" when asked what the next movement should be. I think we've got to keep the tension up in the second act, particularly at the beginning where Da Ponte does a little embroidery. [The first three scenes here are Da Ponte's invention. The Bertati–Gazzaniga Don Giovanni goes straight from the attempt on Zerlina to the graveyard.] The immediate work will be on Ottavio before he goes to America and on finding how to end the first act. I'm sure that when Giovanni hauls Leporello on stage, accusing him of rape and threatening to kill him, the action is for real. Theatre tradition is that Giovanni escapes. I am not sure that is right. I'm intrigued by the fact that Mozart appears to have his chorus on stage but does not give them any music. Besides, there is a Da Ponte direction where Zerlina re-enters from having been rumpled by Giovanni, which indicates that the stage clears apart from the principals.'

The singers had already dispersed for their break of a day and a half. Peter Hall packed his bags for London and left his low-ceilinged apartment in Glynde Place, a stately home midway between the theatre and Glynde station which houses artists in season. The problems of the Act I finale and the National Theatre were to occupy the next thirty-six hours. Stewart Trotter and John Bury stayed down in Sussex to devise the lighting of a pitchy set.

3 Don Ottavio

On his return Peter Hall had only a couple of days with Leo Goeke before the American tenor flew back home to fulfil his concert engagements. In principle an absent Ottavio should not cause too much disruption to rehearsals. He always stands to one side of the action, unwilling to dirty his hands with physical action or even the powder from a pistol shot. Ottavio's connection with the main thread of the action is solely through Donna Anna; he is her not so humble suitor and he never appears without her. Together they form an aristocratic corner of Seville and would never in the ordinary run of events come into contact with the Zerlinas and Masettos of this world; they only befriend Elvira out of chivalrous courtesy to a woman with a semblance of decent upbringing beneath a distraught exterior.

Hall recognised Ottavio's remoteness, but early on thought that it should be questioned rather than accepted. So he decided to spend as many of those hours as possible before Goeke's departure on the scenes involving Ottavio and Anna as well as calling in the Series II Ottavio, Philip Langridge, for the period Goeke was away. The substitution was a risk and slight break in protocol: Langridge as a member of the July cast was officially in Stewart Trotter's hands as far as production was concerned, and in musical background and temperament he was dissimilar to Goeke. Hall took a chance that in two or three rehearsals he could develop his ideas about Ottavio sufficiently to put them on ice until Leo Goeke returned in the middle of May.

From the start Hall had decided to add some twenty years to Ottavio's 'normal' age. There is no guidance in Da Ponte about Ottavio's maturity, or lack of it, and he is simply described as being betrothed to Donna Anna. The age of betrothal knows no limits but that of consent. In all too many productions Ottavio is stripped of identity and treated as a tenor who is lucky enough to have two of Mozart's most heart-rending arias to sing. If he can get his larynx around them to the satisfaction of the conductor and the audience, then his appearance and his birthday are not too important. Ottavios come dapper, like Alfredo Kraus in Karajan's Salzburg production who chose the point on the stage closest to the stalls for both his numbers, or burly and mellifluous like Stuart Burrows. But they rarely appear very involved. Only once have I heard a genuinely aggressive Ottavio and that was when Robert Tear took the part for Scottish Opera. Bald-pated, angrily determined to kill those who had killed, Tear looked like a figure from a Jacobean melodrama and did not hesitate to show his fury when Anna eventually rejects Ottavio in the finale. *Don Giovanni* had become not so much the punishment of a libertine as the revenger's tragedy.

Hall had no intention of turning Ottavio into a bully boy, or man, but wanted to move as far as possible from Brigid Brophy's milksop and even the unobtrusive figure that Hoffmann's narrator notes from his box: 'Donna Anna and Ottavio appear; a neat, well-dressed, well-behaved little man, one and twenty years of age, at most.' The emphasis was to be on authority and the additional years seemed to Hall to be the most effective way of establishing rectitude and control. 'I want Ottavio, contrary to many interpretations, to be very cool and quite able to take command of each situation as it arises. Once the Commendatore is dead Ottavio becomes the moral centre of the story, the man of total integrity who is shocked by those who depart from his own ethical code.'

William Mann in his study of *Don Giovanni** drew attention to the modern production of the opera by Virginio Puecher in which

---

* *The Operas of Mozart*, William Mann (Cassell, London and Oxford University Press, New York).

**Leo Goeke in his first rôle at Glyndebourne,
Tom in *The Rake's Progress*, sets by David
Hockney, production by John Cox**

Ottavio was the one sympathetic person in a cast of thoroughly dislikeable characters. That particular interpretation has rarely been followed and Hall was little concerned with making Ottavio in any way alluring. Courtesy and a very strict code of ethics were to be the cornerstones of the character.

Leo Goeke is a reasonably experienced Glyndebourne hand. He took the part of Tom Rakewell in the new 1975 production of Stravinsky's *The Rake's Progress* and was ready to repeat the part in the 1977 revival when his *Don Giovanni* series was complete; he also appeared as Flamand in *Capriccio* in 1973. The face is round, almost babyish under waves of chestnut hair. Goeke took considerable care of his appearance even in these early rehearsals, and listened carefully to Hall's theories about the character and why Ottavio in this production should be in his late forties. Hall admitted privately that he would have preferred an older singer, but there are very few Mozart tenors of the right age within Glyndebourne's price bracket. Goeke was not too happy about putting on age and greying his hair: most tenors spend time taking age off before facing the footlights. But this argument was tacitly postponed until his return ten days later.

Vocally Leo Goeke showed little fear of the part. The florid, aristocratic style of '*Il mio tesoro*' in Act II, where Ottavio declares that Giovanni will be brought to justice, was well within his compass. So was the earlier '*Dalla sua pace*', a less demanding aria, which Mozart wrote in for Antonio Morella, the tenor who sang the rôle at the Vienna première. Goeke had done the part twenty times or so, first for New York's City Center Opera and then for the Met, both at the Lincoln Center and on tour. On these occasions there had been little dismantling of Ottavio's thoughts and motives.

Ottavio's very first entry, when he is summoned by Donna Anna, prompts speculation on where he has been while Giovanni was upstairs in the bedroom. Anna goes off to fetch him as soon as Giovanni and the Commendatore confront one another; she returns with him a few minutes and several pages of music later. Both, of course, arrive on the scene too late. Has Ottavio been spending the night at the Commendatore's house, or perhaps taking a very late nightcap with him, an irony which Giovanni would surely have appreciated? Or is he just a very close neighbour, as Hoffmann assumes?

'It is probable that he [Ottavio], being Donna Anna's betrothed, dwells in the same street, being so quickly summoned; had he hurried up at the first noise, which he doubtless heard, he might have saved the father; but he stayed to dress, and altogether is not fond of exposing himself at night.' Hoffmann, like so many others, is not fond of Ottavio and implies that he is partly guilty of the Commendatore's assassination.

Hall was more concerned to establish the correctness of Ottavio's behaviour in this opening scene. He dismissed the possibility, often assumed, that Anna really thought that Ottavio was her lover of a few minutes ago. It makes her out to be a liar later in the opera when she describes to him what happened in the bedroom, but it avoids the need, emphasised in some productions, for Ottavio and Giovanni to look roughly alike. 'The first element I want to stress in Ottavio is his great charm and consideration towards his social inferiors. He is very courteous to the servants who arrive with him and Anna. He is also totally practical. When Anna faints at the sight of her father's corpse Ottavio quietly asks for the smelling salts to be brought and, equally quietly, he asks for the body to be removed. There is not a trace of roughness in Ottavio's behaviour just as there is none in the music he is given to sing.'

Tenor and soprano stalked around the dead Commendatore like vultures trying to select the meatiest portion of a corpse. Goeke suggested that Ottavio should recognise the body of the Commendatore before Anna and then break the truth very gently. Hall agrees, although later in the run of the production this move was changed. 'I'm trying to get at Ottavio's compassion and Anna's guilt,' said Hall. She knows that what occurred above led to her father's death and so her cry for vengeance becomes all that more impassioned. Ottavio offers love and readiness to take the place of her father ('*Hai sposo e padre in me*'); Anna is only interested in revenge ('*Ah! vendicar*'). She forces Ottavio into a declaration of retribution rather than fidelity, although his hasty agreement is made in the name of love ('*al nostro amor*').

They experimented with having Ottavio stand on the very spot from which the Commendatore's body was taken for the duet which ends the first scene. The implication is that he is already her father-substitute. But the move was reckoned to be over-subtle and was dropped. Instead Hall proposed that they sing out directly to the audience, confiding their emotions not to one another but to the public. Within a few minutes the idea of Suspended Time was developed, which was soon to dominate so much of the production. Hall wanted the moments to be clearly defined when the characters, individually or together, expressed their thoughts rather than conversed with one another. When the first lighting rehearsals began, he used the brightest possible lighting on the faces while keeping the rest of the stage as dark as possible. Such signposts were unavailable in the daylit rehearsal room and Hall merely moved his Anna and Ottavio as far forward as possible.

'I don't believe at the end of this scene Anna and Ottavio are talking to each other at all. They are thinking about themselves— "*Vammi ondeggiando il cor*" ("My heart is wavering"). Address the audience directly just as Leporello does his opening recitative. I don't want any middle ground. Characters in Mozart either talk directly to the house or to each other. If there is a middle ground, the production descends into feeble generalities.'

Later that day the same technique was used for '*Dalla sua pace*', the only aria in the opera where the singer is unattended by any other character. It follows Anna's sudden recognition that Giovanni is the murderer of her father and her aria '*Or sai chi l'onore*'. Ottavio, the good aristocrat, is taken aback by the possibility that a gentleman could have committed such a crime and he goes on to link his peace of mind and his very life to Anna's contentment. The sentiments are elevated and so are the notes. Critics from Dent onwards have acknowledged the style and dismissed the contents: ' "*Dalla sua pace*", beautiful as it is, falls very flat after the energetic outburst of Anna's exit aria.' Dent as ever is too hard on Ottavio; the effect of the aria depends on who sings it and how.

Peter Hall was concerned with deportment. 'I don't want you to give the impression of a man who is being watched,' he said to

'**Lascia, o cara**': Donna Anna (Horiana Branisteanu) and Don Ottavio (Philip Langridge), of the Series II cast

Goeke. 'When you get to the aria I want a naked sharing of your emotions: here is a man baring his heart and revealing everything that he feels to his closest confidant, the audience. The recitative in contrast is hard and cold. Ottavio is talking of honour and vengeance as well as the need to discover the truth. It's all a little formal—the Spanish nobleman is once again behaving perfectly correctly in the circumstances—and there should be no hint of what is to come. Then the aria arrives and with it the sudden outburst of his real feelings.'

Goeke wonders if it should go that way. 'Doesn't the aria split down? Isn't half of it private and half of it a desire to share my thoughts? After all, the reprise is *pianissimo* and maybe Ottavio should address those words to himself?' Peter Hall disagreed and thought that would be a regression. John Pritchard, who had now come on to the rehearsal stage, sided with Hall. 'Don't worry about the *pianissimo*. More often than not the most important things are spoken very softly. This is the aria which, despite the fact that it was only added at the Vienna première, takes you inside Ottavio.' Goeke replied a trifle tartly, 'I'm trying to get inside him, but it's not as easy as it seems. The point surely is that the recitative is about Don Giovanni, and Ottavio's shock at his behaviour, while the aria is about Donna Anna.'

No one demurred. Goeke took it again and a third time. Hall and Pritchard conferred and agreed that it was 'very honest'. With that the tenor went off to North America and other composers.

Leo Goeke was away until 17 May. Peter Hall worked steadily with Philip Langridge, the Series II Ottavio, but gave the impression of holding back. He was not trying to discover the rôle through Langridge for the basic reason that Langridge, however hard he tried, was not part of Hall's team. Would Ottavio have turned out differently had Goeke been there throughout rehearsals? He might have emerged even stronger because feeling was moving towards Puecher's highly sympathetic interpretation and away from Moberly, who found him insufferable and Shaw who turned him into the flabby Octavius (Ricky Ticky Tavy) of *Man and Superman*. A few tried to argue that Ottavio was gaining too much power, claiming that the only life he had on stage was his connection with Anna; he was another faceless Mozart tenor in the mould of Belmonte in *Entführung* who is only there by courtesy of Constanze. This line of reasoning was rejected by both Pritchard and Hall, with the latter in particular insisting that once the Commendatore has gone Ottavio has to be the moral force of an immoral opera. He may move slowly, but that is because he is by nature cautious and honourable. He does not become totally convinced of Giovanni's guilt until after the sextet in Act II. Before '*Il mio tesoro*' he talks of the forces of law and order seeing that justice is done. Despite Anna's wishes he does not choose instant personal vengeance.

The only change in Ottavio was to age him further. Hall started talking in terms of him being fifty rather than in his late forties, adding that it was much easier to take years off than to put them on. Goeke on his return did not initially much care for the elderly interpretation devised for him any more than he appeared to like the formal black attire for walking out with Anna, which made him look a little like Jane Austen's Mr Knightley.

Finally the last problems were resolved. It was decided for the purpose of the opening scene that Ottavio lived, following Hoffmann's suggestion, a few doors away from Anna. But, contrary to Hoffmann, he arrived unstockinged and with a coat thrown over his nightclothes. After some discussion Ottavio's tiny piece of recitative after Donna Anna's second act aria, '*Non mi dir*', was excised, the only cut in the score apart from the Leporello–Zerlina scene. Hall wanted it in, claiming that it made an effective dissolve to the scene; Pritchard remarked that they were creating an opera, not a film, and wanted it out; Luxon mocked them both by claiming that it was one of his favourite pieces of music and untouchable. Out it went. And back it came in Series II when Haitink took over as conductor.

Ottavio was brought further to the footlights for his final appeal to Anna, '*Or che tutti . . .*', so that his reaction to her refusal of marriage could be made that much more visible to the audience. Ottavio is the loser and will continue his well-heeled bachelorhood while Anna lives on in the shadow of her father.

The portrait of Ottavio, which began and ended by owing nothing to convention, was complete, a Spanish gentleman who lives correctly and judges fairly within a moral code established by his ancestors. Many of the characters in Mozart's operas, led by Giovanni himself, are opportunists pursuing their pleasures at the very first possible chance. Life has taught them to be suspicious and envious. Ottavio in contrast is the good judge who refuses to think evil of anyone until there is total proof. At the very end of the opera he receives all Anna's rebuffs to his declarations of support with apparent equanimity. Christopher Benn wrote that 'Ottavio should be presented as a "dandy", and he should have a large fancy lace handkerchief hanging from his sleeve!' At Glyndebourne Hall and Goeke together made him an almost puritan figure of unimpeachable good manners.

4 Thunder and Lightning

There are two major weather reports in *Don Giovanni*. When Giovanni leaps over the wall into the graveyard he remarks that it is as bright as day, a fine night (*'Che bella notte'*) for hunting girls. Certainly it has to be light enough to see the Statue when he nods his head in acceptance of the supper invitation to come. Earlier the elements have been less kindly. At the end of Act I a roll of thunder goes through the orchestra when Giovanni is cornered by his accusers. In some productions it is almost obliterated by the pandemonium on stage as Giovanni is preparing to fight his way out, but it is there in the score and the libretto. Anna, Elvira, Ottavio and Zerlina all hear the sound of revenge (*'Odi il tuon della vendetta!'*); Giovanni and Leporello hardly need telling. *'Un' orrible tempesta minacciando'*, a terrible storm is threatening.

Mozart for a few moments is using the storm without to reflect the human story within, a piece of musical mirroring which was to be used by many composers subsequently. The scene in the Wolf's Glen in Weber's *Der Freischütz* and the final act of Verdi's *Rigoletto* are but two obvious examples. In *Don Giovanni* the thunderstorm is also used in the classical sense of noting the displeasure of the gods, or the Almighty. For the first time in the opera Giovanni's misdeeds have been noted and the rumbling overhead is a warning to mend his ways. Human justice of a sort has been achieved in that rape has been prevented and lies have been found out, but judgment of another kind awaits above. It is moments such as this which put *Don Giovanni* at the very watershed between the Romantic and Classical movements.

The Series II cast in the Act I finale: Donna
Anna (Horiana Branisteanu), Donna Elvira
(Rachel Yakar), Leporello (Richard Van
Allan), Don Giovanni (Thomas Allen),
Zerlina (Adrienne Csengery), Masetto (John
Rawnsley)

The thunderstorm, brief though it is, has to be seen in all
aspects and with all its implications. Pierre Jean Jouve* analyses
it fully and astutely in his *Don Giovanni* and comes to the
reasonable conclusion that although the *tempesta* is a physical
phenomenon it is also a foretaste of what is to come: the final
punishment of Giovanni, which can only be death.

The two claps of thunder in the orchestra were to provide
Peter Hall with the idea of how to bring down the curtain and
they were also to colour the whole of that first act. But in early
May while he was edging towards a solution he concentrated on

---

* *op. cit.*

Giovanni's state of mind when for a few seconds his grip on the situation is loosened. He has used Leporello as a scapegoat, hauled him in front of the guests at the ball and accused him of rape. The chances of getting away with this impromptu move are slim, although it is more than likely that Leporello had taken the rap a time or two before. Hall took Luxon aside.

'It must be a demonstration, Ben, that you are going to kill Leporello if needs be. Giovanni is at his most dangerous when he has been crossed or is in a nasty corner. He is a man who is more than capable of running people through, as he has already proved with the Commendatore, and he wouldn't hesitate to do it again.

'We need fear in this scene. Giovanni suddenly realises that the three maskers know all about him and what he's been up to in Seville. Anna and Elvira have had first-hand experience and even the incredulous Ottavio is beginning to be worried. For the first time in his life Don Giovanni isn't enjoying living dangerously any more. I want you to play it as though you're scared within your guts and then to recover yourself quickly. Even Leporello, who has had a narrow escape, sees that Giovanni is not himself ("*E confusa la sua testa*").

'Then out of the fear comes defiance. He almost throws down a challenge to heaven. He's prepared to experiment, to take a chance on seeing what it's like to die. At the thunderclap I want the accusers to recognise that God is on their side ("*Trema, trema, scellerato*"—"Tremble, tremble, villain"), which is in a mood quite different from the pleasure they took a few minutes before in telling him that they knew everything.'

John Pritchard looked forward. 'Giovanni is frightened, but only for a moment. In the next act when heaven is heard again in the form of the Statue he shows no fear at all. Quite the contrary. I feel we should emphasise his gesture of defiance, which is a way of telling the audience that there is more to follow. And maybe his accusers, despite their strength of numbers, should fall back.'

Hall called for a complete run-through and then another one, bringing the principals to the very front of the stage, led by Giovanni. It was the very reverse of convention which has Giovanni and Leporello backing away from their accusers so that they can fight or scurry away into the darkness as the curtain comes down. 'We've got to emphasise the anarchy in this scene. It's there when Giovanni proposes the toast to liberty. When he raises his glass in "*Viva la libertà*", he doesn't mean it for one moment and nor do the peasants when they are called on to echo it. It comes even more strongly when Giovanni throws down the gauntlet to heaven. I want to bring out the idea of an individual taking on all comers. It is very *Sturm und Drang*, it's the challenge of Romanticism, and it's all there in the thunderclaps.'

The experiments continued with the principals coming further and further down stage, a flock of sheep under the spell of Giovanni. The whole idea of escape was being jettisoned and replaced by a challenge. Accused and accusers faced not one another but the audience—Suspended Time again. And Giovanni, as Pritchard had suggested, displayed not fear but an almost superhuman arrogance which is precisely the emotion given to him by Da Ponte: '*Se cadesse ancora il mondo . . . nulla mai temer mi fa*'—'Even if the world should fall apart nothing will ever make me be afraid.'

Hall became excited with the solution and one of the most successful rehearsals he had had so far. Days go by when problems are approached, then skirted or shelved. These are the times which feel routine and therefore dull and drear, when the adrenalin for one reason or another ceases to flow and the preparation of even a Mozart opera seems little more exciting than running through a ledger of figures and ensuring that the totals are correct at the end. Pleasure comes when a discovery is made which appears so utterly and totally right that the only surprise derives from the fact no one had thought of it before.

The proposal that the finale to Act I should end on a challenge, not a scurry, completely in accordance with Da Ponte, sent Hall off to the props room. What was Glyndebourne's largest thunder sheet and how much could it be amplified? There were discussions with John Pritchard on just how forceful the sound could be made without upsetting the musical balance, and talks with John Bury on the lighting of the scene.

The 'frozen' address to the audience at the end of the act began to have its effects on the earlier. Stewart Trotter argued that if there was to be no physical action here in the Act I finale, then the

opening of the opera should be equally cool. Suggestions that
Leporello and Giovanni should make a rapid exit after the killing
of the Commendatore, and possibly even be glimpsed by Anna
returning with Ottavio, were vetoed. If there was one frantic
escape then it should be followed by another. Instead there was
an inclination towards a dark tableau, sharply lit from the back,
which pushed the opera far over towards the Romantic
movement.

Having given the production a nudge in the direction of
darkness and judgment from above, Hall was anxious to go
further. There were no rewards in being cautious, in trimming or
in doubting. It was decided that the principals should control the
stage alone. There was no valid reason for keeping on as
spectators the peasants Giovanni had invited to the ball. They
were made to skulk off at the first sign of trouble, followed by the
servants who had been instructed to ply them with food and
drink, and the triple band engaged for the occasion. The
challenge was to be made on a stage stripped of everyone apart
from those who, according to Mozart and Da Ponte, had
something specific to say and to sing.

'*Viva la libertà!*': Don Giovanni (Benjamin
Luxon), Leporello (Stafford Dean) and the
maskers

By the time of the first dress rehearsal there was no reluctance to give the finale its full effect. The stage darkened and the lights flickered at the roll of thunder. The windows at the back of the stage flew open as the first gust of wind attacked them, the curtains billowed and the chandeliers began to swing. When Giovanni and the avengers moved down to confront the audience the stage suggested Castle Dracula in Transylvania rather than Giovanni's well-appointed *casinetto* in Seville. The mood had changed as abruptly as the score: a few minutes earlier the peasants had been imitating their social superiors. Hall had been meticulous about coaching their behaviour at Giovanni's party. He had even insisted, to the temporary alarm of the choreographer, Pauline Grant, that all of them, including Zerlina and Masetto, should arrive in clogs, which they take off when the stage orchestras start playing.

'I don't want you to turn to the audience and say, "Look, I'm a peasant and I don't know how to dance except in my own style!" You've been invited to a strange place so you take refuge in the mockery of those who have brought you here. Imitate the movements of Elvira, Anna, Ottavio. Take the piss out of them, because the musicians are half on your side. When they're playing the minuet you watch, you learn it and then you mock it, then at the moment your own music is played you can show off your expertise. That's why the three stage bands play such socially different dances—from minuet to country dance—all at the same time. So I want the clogs on, off and then on again. [The chorus behaved as obediently as well-trained schoolboys using galoshes to cross the quadrangle from one classroom to another.] The peasants, apart from Masetto, who is constantly suspicious, are only aware of the pleasures of the moment while the aristos, the three maskers, know very well that this is something much more than a Brueghel country dance.'

On Glyndebourne's narrow stage the actual enticement of Zerlina by Giovanni away from the dancers needed a good deal of rehearsal, as did the reaction of Masetto. Both were obscured by too many bodies which had to be thinned out. But the contrast between the two halves of the finale, the apparent jollity at the beginning and the thunderous judgment from above at the end, had been decided. Ben Luxon had devised a mocking bow to the audience at the moment the curtain fell, which left no doubt at all about who was in command for the time being. This solution had its effect on the first-night audience who were taken by surprise but then were anxious to show their appreciation. The critics in the national press for the most part took a contrary view. Some ignored it; others, such as Peter Heyworth in *The Observer*, deplored it. In a generally very complimentary notice he described the first-act curtain as 'unconvincing'. Desmond Shawe-Taylor in *The Sunday Times*, also generally much in favour of the production, complained that it was not explained how Don Giovanni managed to slip the net closing around him. It was left to the playwright Peter Shaffer in a letter to *The Times* some days later to describe Hall's Act I finale as 'one of the most thrilling and satisfying moments I have ever received in an opera house'. His response to the ideas behind the scene is so acute that the letter is well worth quoting in full:

I write in support of Peter Hall and his excellent production of *Don Giovanni* at Glyndebourne. Every review of it I have read has denounced him for wilfully spoiling the all-important end of the First Act—the crown of the arch—by not permitting the Great Seducer a spectacular escape from his vengeful accusers. I was interested in this general response, since Mr Hall's direction of the scene in question had offered me personally one of the most thrilling and satisfying moments I have ever received in an opera house.

Truth to tell this climax, as traditionally played, has always seemed to me to be a weirdly feeble affair. It usually involved a good deal of 'We'll-get-you-yet!' gesturing from three principal singers; a mute ring of chorus members in peasant blouses making 'Whatever-next?' faces for all they're worth; five seconds of 'My-turn-your-turn' swordplay, and five more of muddled escape for the Don set to music quite obviously too brief for the purpose. Mr Hall's version has achieved the near-miracle of changing this pointless carry-on into an immense and coherent climax, simply by respecting the original libretto.

The fact is that the author, Da Ponte, doesn't call for an escape in any form at all. On the contrary, he makes Giovanni stand his ground and cry out for all to hear: 'Let the world fall, nothing will make me afraid!' Faithful as usual to his writer, Mr Hall virtually does make the world fall, and then shows us the Don hurling out an extraordinary gesture of defiance as it does.

I shall long remember the moment after Zerlina screamed in sexual fear and the crowd of peasants, like unwilling guests in De Sade's castle, scrambled away in their clogs. Suddenly lightning ripped the air; the casement at the back flew open; the heavy cartwheel lamps began to sway from the ceiling, and the darkening chamber all at once seemed to pitch like the cabin of a doomed ship in a rising storm. Through that stage window had burst the great wind of Legend. A provincial Spanish saloon was transformed before our eyes into a place of mythical events.

Most certainly this Don Giovanni did not escape through a backcloth, or into wings. Quite the reverse, he stalked *towards* us through the disintegrating world, a desperate figure in a black dream, flanked by black enemies, until he reached the very lip of the stage where he stood, scared but unyielding in the centre of this mental hurricane, to make the audience a savage, crooked bow—the same bow we had seen him make to the women he had seduced and then abandoned. Marvellous!

At one stroke Hall had solved the central problem of directing *Don Giovanni*. By making the scene *demonic*, he could finally link the two disparate acts of this strange piece. By conjuring a surrealist storm in a dining-room at the end of Act I, he could convincingly accommodate a chorus of devils singing under a dining-table at the end of Act II. And by choosing domestic Goya to begin the opera—all those grilles and parasols—he could choose black Goya to fulfil and then end it, and so unify what in my experience has never been unified before.

Typically, this stroke—theatrically beautiful and totally faithful to the libretto—was the one to be singled out for special attack by the majority of critics. On reflection I cannot claim to be too surprised: but I am still, after all these years of reading musical journalism, disappointed by encountering the staleness of response, indifference to aesthetics, and sheer unfairness which seem to characterise so much of it.

The success of the thunder in the finale began to create storm clouds which, it could be argued, are announced in the overture, and even rain in the earlier scenes. Umbrellas sprouted on stage like mushrooms on a warm and wet September morning. In the second act the state of the sky did not matter too much, only the darkness was important, but the climate in the first half of the opera had become unsettled, if not squally. As the weather worsened so the jokes proliferated: Singin' in the rain, *Les Parapluies de Séville*.

The umbrellas were first used as a disguise. At the start of the second scene Elvira arrives in search of Giovanni, the evil man who abandoned her in Burgos, as she announces in her aria '*Ah! chi mi dice mai*' ('Ah! who will ever tell me'). Don Giovanni and Leporello step aside and observe her but fail to recognise her

Don Giovanni on tour: Donna Elvira (Rosalind Plowright), not yet recognised by Don Giovanni (Thomas Allen) and Leporello Malcolm King)

until she has finished what she has to sing, otherwise they would never have been foolish enough to approach her and be recognised in turn. More often than not Elvira's face is covered by a scarf over a broad-brimmed hat and she is accompanied by a few servants carrying her bags from the staging post to the hotel where she is staying in Seville. Hall found this approach unconvincing and determined to have the stage clear of followers. The point is well made by Christopher Benn that if Elvira arrives with a serving maid, then Giovanni would scarcely have waited until the second act before making his attempt on her.

Elvira's natural shield was an umbrella which concealed her face from Leporello and Giovanni. After a number of re-positionings they eventually watched her from well upstage, which allowed the audience full view of her. The umbrella in turn prompted the idea of a rainy morning with a bedraggled Elvira arriving angry and exhausted after a night's fruitless search for Giovanni. The aria was an expression of despair at her total lack of success and a last general plea for assistance. Da Ponte is imprecise about the setting, but Hall decided that it should take place very soon after the killing of the Commendatore, perhaps no more than a few hours later. 'I think it's important to keep the continuity of both the action and the weather. Giovanni has only just escaped from the first adventure that we see, yet he's spry and game enough to have another go at the first opportunity. He brushes aside Leporello's complaint about the life he is leading and immediately gets wind of a woman. ("*Zitto! mi pare sentir odor di femmina!*") I want to keep an element of dark and cloud so that the sun does not really break through until the arrival of the peasants in the following scene.'

The approach cannot be faulted on either the words or the mood of the music. Leporello, when he has been won round not for the last time by Giovanni, announces that it is dawn ('*l'alba chiara*') and there is nothing to suggest that anything more untoward has happened since the Commendatore received a thrust through the heart. Certainly the chorus led by Zerlina and Masetto, '*Giovinette, che fate all'amore*', a variation on the Gather Ye Rosebuds theme, is the first moment of jollity in a hitherto sombre opera, unless the Leporello has been crude enough to milk the audience for too many laughs in the Catalogue Song. In the later rehearsals Hall stressed the continuity by having a flash of lightning split the sky at the beginning of this second scene and by providing Leporello with a further umbrella for the opening words of the opera so that his vigil outside the Commendatore's house appeared as wet and as miserable as possible.

The other umbrellas were reserved for the arrival of the peasants on their way to marry Zerlina and Masetto in what is described without much justification, as John Bury had already noted, as Scene III. Just where they meet Giovanni and Leporello is an open point and just why they have stopped is a matter for the producer to decide. Da Ponte offers no help. Hall once again turned to the weather for inspiration and made a break in the clouds an excuse for a halt for food and drink.

During the first run-through it was decided that the peasants were on the spree, out for all the alcohol and sex available. Giovanni's instructions to Leporello to take them off to his castle and ply them with more liquor were easy enough to fulfil, as Leporello reports just before '*Finch'han dal vino*'. Several of them are fuddled already—'*son già mezzi ubbriacchi*'—by the time Giovanni decides on another party. The intention was to bring the peasants on in two carts, one for the girls and one for the boys, drawn by a couple of donkeys. Stewart Trotter took the first chorus rehearsal for this scene while Peter Hall returned to London to have his sinuses X-rayed. The donkeys, who were being saved for the return to the main theatre stage, were also absentees.

Trotter succeeded in transmitting some of the Hall enthusiasm: 'This is the equivalent of a Cockney wedding with everyone dressed up to the nines on their way to church. The worst thing that could happen is the rain that has been tipping down. Even under the umbrellas they've been getting wet and the donkeys don't like it much either. So there's an impromptu booze-up. The food and bottles are loaded off the carts in a moment of wickedness. It should have been saved until after the marriage service but Zerlina proposes that they should go crazy and have it now.'

There was more than a touch of Peter Hall's film of Suffolk country life, *Akenfield*, about the scene with its pastoral parasols/umbrellas and flowered hats. But eventually both the bottles and the carts and donkeys proved more difficult to manage on stage than on screen. The donkeys were dismissed early on. The rehearsal labelled DONKEY TECHNICAL on Hall's return lasted less than an hour. The two beasts had a dozen humans apiece to tug and they did not much care for it, despite the fact that one had already had operatic experience some years ago pulling on Dr Dulcamara's travelling caravan in *L'elisir d'amore*. They moved slowly and sometimes not at all. In no way could they get on and off stage in the time allowed them by Mozart. They made a great deal of noise and one of the sopranos complained that they were pungent. Peter Hall was quite philosophic about the affair. He wanted donkeys so that the rustic identity of the chorus could be established at once and the only way of knowing whether the idea worked or not was to try it. He had hoped to have a camel on stage at Covent Garden when he was preparing *Moses und Aaron*, but that too went back to the zoo. So the donkeys returned to their pastures while humans pulled the carts.

The unloading of the carts and particularly the bottles, which made almost as much din as the donkeys, also gave problems, disrupting the aggression of Masetto's sole aria '*Ho capito*'. Far into rehearsals it was decided to curtail the picnic and have the wedding party stop at a pub (Elvira's lodgings) so that the stage hands could bring out the drink with a minimum of noise and delay. An inn sign was swiftly ordered from the workshops and slung over the balcony, but on the opening night it was so dark and insignificant that most of the audience would have passed this particular tavern by. The carts stayed and so did the umbrellas and the rain. Seville was in danger of becoming somewhat gloomy after the first dress rehearsal, but Peter Hall had decided for the time being that the lightness should come from the music and singers and not from the skies.

5 *The Stone Guest*

Pierre Thau, the Commendatore, was making his first appearance at Glyndebourne. He gave the impression of a well-to-do French businessman on holiday, immaculately turned out in cashmere sweaters and carefully creased trousers. He was punctual to the minute at each rehearsal and listened attentively to the other singers. The Commendatore only makes three appearances in the opera and his movements are well specified in the libretto, when he is allowed to move at all. Apart from the nods of the head, the graveyard scene demands rigidity and nothing else. While others were rehearsed, changed and analysed, Pierre Thau sat in the stalls or stood in the wings, always smiling courteously and never showing signs of boredom.

Five weeks' rehearsal is a long time for a Commendatore and on his several days off Thau behaved like that businessman on vacation, going to London to shop at Harrods and Marks & Spencer, taking the air at Brighton. He took very little part in discussion on the nature of *Don Giovanni*. To some extent this was because of the language barrier: he preferred not to speak English and confined himself to his own language and very fluent Italian in conversation with Rosario Andrade. There might too have been a reluctance to join in Glyndebourne's *Don Giovanni* exploration. Thau is a bass of considerable experience, with some fifty Commendatores sung in Hamburg, Aix and elsewhere; he was word- and note-perfect in the part and simply did what was required by his producer and conductor with no questions asked and a smile at the ready.

John Bury's sketch for the Commendatore in
the 1977 *Don Giovanni*

Peter Hall's requirements for the Commendatore in the opening scene were modest. He had to represent authority disturbed and then challenged, so Thau made his entrance with a shawl thrown over his shoulders to keep out the cold of the miserable weather which had been building up in Seville during rehearsals. There was no attempt to make him decrepit in the way some producers favour. The Commendatore behaves in the style of a man of his rank and class by challenging the masked intruder and loses to the younger and stronger man.

The two demands in this opening scene were the urgency to fit in with the requirements of the agitated score and the establishing of the idea that a ruling class was threatened. The Commendatore has to behave with total correctness (*'Lasciala, indegno, battiti meco!'*—'Leave her be, wretch, and duel with me!')

in exactly the same way that a few moments later Ottavio orders the servants, courteously but firmly, to carry away the corpse. Hall made sure that the Commendatore knows the identity of his assassin so that he can take suitable measures when he is turned to stone. Giovanni takes off his mask and looks straight into those dying eyes. Hall also tried to emphasise the dishonouring of the dead, which the Victorians considered to be high up on the list of Giovanni's crimes, by having the murderer roll over the corpse with his foot and wipe his bloodied sword on the dead man's white nightdress. There was a danger in pressing the macabre a shade too far, but Hall, as in the case of Seville's weather, preferred to push his ideas to the limit rather than take the side of caution.

The disdainful cleaning of the sword was followed by a good deal of argument on how Giovanni and Leporello make their escape. Peter Hall wanted the courtyard in which the Commendatore is killed to be as intimate as possible, so bringing the events close to the audience. This was emphasised by the high wrought-iron gates, the first row of 'sliders' in John Bury's set. Anna locks the door to the street as she rushes off to Ottavio for help. Leporello and Giovanni could have scaled the wall and made off, but there is scarcely any leeway in the music before their final words and the return of Anna and Ottavio. Hall wanted no chance of one pair being distracted by the sight of the other. The idea used in some productions, of having Leporello taking refuge *outside* the courtyard while the duel is in progress, was probed but it did not solve the problem of the key. *Il faut qu'une porte soit ouverte ou fermée.* If Anna locked the gate then it had to be opened somehow.

Hall turned to the Commendatore and decided that he would carry the keys to the house on his person. So Giovanni's final victory was to search the corpse, find the key-ring and toss it delightedly to Leporello so that they could make an easy and unhurried exit. Some murderers feel distaste at touching the body they have just despatched, as Tosca did when she had to uncurl the fingers of the dead Scarpia to get her official pass to freedom via Civitavecchia in Puccini's opera, but for Giovanni the feeling was one of triumph not queasiness.

The Commendatore's entrance and death vary little from one production to another, but the shape, form and placing of his statue in the graveyard are open to debate. So too is the quality of the whole scene. Those who question the excellence of Da Ponte's libretto note that this is the point at which he returns to the Bertati–Gazzaniga plot after inventing the adventures for Giovanni and Leporello which have formed the first part of the second act. Yet the opening duologue in the graveyard, where Giovanni and Leporello bring one another up to date on their exploits like a pair of salesmen comparing successes in a saloon bar, adds little to plot or to character. It is basically lighthearted chat to contrast with the moment of chill when Leporello reads the inscription on the plinth.

Tradition has it that the Commendatore as a Spanish grandee is allocated an equestrian statue, although there is no specific instruction in the text that he should have one, as Christopher Benn has noted.* Some of the other dead in the cemetery are honoured by horses and it is reasonable to put the Commendatore in the same class. From the producer's viewpoint it helps the scene because Giovanni and Leporello are in the graveyard for several minutes before they realise they are by the side of the Commendatore's tomb. It is useful for him to be above human life quite literally so that his voice, when it is eventually heard, comes from the direction of heaven. Hall for once strayed from the stage directions in having only a single statue on horseback, that of the Commendatore; the others were represented, despite John Bury's worries about last-minute changes, by 'frozen' extras.

Sometimes the Commendatore stands almost alone, as he did, to judge from photographs, in one of the most famous of *Don Giovanni* productions, that designed by Alfred Roller for the Vienna State Opera when Gustav Mahler was in command. Roller's figure is gothic and squat in what appears to be the vaults of the Ulloas, the Commendatore's family. More recent designers, led by Piper and Holzmeister (Salzburg, 1950), have taken a romantic view of the cemetery, setting it about with

* *op. cit.*

Emanuele Luzzati's interpretation of the
graveyard scene in the 1967 production

southern European cypresses. Josef Svoboda in Prague tried to
diminish the power of the horse so that it presented its
hindquarters to the audience, according to John Bury, and the
Commendatore's acceptance of the invitation to dinner was
boomed on to the back wall of the stage. Salzburg in 1934 went to
the other extreme and gave the Commendatore a horse both in
the graveyard and in the final scene where he comes to attend on
Giovanni. One of the first and most quoted remarks on the
Statue's nod of acceptance to his invitation came from the lady
who did not much care for this element of the supernatural in
Molière's *Don Juan*. '*Votre figure de Don Pedro* [as he is called by
Molière] *baisse la tête et moi je la secoue*'—'Your Don Pedro lowers
his head and I shake mine.'

The danger of disbelief and even more of the laughter of disbelief overshadows this scene. Peter Hall rehearsed time and time again with Thau mounting and remounting the grey-green statue that had been waiting at Glyndebourne since the first day of rehearsals. Thau remarked phlegmatically that he had been on any number of stage horses during the course of Commendatore duty and in one house had not even been on stage at all—he had intoned the Statue's words down a speaking tube while a technician tugged at the 'stone' head, not always at the right moment.

Hall was less concerned with the Commendatore than with the movement around his statue. He began by getting the interchange between Leporello and Giovanni running as fast as possible, partly out of fear that it would be of little interest to the non-Italian-speaking section of the audience. 'It's got to be very light and ironic, almost a ping-pong match between the two men. What's happened to Elvira? Giovanni hopes to hear that she's been thoroughly humiliated. Leporello wants to know how his master has got on ... is there another name to go in the catalogue? It's all banter so that the atmosphere can change like THAT!' Hall's right hand describes the drop of a guillotine or some other equally sharp instrument.

Luxon, ever practical, wonders where he and Leporello should *be*. Do they sit on the plinth for this news-exchange session? It is tried and Luxon does not like it. As always he works by his instincts while Stafford Dean tries to analyse the music in the hope that it will tell where he should stand on stage. The pair of them circle the Statue like a pair of mating peacocks, or peahens. Dean is concerned that the Statue is the first thing that anyone would notice when he hops over the graveyard wall. Luxon, although his crutches have gone by now, worries that his ankle is in no state to hop over anything at all and pretends that he has caught his testicles while scrambling over Bury's set. Dean, not to be outdone, reckons that the graveyard wall effectively blocks out any musical cue and to Giovanni's cry '*È desso!*' ('It's he!') replies, 'No, he's not because he can't hear a bloody thing!' Stewart Trotter suggests the Prague solution of having the horse face away from the audience so that it will not be obvious that Leporello and Giovanni deliberately ignore it when they come on stage.

This suggestion is rejected, but the Statue is to be raised another foot or so higher—swift words with the workshop—so that it stands well above the heads of the two night visitors. This has the advantage of elevating Pierre Thau by a similar amount so that his voice appears to come from a point rather closer to heaven. Peter Hall returns to the feel of the scene and suggests that it is about various grades of terror. Giovanni is in good humour and afraid of nothing. His insistence that Leporello issue the supper invitation provides him with sadistic pleasure in seeing his servant caught between fear of the unknown and terror at disobeying his master. The audience should share some of Leporello's fear, which Mozart induces by the trombones associated with the Commendatore at this point. As Dent has written,* trombones were not generally part of the eighteenth-century opera orchestra and their use should bring a *frisson* into the house. Hall tried to stress the dichotomy of the scene: 'It is chilling and grotesque at the same time. There is a power struggle, with Leporello desperate to leave and Giovanni rather enjoying an entirely new situation. Giovanni wins without knowing that this will be just about his last success.'

The graveyard scene ended as one of the more conventional episodes in the production. Sometimes the sections which superficially appear to present the greatest possibilities finish by offering the least. Hall's ideas about Don Giovanni's last supper were far more definite. He wanted a demonstration of physical and aesthetic pleasures without any sense of ridiculous luxury. A tradition grew up in Germany, and was followed in Glyndebourne's pre-War production, of having Giovanni surrounded by courtesans as well as by food and drink. The English National Opera follow suit in their current *Don Giovanni*, and Jean Pierre Ponnelle carried the idea to extremes in his 1977 production at Salzburg. Hall objected to the idea because Giovanni has never given any indication of *paying* for his sexual satisfaction. His principal delight in the scene was eating while Leporello went hungry.

---

* *op. cit.*

**Giovanni's last supper: Benjamin Luxon with
Stafford Dean**

'Giovanni is indulging all the sensual pleasures—food, drink,
music—bar one, and he makes up for that by relishing
Leporello's complaints of starvation. Giovanni does not enjoy
anything that is not mirrored and the joy he gets from gluttony
stems from the fact that Leporello hasn't got anything until he
steals that pheasant bone. Stafford, you've got to play bloody
hungry. Giovanni has kept you that way all day. He is at the end
of normal appetites and sadism is one of the ways he diverts
himself. I don't want the scene played for laughs, because that
will destroy the tension before the entry of the Commendatore.
It's far more devilish than jovial and Ben must bring out all the
cruelty in Giovanni.'

Later in the month there was a slight move away from this
rather sombre spectacle. Leporello was allowed his asides to the
audience on the music played for Giovanni's pleasures—two of
the operas quoted were to Da Ponte librettos which shows that

he was not reluctant for publicity—and to splutter out his mouthful of meat at Giovanni's intervention. But Hall was insistent that the comedy should be kept within modest bounds. 'This is the most anarchic section of the opera. Giovanni is positively enjoying himself by rejecting all those who come to save him. Elvira rushes in and kneels in a final plea to him, but she is tugged to her feet as Giovanni scorns her (*"Io te deridere!"*). He turns back to his food and his wine and proposes a toast to the good life, *"Vivan le femmine"*. Perhaps he feels a moment's tenderness for her, but that is only so that he can make his rejection the more hurtful. Her love has now changed and moved to a more spiritual plane. She has come as a saviour, not as a spurned wife. Even Leporello realises just how vicious Giovanni is when he sees this heart of stone (*"Di sasso ha il core"*).'

The Commendatore, who at Glyndebourne arrived on foot not horseback, was also seen by Hall as more saviour than avenger. Molière had much the same idea in *Don Juan* where the Statue arrives at the end of the fourth act and asks Juan if he has the courage to dine at his place the following evening with Sganarelle/Leporello. Sganarelle pleads that it is his fast day, but Juan accepts and the Statue leaves, declining a candle to show him to the door, saying very piously that he who has God for guide needs no other light.

Dent derides the Statue gently, commenting that 'the old gentleman has a great deal to say, and like most people of his age is very slow in delivery, so that in practice his supernatural impressiveness is very liable to break down before he has come to the end of his part, with the result that the audience finds him as much of a bore as Don Giovanni obviously does.'* That is all a little hard on the bass who has been waiting almost three hours for his big moment in the opera, although the onus is placed squarely on the producer to keep up the tension at this point.

The stressing of the neutrality of the Statue was a new concept to Pierre Thau: he had always played the avenger who lived up to the inscription on his plinth and was determined to throw Giovanni into the fiery pit. Hall on the contrary saw him as both

---

* *op. cit.*

the agent of heaven and a man of compassion. 'He is the last in the line of those who try to save Giovanni. That is why he offers his own supper invitation—"I have accepted your request to come to dinner, now will you accept mine?" Where would they have gone? The Statue does not say but the implication is that it will be in heaven. At Giovanni's refusal the Statue's demand *"Pentiti"* becomes more insistent, but quickly he realises that the cause is lost.'

The religious nature of the finale, which so many producers duck, just as they are leery of having Marguérite float up to heaven in *Faust*, was heavily underlined by Hall. A fiery red cross rose vertically over the back of the stage as the Statue made his final call for repentance and then faded as Giovanni to the very last refused to budge from his life style. The walls fell back and the floor dipped down as the red-eyed demons specified by Da Ponte tugged Giovanni, screaming in terror for once in his life, to the nether regions. Pierre Thau was instructed by Hall to look as sorrowful as a Statue can in these final minutes. He led Giovanni up to the edge of the volcano very slowly and then relinquished him as the devils took over. The walk back, after a look into the flames, was tragic and disconsolate as though a battle was lost. This tableau was as defiantly Romantic as the one which ended the first act, an almost Catholic view of an opera which takes no religious sides.

Peter Hall said, 'I don't want the Statue to represent heavenly vengeance. He isn't out to destroy Giovanni but, like Elvira, to ask him to change his ways. He comes to supper to praise the hereafter, and to demonstrate that there is more to the world than human life. Da Ponte and Mozart, the men of the Enlightenment, are looking back towards mediaeval Catholicism. Or is it forward to the religiosity of the nineteenth century. Perhaps Giovanni gets a flash of pleasure at this new experience, but he loses because he never refuses a challenge. Never.'

6 The Ladies

When Joan Carden in Sydney received the telegram from Glyndebourne asking her to change from Elvira to Anna, her first reaction was to say no. 'I'd just come off a rehearsal for *Lakmé*, in which I was sharing the title rôle with Joan Sutherland, and I did not feel like taking on anything else. I'd given up my holiday to learn that one, my third new part of the season, and reckoned that enough was enough. Elvira looked just right. I'd sung it, moderately successfully, with John Pritchard conducting and Glyndebourne provided the ideal opportunity to polish it.

'It was John who persuaded me to make the change. I'd been very much in his hands during that Australian *Don Giovanni*, where I could have done with more stage direction. We worked on that interpretation together within the limitations of the casting—the Anna was an older and bigger woman, so we turned Elvira into a spurned creature, a firebrand who was on a much lower social level than Anna. John made the music dictate what I did on stage and forced me to act with my voice. His influence must have been powerful because when he began to talk me into Anna and assured me that it was well within my range I simply gave way.

'Now there are no regrets, although I'd like to have another go at Elvira and make her a much sadder and more sympathetic character than I did with the Australian Opera Company. Anna is certainly coming that much more easily because of what I had absorbed already from the Anna–Elvira encounters. Although

most of the ideas I brought with me to Glyndebourne were rubbed away by Peter's interpretation. I knew England—I'd been a music student at Manchester and I'd sung one rôle at Covent Garden, Gilda in *Rigoletto*, but that didn't exactly prepare me for Sussex rehearsals.'

Changing from Elvira to Anna is by no means unusual. Sena Jurinac after her disappointing Elvira in 1954 became, as George Christie has recalled, one of the house's most distinguished Annas. It was obvious from the first days that Joan Carden too was going to make a success of the part. Off stage she cut a friendly, slightly housewifely figure with a bag of knitting from which protruded an unidentifiable piece of red clothing which became longer as the rehearsals progressed. She was constantly ribbed by the English members of the cast for an Australian accent which she made no attempt to shade. She took it all as a good sport, to use the word most frequently used in affectionate mockery. On stage there was a totally different Carden, a gritty figure who was determined to succeed. In Australia she had played tennis to championship standard and guts as much as strength had obviously helped her to win. Concern that she should reach the first night in the best possible vocal condition bubbled just below the surface.

Anna's character is in part determined by that opening scene. Hoffmann had no doubts that Giovanni aroused violent sexuality in her. No longer could she be the same woman. Giovanni is at the same time her saviour and her destroyer. 'She feels that only Don Juan's destruction can bring peace to her soul, martyrised by deadly tortures. But this peace will bring her own spiritual annihilation.'* This is why, as Hoffmann continues, she will never marry Ottavio. The demand at the very end of the opera for a year's delay is not so much a promise as a rejection: after Giovanni no one else is worth consideration. The Hoffmann conception was taken over by possibly the most famous of all Annas, the German soprano Wilhelmine Schröder-Devrient (1804–60), who, according to William Mann, 'appreciated the possibilities of the rôle and, having made it her own, persuaded

---

* *op. cit.*

Sena Jurinac, the only artist to have sung both Donna Elvira and Donna Anna at Glyndebourne, in the latter rôle in the 1955 production

'*Padre, padre mio!*': Donna Anna (Joan Carden), Don Ottavio (Leo Goeke) and the Commendatore's corpse (Pierre Thau)

posterity that Donna Anna is the *prima donna* in *Don Giovanni*'. Casting directors tend to agree with Schröder-Devrient because her music is the most taxing of that given to the three sopranos, but Hoffmann's interpretation has found plenty of challengers including Dent who asserted with typical assurance that Elvira was by far the most interesting character in the opera after Don Giovanni.

Peter Hall and the cast continued to argue throughout the rehearsals over what went on in Anna's bedroom, but all agreed that she had been mightily aroused while the overture was being played. This was supported by the fact that in the first scene Anna is trying to hold back Giovanni and not vice versa. Her first desire is to know who he is and Giovanni is not prepared to let this happen (*'Chi son io tu non saprai'* — 'You shall not know who I

Joan Sutherland as Donna Anna in the 1960
Don Giovanni

am'); he uses his superior strength to guard his identity. Anna's next thought is to prevent him from going, so Hall after several experiments had her kneeling in supplication and at the same time grabbing Giovanni's legs. Giovanni is given plenty of time by the music to shake himself free, or even to call the waiting

Leporello, but he delights in the piquancy of the situation until the arrival of the Commendatore. Anna then is shaken out of her romantic transport and has regained enough of her wits to rush off for help.

Joan Carden had conceived a quite different interpretation of the scene while she was preparing the rôle on her own. 'I thought of that first entry as being much more aristocratic and that the core of Anna's character was her chill treatment of Ottavio. Now I feel that something happened in that off-stage encounter with Giovanni to make her guilty. Anna probably had a pretty uneventful life before that particular night, as one would expect for a well-brought-up lady in Seville. For the moment she is unable to cope, especially as she begins to feel that she is responsible for the death of her father. So she needs Ottavio and turns to him for his manliness and his firmness.

'I've also completely reconsidered that narration to Ottavio before "*Or sai chi l'onore*". Once I accepted that Anna was telling the truth about her midnight visitor; now I believe that she was being far from honest with him. She is crying out for vengeance to expiate her own feelings, those awakened emotions which she did not know were there and which she has not come to terms with. I've an idea that after that year was up and all her personal turmoil had settled down a little Anna would eventually marry Ottavio. Mozart does not always treat his ladies too well: Fiordiligi and Pamina are both called on to prove themselves and I see Anna as forced to go through her personal fire.'

As the rehearsal progressed Hall moved further and further away from the chill and haughty lady Anna is often seen to be. He drove hard to begin the opera at a high pitch of tension and looked to Anna to provide much of it. The first of the several occasions on which she rounds on poor Ottavio ('*Fuggi, crudele*'—'Get away, cruel one') was spat out, although the suggestion that at this moment Anna mistakes Ottavio for her father's murderer was firmly rejected. Anna always uses Ottavio and within minutes they are swearing vengeance. Hall here used his Suspended Time to indicate that Anna has little or no affection for Ottavio. She turns to him not as a lover—Don Giovanni for the time being has that rôle—but as an accomplice.

Once he has agreed, Anna's thoughts come back to herself and she shares them with the audience.

Donna Anna's next appearance comes at one of Don Giovanni's rare moments of depression and irritation. Donna Elvira has found him trying to take Zerlina off and has foiled the attempt in her aria '*Ah! Fuggi il traditor!*' ('Ah! fly from the betrayer!'). Giovanni reflects that this is just not his day and that the devil is impeding him at every move, a piece of recitative much quoted by those who claim that Giovanni is sexually unsuccessful throughout the opera. He turns round to find Ottavio and Anna, who are just about the last couple he would want to encounter at this moment. The scene is the turning point of the first act and written with consummate skill by Da Ponte who delights in the irony of the situation as indeed Mozart does. It is not specified that Anna and Ottavio should be in mourning at this point—Benn rather flippantly suggests that their clothes might not have been tailored in time—but Hall and Bury had no doubts that this should be a sombre moment for the pair of them, sartorially and emotionally. Anna was dressed from head to toe in black and in mid-rehearsal it was decided that she should enter weeping on Ottavio's arm. Ottavio himself, also in formal black, was to resume his Jane Austen stance.

Hall first of all worked on the reactions. The viciousness of Giovanni had to be emphasised as he claims that Elvira, who has returned to the scene after putting Zerlina in safer hands, is mad when she makes her accusations of infidelity. The first moves were as always worked out through the singers and Hall arrived at the notion that Giovanni should be clutching Anna's hand at the moment of Elvira's return. Ottavio and Anna have both come for help in tracking down the murderer of the Commendatore; Giovanni, as soon as he realises that he is not suspected, gives the warmest of verbal agreements, promising his hand, his riches, his sword and even his life. Hall stressed the mockery in the words.

'It begins as a gracious social encounter. Ottavio is glad that he spots Don Giovanni, who should be just the man to help him. Giovanni has to pass himself off with total honesty and aristocracy, but he probably cannot resist giving Anna's hand an extra squeeze as he offers total support. [The gesture contradicts those who argue that Giovanni shows no interest at all in Anna after the opening scene.] At this moment Elvira returns and is horrified to find Giovanni apparently being affectionate with yet another woman only seconds after she had got the first one out of his clutches. Giovanni realises that the only way out is to say that Elvira is touched (*"È pazza, non badate!"*—"She's mad, don't pay any attention!"*) and then as always in the most dangerous moments he stands back and observes ironically the reactions of Anna and Ottavio.'

The next step, which came about a week later, was to stress the comedy in the scene. Peter Hall slowed down Ben Luxon and made him savour the situation. 'Don't be too hearty when you claim that Elvira is off her head. And when you appear to offer everything you have to Anna put a little irony into it and emphasise the aristocratic exaggeration—*"questa* man . . . *questo* ferro . . . *il* sangue"*. It is not often the quarry is asked to hunt himself down and Giovanni enjoys anything novel. Make the moment when you take Anna by the hand almost physical, her tears will dry at this moment of contact and Elvira will be that much more outraged when she sees it.'

Hall was working the singers in exactly the same way that he wanted them to 'work' the audience. There was always gentleness, particularly with the Elvira, Rosario Andrade, whose translator was putting in double time to achieve the necessary subtleties of the scene. There was nothing of the autocrat, the producer who knows *exactly* what he wants; Hall's method was to suggest that the solutions came as much from the singers as from himself. After a number of experiments the ensuing quartet was played in Suspended Time directly to the audience.

'It's a moment of bafflement for Anna and Ottavio. Elvira, whom they do not know, is claiming one thing; Giovanni is brushing aside her words. Anna is half-inclined to take the feminine viewpoint, while Ottavio cannot concede that a gentleman, such as Giovanni, can be a liar. Together they're all saying "Here's a how d'ye do" and appealing for help. Gradually the bewilderment turns to suspicion as far as Anna and Ottavio are concerned and this is compounded by the sexual implications

of Giovanni's words of farewell: "*Perdonate, bellissima
Donn'Anna! se servirvi poss'io, in mia casa v'aspetto. Amici, addio!*"
("Pardon me, most beautiful Donna Anna, if I can serve you, I
shall await you in my house. Friends, goodbye!")'

Ben Luxon at this point was made to give an extravagant bow
and Anna suddenly realised that Giovanni was the masked
murderer, as she exclaims in her cry '*Don Ottavio! son morta!*' —
'Don Ottavio! I am dead!' After stressing the irony Peter Hall,
supported by John Pritchard, took another tack and concentrated on the danger of the quartet. 'The feeling of the

ensemble, despite the delicacy of the music, is electric. Listen to the orchestra and the underlying tension there. Make it dangerous . . . more dangerous. This is the moment when the ice is really beginning to break and Ottavio at last will be forced to pick up his sword. His first reaction is one of class incredulity, if you can't trust a nobleman then what *is* the world coming to. Yet it is just conceivable that a pillar of society might be telling lies. Ottavio doubts everything because it is most unlikely that he has ever been exposed to a situation like this before. Elvira's comments are marked sometimes *pianissimo*, but she is quite determined to be heard and so the seeds of suspicion are sown in the minds of Ottavio and Anna ("*Incomincio a dubitar*"—"I'm beginning to have doubts").'

Much of the style of the production was created from the analysis of scenes such as this. Characters were established more through recitative and the breaking down of ensembles than through the arias. The solo numbers tended to be polished in the small rehearsal rooms and not altered a great deal on stage, another trademark of the Hall approach. Most directors have a habit of concentrating on the arias and fitting in the recitatives later. Hall followed his own precepts in Anna's first big number, '*Or sai chi l'onore*', which comes immediately after the quartet and in which she demands that Ottavio shall join her in vengeance. More time was spent on the preceding recitative than on the solo. The cry '*Son morta*' was acknowledged as the turning point. Anna watched Giovanni depart, taking his time, before she uttered the words and then did a slow about-face to Ottavio before looking him straight in the eye at '. . . *è il carnefice del padre mio*!'—'my father's murderer!'. These words were uttered with equal deliberation.

Joan Carden at first made the *racconto*, in which Anna tells Ottavio of her encounter with Giovanni, too fierce. She was trying to convey some of the horror of that night and made a violent story of it. Hall steadied her down, suggesting that the tale might not be true. Ottavio, with his devotion to her, would not need much persuading. The recitative gradually became much softer and more calculating. The aria itself was fined down so that it started quietly, following the *pianissimo* marking for the strings in the orchestra, and menacingly before building to a demand for revenge. Hall said that he wanted this particular vendetta to resemble cold steel and to be almost unemotional. 'Don Ottavio as a Spanish man of honour has got to respond to Anna's request. He will do it automatically as part of his moral code, even though he is not yet totally convinced that Giovanni is guilty. Anna will get what she wants and she doesn't even have to be sly to do it.'

Anna's second act aria, in which she responds to Ottavio's reproach '*Crudele*', one of the rare moments when he questions either her words or her actions, has its detractors. Berlioz found the *coloratura* shameful; Dent, against the aristocrats to the end, declared that there was no reason at all for this scene in which Anna reaffirms her faithfulness to Ottavio and hopes that heaven will take pity on her; Benn takes the same line and claims that this brief interlude in Anna's house tells us nothing new about either her or Ottavio. More recently the aria, which few would deny is heartrendingly beautiful, has had its supporters. Brigid Brophy sees Anna in the early scene as the wronged woman, who much like the wronged Ghost in *Hamlet* is constantly nagging away for justice. She goes on rightly to admire '*Non mi dir*' as the core of the only domestic scene in the opera and describes it as 'incomparably moving', suggesting that it needs a Queen of the Night to sing '*Or sai chi l'onore*' and a Countess to tackle '*Non mi dir*'. Alfons Rosenberg, who has written one of the most exhaustive recent studies of the character of Donna Anna,* puts it on a level with the slow movements of the symphonies and quartets of Mozart's maturity.

It has been established that Mozart composed the aria so that the scenery could be changed at Prague between the graveyard and Don Giovanni's supper table. Yet it is far more than the conventional display piece that Anna as the representative of *opera seria* in *Don Giovanni* might require. It takes us to the heart of her condition. At last she has stopped crying for revenge, probably because Ottavio has just told her that justice is on its way, although rather evasively he does not say just whose hands

---

* *Don Giovanni*, Alfons Rosenberg (Prestel Verlag, Munich).

are going to administer it. Although she tells Ottavio that he should not doubt her love, the protestation is not all that convincing as she turns to heaven to help her out of the tribulations, and almost certainly the guilt, that have surrounded her for the whole course of the opera. This final section, so derided by Berlioz, prepares for that sentence in the finale, which he also abhorred, when Anna sends Ottavio off for a year. The sadness in the song comes from the realisation that Ottavio will not do, although the moment is not quite right for telling him, and the hope that God might provide a little light at the end of her horridly gloomy tunnel.

At Glyndebourne the scene was set as simply as possible: a small chair for Ottavio and a larger one for Anna. After an initial reprimand at the word '*Crudele*', Joan Carden's Anna retired into her own shell, developing the contrast between the brilliance of the music and the despondency of the thoughts. She trudged off the stage as the woman who had loved neither too wisely nor too well.

*   *   *

Peter Hall waited until rehearsals were well advanced before he began intensive work with Donna Elvira, Rosario Andrade. To some extent this was out of consideration for his soprano. Miss Andrade spoke only a few words of English and despite the constant attentions of her translator, Gabrielle (who flitted around the wings knowing instinctively when she was wanted and when she should disappear from sight), was finding adjustment to Glyndebourne life more difficult than the others. The dissection of an opera, during which its components were looked at from a multitude of different angles, was not within her range of experience. Rosario Andrade looked on while Hall and Trotter, Luxon and Dean argued and explored; she smiled winningly and was constantly anxious to please, but it was not her world.

There was, too, considerable delay in deciding just what sort of person Donna Elvira was. At the beginning there was a move towards making her an almost comic figure, the mad woman of Burgos who is constantly duped. Andrade's strong Mexican face and her expressive eyes, capable of both sadness and considerable fury, told against this approach and Elvira became a more solemn and a more sympathetic figure.

The style of her entrance aria, '*Ah! chi me dice mai*', in which she asks *someone* to tell her where Giovanni might be, changed constantly. At first it was very physical with Elvira coming in through the early morning rain and rattling all the doors in the square. Hall said: 'Elvira is exceptionally tense. She hasn't slept all night because she's been searching for Giovanni. The music asks the question "Where is he? Where is he?", but Elvira has almost given up, as she indicates in that opening sigh of resignation, so she turns to the audience instead.'

The switch in the aria to the final section of *coloratura* in which Elvira threatens to rip out Giovanni's heart the moment she finds him was made deliberately extravagant. Hall urged Andrade to probe the extremities of Elvira's emotions: her fury at being deserted by Giovanni and her probable readiness to make love to him should he ask. There was no harm in appearing a little ridiculous at this point.

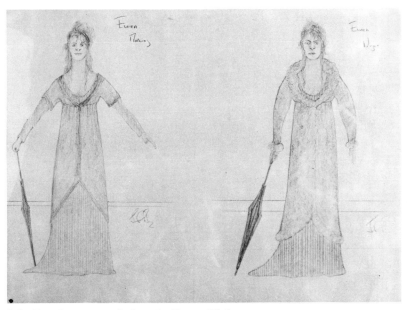

John Bury's costume designs for Donna Elvira

Then the approach began to change colour in the face of Elvira's actions later in the opera. The wronged woman took the place of the slightly deranged one and the aria became much more a cry of personal loneliness and despair which Don Giovanni by chance happens to overhear. Elvira begins to live off insults. When she eventually discovers Don Giovanni she is fobbed off with his servant, this *gentleman (questo galantuomo)* as Leporello is ironically described by his employer, who further upsets her with the catalogue of Giovanni's conquests. The sight a little later of Giovanni in the arms of Zerlina and then apparently paying court to Anna round off a morning which could hardly have been blacker.

Her situation scarcely improves in the second act as she is gulled by Leporello into thinking that he is Giovanni once more in love with her. The unmasking of Leporello in the famous sextet only compounds the misery which she is suffering, although it is to Elvira that Leporello turns with his plea for leniency. In the aria '*Mi tradì*' Elvira really reaches the turning point. For some time it was the practice to deride this number also as adding nothing to the opera. It suffered much the same fate as '*Dalla sua pace*' and was too a Vienna addition. Caterina Cavalieri, the Elvira there, persuaded Mozart to compose an additional piece for her. The request was reasonable for, although Elvira has a considerable amount to sing, her arias tend to move into concerted numbers and give the audience no chance to show appreciation. '*Mi tradì*' has been moved about the opera and there was a German tradition, quite unjustified, in the last century which put it into Act I. It is now almost always given after Ottavio's '*Il mio tesoro*' despite the objection that two 'display' arias in succession slow down the pace of the opera.

Brigid Brophy in *Mozart the Dramatist*, supporting the ladies again, argues persuasively that '*Mi tradì*' is the turning-point not only of the second act but of the work as a whole. She describes it as a Hamlet-like soliloquy in which Mozart is hesitating just as much as Elvira because he cannot bear to have Don Giovanni's crimes punished by human hands. Miss Brophy pushes her case rather too far but she is right in pointing out that both words and music tell us a great deal more about Elvira than we know so far.

'*Ah*! *fuggi il traditor!*': Don Giovanni (Benjamin Luxon), Donna Elvira (Rosario Andrade) and Zerlina (Elizabeth Gale)

It is by no means a display piece composed for a pushy soprano; instead it reveals that Elvira's character is changing. Her feeling for Giovanni is no longer that of lust or jealousy or vengeance but of pity. She has been deserted and betrayed, as she announces at the end of the aria, but her attitude to Giovanni is still one of profound sympathy—'*provo ancor per lui pietà*'.

Hall needed to concentrate on bringing out all the conflicting emotions of '*Mi tradì*', culminating in that surge where sexual love turns into pity, in order to make the point in the supper scene that Don Giovanni is visited to be saved and not roasted in hell. A few days before the first night he took Rosario Andrade and her interpreter into one of the small rehearsal studios to give his last production notes on the character of Elvira.

'Before this final aria I want you to give the impression that Elvira has been through a night of purgatory. She has lost her husband, found him and then lost him again, this man for whom she had an overwhelming passion. She's even fallen in love with a figure who mimes a serenade intoned by Giovanni. It's happened all over again. But this is the very last time. She sees the wrath of heaven ("*l'ira del cielo*") approaching, so her own desire of vengeance turns to pity.

'The aria follows Elvira's change of heart in a question and answer pattern. She begins by asking why she should feel pity when she has been treated so badly and she answers herself by understanding that any human being must show compassion.

'Elvira is the person who changes most in the opera and generally for the better. At the end she reaches a strength and clarity which completely pass Anna by. Indeed the two women cross, moving in totally opposite directions. Anna begins strong and ends in considerable bewilderment and alone; but is much more human; Elvira begins alone and emerges from it all a far more considerate and mature person simply because of what she has been through. I think in "*Mi tradì*" she realises what a hopeless mess Don Giovanni is in. She is unhappy but there is Giovanni in a far worse plight. That is why she comes to him at the last supper in a spirit of entreaty begging him to change his ways ("*Che vita cangi!*"); he may be playing games with her but she could not be more in earnest with him. Elvira does not get angry with Giovanni as she might well have done earlier in the opera when she would probably have shouted and screamed at him. Her pity and her entreaties form the last proof of her love ("*L'ultima prova dell'amor*"), and when they are rejected she finally gives in.

'In the Epilogue Elvira, unlike the others, is calm and collected. This is a woman quite different from the distraught figure hunting through the streets of Seville for Giovanni. Her decision to go off and end her days in a cloister is the firmest and most credible of all those resolutions expressed at the end.'

Peter Hall and his répétiteur spent about two hours with Rosario Andrade and this almost private tutorial set the seal on the character.

*   *   *

Elizabeth Gale, the Zerlina, had previously had quite a lot of experience with Glyndebourne, both with the Touring Opera and in Sussex. She had just finished singing the same part in the revival of John Copley's production at Covent Garden. She had not though worked with Peter Hall before nor had her Masetto, John Rawnsley, who only a year earlier had been in the chorus at Glyndebourne.

The Hall method began by sapping some of the Gale confidence. 'I'm used to long rehearsals and being one of Glyndebourne's "captives", as we think of ourselves. When we were doing *Falstaff* [Gale was Nannetta, a rôle she repeated in the 1977 season] we immersed ourselves entirely in the opera and thought about virtually nothing else. *Giovanni* has been more exhausting because we are constantly investigating, exploring and doing things quite differently.

'At times I confess that I have been a little dispirited because I've been confused about the way we are supposed to be going. Take, for example, the Zerlina–Giovanni duet, *"Là ci darem"*. Everybody knows it so well that we had to begin by turning it virtually upside down so that each phrase was insincere, almost the reverse of what it appeared to say. Now that has been changed and it is agreed that Zerlina is attracted sexually to Don Giovanni as well as by his wealth. On the other hand I think she gets quite quickly out of her depth, which is why she screams so quickly for help when he tries to seduce her in his castle. Zerlina has an optimistic vision of silk sheets and a lot of servants — a rough and tumble in the dark outside the ballroom is quite a different matter.'

Hall concentrated on bringing out the sexuality, but most of all Zerlina's native wit. She is very much the *contadina astuta*, to steal Jani Strasser's expression, and it is worth recognising that she is the only one of the three women in the opera to remain unscathed after contact with Giovanni. Both Masetto and Zerlina were intended to be aggressors in their totally different ways. He was pulled far away from the normal peasant clod, who bumbles and stumbles his way through the opera to provide a few easy laughs. Hall was constantly encouraging John Rawnsley to be dangerous, particularly in his aria, 'Ho capito'.

Elizabeth Gale as Susanna in Peter Hall's Glyndebourne production of *Figaro*

'*Vedrai, carino*': Masetto (John Rawnsley) and
Zerlina (Elizabeth Gale)

'You are the one person after the death of the Commendatore
to stand up to Giovanni. You're quite shrewd enough to know
what he's up to and you tell him so. That takes some courage in
the social structure of Spain at the time. The other peasants will
withdraw—there's nothing in the libretto to indicate that they
must stay—so that they do not get involved in what could be an
ugly squabble. Masetto remains sober at the party while
everyone else is thrusting all the free booze available down their
gullets because he is suspicious that his property—Zerlina—is at
risk. His precautions are justified and he is one of the first to
answer that scream for help.

'Zerlina's aggression is much more sexual. She knows that she
is attractive and she plays on this. I think she's also an
opportunist who will move up the social ladder if there's a
glimmer of a chance. After all she reckons that she can always
return to Masetto, as she does in "*Batti, batti*".'

Neither of Zerlina's arias is simple to stage because both are fairly lengthy and less inventive musically than the other solos in the score. Comment has been passed on the streaks of apparent masochism in '*Batti, batti*', where Zerlina asks Masetto to whip her, tear her hair and dig out her eyes. Dent even goes so far as to suggest that Da Ponte was influenced by an incident in Venice where a certain doctor spanked a noble Paduan lady by the Riva degli Schiavone while singing a students' song. The bubbling and conniving orchestra though suggests that Zerlina is merely getting a lot of pleasure out of seeing Masetto quickly coming under her influence again. After trying various parts of the stage, Peter Hall ended by placing Zerlina under the right-hand balcony where she could finger the wooden upright much as Masetto later hoped he would be fondled.

'*Vedrai, carino*', in which Zerlina comforts Masetto after he has been thwacked by Giovanni and prescribes the best and most natural of remedies, feminine care, is a more appealing number. Da Ponte's words are honeyed and direct. Zerlina says that she carries balm with her and keeps it in only one place, her heart, which also happens to be her left breast, and that is where Masetto's hand is placed. Mozart wrote the number for Caterina Bondini, who was considered the leading soprano of the three taking part in the Prague première, and his music is as sensuous as Da Ponte's lyric.

For it Peter Hall allowed himself the only moments in the production which could possibly be described as pretty. Dappled moonlight covered the stage as Zerlina's hand guided Masetto's arm over her body. Earlier Hall had growled that he would have no Dresden shepherdess nonsense around this production, but here he relented possibly because the shepherd and the shepherdess were genuine peasants.

Elizabeth Gale remarked that the one sure thing about a Hall rehearsal was it was never boring and she was afraid the scene might be changed at the last moment. As it turned out Hall had no last moments to alter anything and in all probability he would have left it just as it was.

7 *Interlude with Stafford Dean*

Leporello and Don Giovanni acted as foils to one another throughout rehearsals. Ben Luxon usually looked as though he had come off the Cornish beaches of his childhood: jeans were rolled up around the ankles and loose blue sweaters flowed full over the hips. While Don Giovanni could have taken to sea with the fishing fleet, Leporello would not have been out of place having Sunday cocktails on a Surrey lawn. Stafford Dean was conspicuously neat with every hair on his head in place; he even wore a tie from time to time, a piece of clothing as rare at an opera rehearsal as a cloth cap in the Stock Exchange.

Ben Luxon fretted over the progress of his strained ankle. He was always volatile, cursing himself for that leap and worrying that he should have rested at once rather than continued with rehearsals, constantly afraid that his own immobility was holding back the work of others. Then when the strength returned the exuberance came back with it. Don Giovanni on two firm feet was apt to sing Richard Rodgers in the wings and he burst into farmyard noises at the first sight of the three maskers in costumes that turned them into a trio of white-beaked roosters. The Luxon reactions were always instinctive, a clear-cut reflection of the mood of the moment.

Stafford Dean by contrast always played the rôle of rational man. He had worked out the benefits of returning to Glyndebourne for the first time since singing that tiny rôle in *Werther* a decade ago. It made a break in the circuit of European opera houses and it paved the way to the Don Alfonso which he was contracted to sing under Peter Hall's direction in the 1978 *Così*. Dean was word-perfect as well, rather rarer as singers tend to get lazy like the rest of us when they think they know everything. He was consistently courteous. There was never any reminder in rehearsals that he had sung over a hundred Leporellos before Luxon had even begun to prepare his first Giovanni. At the beginning he was ready to throw away all his acquired ideas about the part and fit in with the view of the opera Hall was evolving. Leporello spends very little time off stage and Dean knew everybody else's part almost as well as his own, but he rarely paraded that fact after the first few days when the répétiteurs were still finding their way through the work.

Two-thirds of the way through rehearsal Stafford Dean talked about his return to Glyndebourne.

'In just over three weeks Leporello has changed a lot. Peter's initial view was that he should not be far removed from Papageno, so we worked on him as being Common Man, constantly tempted and going the way of all flesh. We started by making Leporello very resentful of Giovanni and stressing that in the Catalogue Aria. Leporello kept that list under duress and brought it out very reluctantly. When he was left with Elvira he didn't really want to show it to her—the feeling was "Look I've got this awful book in my pocket and I suppose that I'd better tell you all about it."

'This was at the time when Peter was trying to turn Elvira into a more sympathetic character. I wasn't sure about that. I've played in productions where she is portrayed as a pathetic creature, which tends to make life hard for Giovanni and Leporello. The three of us are the dramatic keys to the opera and it is essential that the balance is kept right. I put it to Peter that perhaps we were going wrong, that Leporello admires Giovanni and that he feels nothing but relish when he thumbs through the catalogue with Elvira. Stewart Trotter supported me and almost without hesitation Peter said, "I'll buy that." So we started to reconstruct the scene and part of the character as well.

'Peter is the only producer I know who experiments to the extent that he is prepared to throw right out of the window an interpretation on which he has worked for some time. He once told me that the only thing which had got him to the top was

A dress rehearsal of *Werther* at Glyndebourne:
Sir Michael Redgrave, the producer, shows the
way to Stafford Dean, the Bailiff

The graveyard: Benjamin Luxon threatens
Stafford Dean; the statue, Pierre Thau, remains
impassive

knowing when things felt right. I respect that remark. One of his great qualities also is to know when he has gone up a blind alley and to admit it.

'The sympathy for Elvira is now being drawn by emphasising her dramatic side—it's worth remembering that the Italians tend to cast Elvira heavy and Anna light. Leporello is moving back towards the interpretation that I basically learned from Günther Rennert. He is on Giovanni's side when his master is seducing the birds and against him when he starts to beat and to kill. But we will not go nearly as far as Rennert, who made Elvira almost a buffoon and told me to emphasise the scruffy, messy side of Leporello. When I did it for him in Stuttgart I was virtually a gypsy. Rennert too tried to bring out the semi-physical relationship with Giovanni and had Ruggero Raimondi throw me around as though I were a battered suitcase.

'Perhaps that's a little extravagant, but it is essential to bring out the master–servant relationship. Some Leporellos have too much Giovanni in them [Dean names a well-known European baritone] and that's why it can be dangerous to switch rôles, quite apart from the fact that I see Giovanni as a baritone whereas Leporello is really a bass part. There are a few moments when they approach verbal equality, at the beginning of Act II for instance when Leporello hands in his notice and is won over by the purse of four doubloons, *quattro doppie*, tossed to him by Giovanni. Leporello is constantly at the mercy of his master's money and sword.

[Leporello at the end of the opera is apparently one of Seville's losers. Giovanni goes off to hell without having paid Leporello any more wages and it is no surprise when in the Epilogue he announces that he is going off to the tavern to find a better master.]

'The balance between the two has to be carefully weighed in the graveyard, which I reckon is the most difficult scene in the opera to play. You have to convey a trembling Catholic peasant who is caught between Giovanni and the Statue, the sword and supernatural. All too often it falls flat and it is no good looking to the audience for help: they are meant to share some of Leporello's fear and unease does not exactly stimulate applause.'

Does Stafford Dean approve of the Peter Hall approach?

'I'm not sure I like that word "approve". Look, opera is changing fast, not only here in Glyndebourne but all over Western Europe and in the States. There was a time when the singers were the bosses, they did what they liked and very few people said nay to them. Then came the rule of the conductors, who were the autocrats. Now the directors have moved in.

'With Peter you come down to the very fundamentals of a work. He invites you to make suggestions so you go along with that. Most producers are very suspicious of other people's ideas and feel that in some way their position might possibly be usurped, although there are exceptions, such as August Everding who directed me in San Francisco. Everding used to take me aside from time to time so that we could assess the way things were going, but it was not the day-to-day interchange we have here. I've taken my cue from Peter's remark on the very first day when he looked round the cast and said, "There's a wealth of experience here, let's make the best use of it." I suppose that I've never discussed an opera in such detail with a producer, but that is simply because I've rarely, if ever, been invited to do so.'

8 Master and Man

Christopher Benn had no doubts about the importance of the servant. 'Leporello is the central figure of the opera,' he wrote and continued in the same paragraph to say that the work '. . . rests more on his shoulders than on those of his master.'* Those are fighting words, particularly as Benn sees the whole of *Don Giovanni* as possibly being no more than a dream of Leporello. Such a view might make for a fanciful production, but it would not cheer those who have spent days and weeks psychoanalysing Giovanni. The opera has always attracted the theorists. Benn's claim is no more extravagant than the suggestion that Don Giovanni is a suppressed homosexual who chases women, successfully and unsuccessfully, to allay the suspicions of his fellow aristocrats, although if this were true, then Don Giovanni would have had little time to indulge in his real pleasures if Leporello's book is to be believed.

Leporello's character has to be defined through his relationship with his master and with Elvira. His attitude to both Anna and Ottavio, Zerlina and Masetto is neutral; before the Commendatore, alive or dead, he feels awe. Da Ponte allows Leporello to reveal little about himself. We know nothing via the libretto of his upbringing, how he learned to read and write, how long he has been with Giovanni or with whom he was in service previously. It is typical of Leporello that his single extended aria, the Catalogue Song, is about someone else and his attitude is so carefully concealed by the words that it has to be a matter for

---

* *op. cit.*

debate between the singer and the producer. Indeed just about the only fact we have about Leporello is that his arithmetic is a little slipshod. He tells the audience that Giovanni has 'consoled' eighteen hundred ladies (*'consolo mille e otto cento'*). That figure scarcely tallies with the number in his little book. Leporello lists the countries individually and leaves Anna and the audience to tot up the figures, which come to 2,067.

Peter Hall began by rehearsing the Catalogue Aria as solemnly as he could. In part it was reaction against the over-used production gag where the book becomes a string of linked view-cards tossed across the stage; in part it was an attempt to turn Leporello into a harder and more embittered figure. He had asked Stafford Dean to make the opening scene *'Notte e giorno'* less cosy; the umbrella and the rain had not yet been introduced but the chill and the frustration were already there. He was also trying to devise the way Elvira should react. Ten days into rehearsal he saw the Catalogue Aria as a continuous story and warned Rosario Andrade against a series of different reactions:

'You've got to see all these women listed by Leporello in a long line. The catalogue fills Elvira with despair because the competition is on so vast a scale ... there's the little girl (*la piccina*), she can't compete with her ... the tall, stately one (*la grande maestosa*) ... you're not a baroness, a marquesa or a princess, you're not even a blonde. Elvira would like to be them all, young and old, tall and tiny, rich and poor, white-haired and brunette. What if she could be all women rolled into one? But of course she can't and so she despairs.'

Once the right reactions were drawn from Andrade, Leporello's approach was modified. The list, which Leporello began by pulling out regretfully, almost shyly, as though it were some kind of Black Book, became a much more cherished document, although it never achieved the status of 'Leporello's masterpiece', to filch Benn's phrase. The first of the dress rehearsals had been theatrically heavyweight and over-sombre and Hall had taken Stafford Dean's point that Leporello was in danger of losing his native wit. Dean took his cue from Giovanni's command to tell Elvira the lot (*'Dille pur tutto'*) and dangled the catalogue before her as a bone is shown to a

Donna Elvira (Rosario Andrade) checks Leporello's arithmetic (Stafford Dean) during the Catalogue Aria

'*Madamina: il catalogo*': Ilva Ligabue as
Donna Elvira and Geraint Evans as Leporello
in the 1960 production

frightened and suspicious dog. Leporello now became intrigued by his own record of his master's virtuosity, emphasising the new theme of Giovanni-admiration in the servant and fascinating the reluctant Elvira, who waits until mid-aria before she seizes the book.

The performance was coming closer to Dean's normal Leporello, who is captivated by the style and glamour of Giovanni, and moving away from Hall's original conception of Everyman succumbing to temptations, yet between whiles trying to sustain some moral standards. The suggestion was that although Leporello would prefer a quieter life, where his skin was not always so much at risk, it only takes a little encouragement or a few coins from Giovanni to persuade him back to the fray. It also built up the importance of the aria itself, the one number likely to bring Leporello a round of applause, which was in danger of becoming too solemn. Dean under John Pritchard's guidance began to pace it very slowly, shaking his head in sanctimonious regret at the Spanish figure of 1,003 and showing the evidence to Elvira in confirmation. Leporello begins in slight sympathy with Elvira, yet ends dazzled once again by the achievements of his master. This is then overtaken by a feeling of humanity towards Elvira, who turns away in anguish, overwhelmed by her own thoughts about the most dispiriting catalogue it has ever been her unhappy lot to see or hear.

Stafford Dean felt vindicated. 'Basically there are two Leporellos, the *buffo* interpretation and the character one. The audience laugh at the first and smile at the second. Obviously when you are taking your Leporello around with you from place to place and to unfamiliar productions, you use the first because it is the easiest way of making an impression. In a Peter Hall production only the second is possible and I think we're getting the smiles in now.'

Leporello again has doubts about the life he is leading when he comes back to Giovanni after filling up the peasants with food and drink and being surprised in the act by Donna Elvira with Zerlina in tow. Leporello announces that he has been given an earful by Elvira but in view of the length of the Catalogue Aria the complaint is unreasonable and in any case he gets his own back by locking her out of the palace gates and leaving her on the street. This is the prelude to the misnamed Champagne Aria. Giovanni in his song does not specify the wine he will be serving at his ball and is far more concerned with adding a dozen names to the catalogue by tomorrow morning ('*Ah, la mia lista doman mattina d'una decina devi aumentar!*'). The name has simply been tagged on by various interpreters who have flourished a champagne glass above their heads while delivering the aria, and the tradition was encouraged by a German translation which fed '*Champaganer*' into Da Ponte.

The location of the scene is not specified. Several producers favour a room in Giovanni's castle, which makes for a visual break. (This section of the opera has been accused of inertia because three solos follow in succession from Donna Anna, Don Ottavio and finally Giovanni. Such criticism takes little note of the quality and totally differing emotions of the numbers concerned.) Rennert in Munich had the imagination to put the aria in Giovanni's dressing-room where Leporello set about his valeting duties, shining boots and adjusting lace cuffs. But changes of scene require a pause. Hall and Bury, anxious to keep the action going without a break, stayed on the same Seville street where they had been for nearly an hour.

Hall was anxious to keep the barriers between the two men and build the opening mood of disgruntlement from Leporello. 'Stafford, you're making him too perky. He comes on complaining, almost disgusted with himself. Another shady mission is accomplished: he's got the peasants drunk, dealt with Elvira once more and yet here is this man giving him more orders to serve wine and condescendingly saying that he can pick up a girl in the square and bring her along too.'

In the early rehearsals the opening was played as another crisis of confidence between the two men, with Leporello on the verge of handing in his notice. This changed under the influence of Leporello's opening aside to the audience that he *ought* to leave Giovanni . . . ('*Io deggio . . . per sempre abbandonar*') because he has had enough of trying to flatten each obstacle in the way of Giovanni's next seduction. It was decided that Leporello was going to stay but that he was in complaining mood. According to

Paolo Montarsolo and Kostas Paskalis as
Leporello and Don Giovanni in the 1967
production

Hall, 'Leporello begins by grumbling and then is won round by "*Finch'han dal vino*". It's most important that he does not fall under Giovanni's spell again before the aria starts because then it becomes a static piece. He comes in angry and fed up, not whining, but critical of Giovanni who senses at once that here is one of the moments when he has to win Leporello over. This he does by half taking the piss.

'Leporello arrives saying "D'you know what I had to put up with? First Zerlina . . . and then do you know who was with her—Elvira." ' Hall demonstrates on stage for once, apeing a Levantine stallholder claiming that business is bad. Dean suggests that Leporello is converted back to Giovanni's service before the aria starts. Hall disagrees. 'The curve of the scene is that Leporello is morally in the right, but once again he gets corrupted. He changes from a man who is aggrieved and bitter to one who leaves metaphorically arm in arm with Giovanni as they set off on another adventure. The crux of the drama between the two men is just where that moment occurs. I believe that it is at the beginning of the aria, which is not the conventional display piece for the baritone but a song of persuasion aimed as much at Leporello as at the audience.'

Moods and opinions vacillated for well over an hour. Luxon changed the aria, which he had previously been interpreting as another outburst of anarchy. Leporello brought out a notebook to take down Giovanni's instructions and then put it away as a useless prop. Luxon re-thought the song as a list of commands rather than a premature celebration and suggested that whichever way it came out Leporello would have to be back on Giovanni's side from the start. Leporello and Giovanni began to take one another's sides with Dean claiming that '*Finch'han dal vino*' had to be a fire-cracker tossed out at the audience while Luxon wanted to point up Leporello's recitative. Hall was still looking for the moral conflict.

Stafford Dean suggested the compromise. 'I think it's a case of Leporello being half won over without leaving all his conscience behind. Midway he reverts to being the servant taking orders once again.'

Hall: 'Does that approach to the aria worry you, Ben?'

'*Là ci darem*': Zerlina (Elizabeth Gale) and Don Giovanni (Benjamin Luxon)

Luxon: 'No, no, nothing worries me apart from singing the bugger.'

It was resolved. Benjamin Luxon addressed the opening to Leporello and then turned to the audience as he retired into his own thoughts of sexual conquests. John Pritchard modified the pace and the volume so that the number did not become the regular two-horse race between baritone and orchestra. Hall continued to insist throughout rehearsals on precision. 'It should be devilish, daemonic in its accuracy; if you allow too much energy to explode early on then you take away precision and the whole piece becomes a generality. That is just what it should not be. The aria is a dangerous prologue to more anarchy.'

Throughout the middle period of rehearsals Peter Hall concentrated on making Ben Luxon's Giovanni fiercer and fiercer. As Elizabeth Gale had noted, the mood of the Zerlina–Giovanni duet was changing and was to alter again when the Series II cast came in. The irony was left to the orchestra and John Pritchard, so that the suggestion of complicity between seducer and victim was a matter for the instrumentalists. After the opening both Zerlina and Giovanni turned to the audience to ask just how far the other was to be trusted. Would Zerlina's lot really be changed (*'Io cangierò tua sorte'*)? Physical contact was left until quite close to the end of the number when Giovanni runs his swordstick first down Zerlina's hair and then along her arm at the moment when she confesses, again in Suspended Time, that she will not be able to resist much longer. That gesture, once devised, remained and it was followed by *'Andiam, andiam, mio bene'* ('Let us go, let us go, my dear') sung with lips almost touching and a final embrace to spark off Donna Elvira's *'Ah! fuggi'* a few moments later.

The duet was used to summarise Don Giovanni the opportunist, who seizes each moment for his personal pleasure, but has no real aim in life apart from instant self-satisfaction. Alfons Rosenberg's description *'Der ziellose Mann'* is in exact parallel with the character Hall was trying to develop and Rosenberg astutely goes on to suggest that Giovanni always has to catch the moment because he is a man with no future. He has little past either, apart from that catalogue.

The vicious streak in Giovanni was being emphasised, often at the expense of the humour in Da Ponte, in order to separate master from man, Luxon from Dean. In the middle of May, Peter Hall reckoned that he was moving in the right direction:

'The strength of the production at the moment is that there's something happening between Ben and Stafford. I'm trying to stop Ben confusing energy with intensity. He's got to eliminate his own natural, extrovert heartiness, which has no place in *Don Giovanni*, and replace it with a hardness both sadistic and chill. That's now coming along swiftly. I've learned over the last few days through analysing the text word by word with Ben that Giovanni spends a great deal of time provoking Leporello. I think they like one another, but Giovanni's real pleasure is malicious, and that adjective is far too weak. His joy comes from manipulating Leporello. It was by working along these lines that we found the way into the Catalogue Aria. Is Leporello there to laugh at Donna Elvira or to warn her? I think he warns her.

'By bringing out the destructiveness in Giovanni's character I think we are making other scenes work. The beginning of Act II with the disguises and the mockery of Elvira is now *painfully* funny. The humour, which is not yet as strong as it should be, will develop, I hope, from the intensity. It'll come from Giovanni because he is outrageous; it'll come from Leporello grumbling; it'll come from Elvira's rapid changes of mood; it'll come above all from the orchestra which provides a running commentary of mockery.

'I'm anxious to eliminate that bogus Casanova overlay which sticks to Giovanni. He is not a character from Fielding, guzzling and whoring, but a figure from the Enlightenment who won't believe in anything until it is put before his eyes, and sometimes not even then, as the graveyard scene proves. In many ways Giovanni is modern, rational man being sent to a hell whose existence is proved by his actions. But it must be recognised that his appetites are completely jaded. He derives a certain delight from thinking that every unpleasant and selfish step he takes moves him a little further down the road to proving the existence, or the non-existence of God. He is sadistic to everyone, including himself.'

The Luxon–Hall Giovanni, which was well established by the middle of May, showed quite a lot of similarity with Molière's Don Juan, who is described early on in the play by Sganarelle as being the biggest scoundrel the world has ever known. He believes in neither heaven nor hell, goodness, nor even in werewolves! Juan's own philosophy was equally direct in Molière: 'Life's supremest pleasure is making a woman do what she thinks she doesn't want.'*

While sadistic aggression was being fed into Don Giovanni the outlines of Leporello were softened. Peter Hall half accepted that he had been moving towards the unfunniest Leporello of all time. 'Stafford has a strong comic instinct, but in the early days he was giving too much of a *buffo* interpretation. We've been out to remove all those pieces of business which make the audiences laugh in German opera houses. Perhaps we've gone a little too far. I want a rueful Leporello, who feels sad about the bad things happening round about him. But above all he is Common Man, open to temptation and, like a good Catholic, rushing off to confession to clear his conscience. He is also out on every occasion to save his own skin, which he becomes pretty adept at doing. There's a good deal of resilience there too. At the end of the opera he has come closer to death than any of those who join him in the finale and yet he appears almost unscathed by this encounter. He's lost a master, he's lost his job and his money; he's had a sight of hell but he does not seem too worried.'

The skin-saving aspect of Leporello, much emphasised by John Pritchard during rehearsals, is seen most strongly in the sextet of Act II. Masetto and Zerlina push him before Donna Anna and Don Ottavio, who believe for a moment that Giovanni has been cornered at last. Leporello throws off his cloak and begs forgiveness, although those around him, and particularly Elvira who realises that she has been duped again, have plenty of cause to attack him. Mozart builds up the situation into a sextet of consternation and bewilderment which, Dent argues, forms a typical operatic finale. Dent's case is not wholly convincing because he finds no corresponding break in the first act. It seems

---

* *op. cit.*, Fowles.

far more likely that Mozart and Da Ponte wanted to give Leporello a chance to *sing* himself out of trouble, which he does by grovelling before his accusers and then slipping off into the night while their attention is distracted for a moment.

The scene is probably the most difficult to stage in the whole opera. The direction by Da Ponte is that it is set in Donna Anna's courtyard, although it seems unlikely that Leporello would choose this particular place, which has memories in plenty for him, for ditching Elvira. It is scarcely more probable that Masetto and Zerlina should turn up here during their torchlit hunt for Giovanni. Donna Anna is specified as being in 'deep mourning' although it is far enough into the night for Leporello to be confused when he tries to find the door out into the street — putting Elvira the wrong side of the wall in Giovanni's castle was easy enough but here it causes immense difficulties. Christopher Benn has noted that some producers, prompted by Anna's dress, have placed the scene close to the Commendatore's grave to imply that she and Ottavio have just returned from paying their respects to the dead. But he goes on to point out very reasonably that this mutes the effect of the graveyard scene itself, following Ottavio's aria. Bury and Hall chose a walled courtyard, very close in shape to the beginning of Act I but with windows through which the flares of Masetto's search-party can be seen.

This section of the opera needs almost as many doors as a Feydeau farce. Leporello and Elvira have to make their entry through one gate; Anna and Ottavio in this setting had to emerge from the house of the late Commendatore; it is arguable that Masetto and Zerlina should appear through yet another entrance. Hall reckoned that he needed a fourth gate in the scenery, but the workshop which was in the middle of preparing Strauss' *Die schweigsame Frau*, the second of the season's new productions, was unenthusiastic. The request was withdrawn, but the element of farce remained and the upper dimly-lit windows at the back suggested a labyrinth in this corner of Seville.

The irony of the early part of the scene is that Leporello manages to lose Elvira but then gets lost himself. Hall wanted both the orchestra and the singers *molto agitato*. 'When Elvira is singing "*Sola, sola in buio loco*" she's reflecting not only her fear but Leporello's worry that now at last he's on his own he can't even get away. The doors he tries are either locked or else they are recesses in the walls of the courtyard. The comedy comes from having two people almost side by side both looking for a door.'

The darkness of the scene did not help. Pritchard complained gently that if he could not see the singers then he could scarcely conduct them and he was not reassured by a cheery reply from the stage that they could not see him either. Light was gradually brought in, first by the flares of the search-party and then by a shaft which pierced the gloom when Ottavio opened the door to lead Anna outside—there was no implication that they were just on their way back from the cemetery. Leporello slid round the set like a lizard, feeling for exits, until he found the only unbolted door which was the one by which he had entered. There, logically, he came face to face with Zerlina and Masetto as this was indeed the exit to the street.

Acting in the dark is not easy and few members of the audience care to strain their eyes in an effort to make out what is going on. As soon as Leporello reveals himself to general amazement ('*Dei! Leporello!*') Hall moved into Suspended Time and brought the lights full on to the faces of the singers. The principle of dividing the moments when the characters address the audience from those where they are talking to one another was here taken to its extreme. Mozart, according to Peter Hall, does not keep to conventional dramatic timing. When he has something important to say, or when emotions are stretched like a piece of elastic, he can stop the clock so that the audience can be addressed. Hall brought the band of accusers and their victim to the front of the stage and encouraged them to grab the public by the ears in exactly the way he had asked Stafford Dean to behave like Frankie Howerd in the opening words of the opera.

'When there is an ensemble everyone tends to abdicate his or her rôle. We need the reverse. It's essential to keep up the questioning direct to the audience and express whatever you as individuals are feeling, whether it be puzzlement, bewilderment or shock. This ensemble, "*Mille torbidi pensieri*" ("A thousand confused thoughts"), consists of five people, and Leporello,

The last handshake: the Commendatore
(Pierre Thau) and Don Giovanni (Thomas
Allen) of the Series II cast

singing much the same words but from their own viewpoint. You've got to address the audience individually as though you, and you alone, were asking for their endorsement and approval. You're a gospeller, a Marble Arch orator, complaining that you're in a terrible state and asking for—no, demanding—attention. I want you to shed all trace of operatic stiffness. Relax your bodies as much as possible.

'The difference between being an ensemble and a group of six people singing separately is a very fine one. That's why each and every one of you has got to make his own personal appeal.'

Hall rarely made speeches in rehearsal, preferring to take individuals or pairs of singers to one side to analyse music or movement with them. During this explanation of Suspended Time he became more and more animated, gesturing and even persuading himself that the singers were intended to buttonhole the audience. John Pritchard, in contrast, was very cool at this heated noon, sipping from a china cup which contained not coffee but chilled *Orvieto secco*. Hall built up the enthusiasm, Pritchard acted as the tempering agent, calming the pace and quietening the orchestra.

The idea of bringing the sextet forward to engage the audience made Leporello's escape possible. The blackness at the back of the stage coupled with the brightness at the front distracted the eye from the possible routes into the night. Conventionally, Leporellos edge, usually rather too obviously, out of reach of their accusers and then make a run for it. Stafford Dean, after a number of experiments in escapology, behaved like a secondhand-car dealer and vanished in the middle of his spiel. The method of his departure was almost as surprising to the vengeance brigade as the manner of his discovery. It was in many ways a reflection of the solution to the Act I finale.

Getting the balance between Leporello and Giovanni right leads to the correct weighting of the whole opera. The servant became more adept at slipping out of tight corners and the master more inclined to court danger. Stafford Dean had no wish to equate Leporello with Figaro (another of his regular rôles) who is out to challenge authority. When the Statue comes to supper he hides behind the chair and burrows beneath the dinner table, showing deep terror at this brush with vengeance just so long as it lasts. He emerges unscathed at the end and is justifiably pleased, but there is no question of him supporting Giovanni in those final minutes.

Peter Hall was anxious that nothing in the supper scene should distract from the awe evoked by the arrival of the Statue. The traditional gags, apart from the filching of the piece of pheasant which is referred to in the libretto, were removed and even Leporello's scramble to hide beneath the table cloth was considered dubious. In the end Leporello went under the table for a moment out of sight of the audience and then peered at them. Giovanni should grow in strength and determination as his time on earth came to an end. He was to mock and rebuff those who came to save him as befits a man at the end of the eighteenth century who has taken Enlightenment just as far as he possibly can. The human cry of terror, the only one from Giovanni during the whole opera, uttered as he is dragged down to hell by the demons reveals him as the last opponent of a civilisation which is moving back towards God.

So the end, with the cross of red moving across the sky and the equally fiery pit with its horned demons gripping Don Giovanni, was an almost Blakeian vision of heaven and hell. It echoed the Romantic freeze of the Act I finale with the billowing curtains and swaying chandeliers. Only the Epilogue, with its glib moral and almost unfeeling dispersal of those who remained on earth, returned the opera to the eighteenth century.

9 Interlude with Benjamin Luxon

Before he came to Glyndebourne at the end of April Ben Luxon had sung Giovanni in one other production. That was in Bern where he stepped into a routine staging in which he recalls having a lot of Errol Flynnery and buckle and swash. Luxon had his difficulties, first with the ankle which took so long to heal, and then with a rearguard action against Hall and the wig department defending the right to keep his luxuriant blond beard. Hall claimed that gentlemen at the beginning of the nineteenth century did not wear beards and Luxon replied that fashion was less important than his appearance. He looked better with a beard than without one. Wigs reckoned that Luxon would win that one and prepared a false beard for Leporello so that the disguises could be maintained. They lost that wager when Luxon gave way just before the final dress rehearsal, first of all trimming his growth of hair, then cutting it to the correct Jane Austen length, and shaving his beard.

Both *The Sunday Times* and *The Observer* used the same adjective 'debonair' to describe his Giovanni and Peter Heyworth went on to suggest that he looked rather like Puccini. Luxon during rehearsals had not consciously worked towards the smooth, elegant Giovanni portrayed by Cesare Siepi and, to a lesser extent, by Roger Soyer, but he had responded to Peter Hall's call for ice in the soul. A couple of days before the première he was typically critical of what he had achieved so far:

'I don't think I can do Giovanni yet, although I certainly hope to one day. The point is to realise the slickness, the silkiness and

Elizabeth Gale, Benjamin Luxon and Stafford Dean rehearse

A break on the way to church: Zerlina (Elizabeth Gale), Masetto (John Rawnsley), Leporello (Stafford Dean) and Don Giovanni (Benjamin Luxon)

the driving force behind the man. When I arrived here on 26 April, I had little idea where to begin. You could say that I was open-minded but that would only be half the truth because as a singer I've always found it extremely hard to go against my instinct.

'I knew from working with Peter before that he would have no shortage of ideas about either the opera or the rôle. There would be a constant flurry of suggestions. I realised too that there would be a mixture of frustration and exhilaration. He is marvellous when he has the right material and he always knows the general direction that he wants to take, but the backwarding and forwarding on specific points too easily becomes confusing.

'Take the opening scene. We've argued about the pacing of that and on whether Giovanni actually enjoys fighting and killing the Commendatore. We've altered the entrances and exits so that Ottavio now comes in from the street in his nightgown. We've had locks fitted to the door so that Anna can shut Leporello and myself up inside the courtyard and then we've had to work out just how we free ourselves.

'There's almost a farcical side to the experimenting. Take the donkeys which were meant to pull the peasants' carts. In no way could they ever have worked satisfactorily, but we had to spend an evening proving that. It had to be seen that it couldn't be done.

'You become depressed that time is being wasted and the hours you have spent developing a false theory have gone for nothing, but then the exhilaration suddenly breaks through. The Act I finale strikes me as masterly. Peter had no clue how to handle that when rehearsal began and it suddenly evolved. It was shaped by stripping off all the years of operatic crap obscuring the scene and seeing at last what is there underneath. That is something very special.

'I'm grateful for all the work that has gone into the recitatives. There is very little in Giovanni's arias on which to build a character—the music just skates away. You can only discover the man in his asides or his comments to Leporello; we've pulled each sentence apart in a way few, if any, other houses would do. That's why the relationship between Giovanni and Leporello has been altered and why it is now so convincing.

'We've passed out of the period when Leporello was seen as Moral Man. I wouldn't be surprised if Peter planted those seeds so that he could root them out later. It couldn't work because Leporello is a rascal, he's funny and he's a foil to Giovanni. Stafford became frustrated when he was pointed in the wrong direction after singing the rôle a couple of hundred times. Now we've got the two men back together.

'I think one of the troubles with Giovanni is that he has no security and no background that he speaks of. The nearest he gets to stability is with Leporello who acts as a kind of human travelling home for him. That's why their happiest moments are the ones they have together, even those brief moments of semi-equality such as the prelude to the Champagne Aria. And there's that shared excitement which I want to establish in the final scene. Giovanni turns to Leporello when the Statue arrives. They've been together for a long time and they know that it is the end of the line. Leporello is afraid because he does not want to lose Giovanni, who is his very life. Leporello is totally loyal and at this moment there is real knowledge shared between the two men. Leporello is the only man Giovanni trusts or needs to trust.

'The Champagne Aria is the most difficult number in the score for me. No one seems to know quite what to do with it or how to sing it. A friend of mine recorded it privately imitating fifteen different Don Giovannis and they all sounded bad. In a way it's non-music because there is nothing to get your teeth into. It is a steady crescendo of fury, potency and sheer driving power and yet it all has to be sheathed in elegance. Siepi sang it well on record—I used his set when I was learning the rôle. A lot of the interpretation I found uninteresting, lacking colour particularly for an Italian, but he had the measure of that number alright.'

Ben Luxon intends to spend more time at Glyndebourne.

'The strength and weakness of the place is that there is no star system. No one is down here for the money, indeed some of my colleagues will not come because of the level of fees. But the compensation for this is the identification with the singers. It was the same with the English Opera Group, where I spent seven or eight years. They were concerned with you and thought carefully about how to cast you. They also force you to go to the roots of whatever you're performing in. It's a bit like being at school— and I speak as an ex-schoolmaster—where you are made to learn all your lessons and you don't get any days off without a top-class excuse.

'Above all I'm attached to the house because most of the best productions I've been in started here. *Ulisse* was special— everyone who saw it remembered it. *Figaro* was special and so in quite a different way was *Vixen*. Perhaps *Giovanni* will be special too.'

10 The Conductor

John Pritchard arrived first at Glyndebourne in May 1947. The facts are there in Spike Hughes' history of the house where the name is listed under the musical staff for both the Sussex and Edinburgh seasons that year. The Pritchard progress is charted in Hughes' orange endpapers: Chorus Master in 1949, Assistant Conductor a year later, and then in 1963 came the unwieldy title of Music Counsellor. Pritchard has given a large slice of his operatic life to Glyndebourne but in the mid-Seventies he decided that he had to relinquish his musical home there, comfortable though it was. The Cologne State Opera offered him the post of Musical Director and Pritchard accepted. Bernard Haitink was appointed as Musical Director of Glyndebourne (and in order to do so cut back on his administrative commitments with the London Philharmonic Orchestra).

Pritchard's last performance as Glyndebourne's Director of Music was *Falstaff* on 11 July. For the sake of symmetry it should have been *Don Giovanni*, the opera which he learned by the side of Fritz Busch and which he took over when Busch was ill. But calendars sometimes get out of shape.

He told the story of his initial engagement in an affectionate, bland reminiscence of his youth in the 1977 Glyndebourne Programme, the only time he has been persuaded to write for the publication. Roy Henderson was among the singers in a performance of Mendelssohn's *Elijah* which Pritchard had conducted at Uttoxeter, a small town better known for its racecourse than its music. Henderson, who had sung the Count

A serenade from John Brownlee for Rudolf
Bing and Glyndebourne's first Masetto, Roy
Henderson

in Glyndebourne's very first production of *Figaro*, recommended
Pritchard to the Christies. A card followed from John Christie in
response to a letter from Pritchard, who had not been slow in
following up the Henderson endorsement: 'You sound the right
sort—go and see my man Bing, at the Baker Street Office.' As
John Pritchard remarks, only John Christie could have referred
to the 'redoubtable future head of the Metropolitan Opera and
the Edinburgh Festival as though he were a kind of head
gamekeeper on the estate'. Bing engaged him and told him to
take the 8.45 a.m. train to Lewes on the opening day of rehearsals
in early May. Pritchard joined the other young répétiteurs and
moved into his room in the Christie house in much the same way

that the 1977 crop settled down in Sussex in late April. Glyndebourne tends to distrust change.

With six previous seasons of conducting *Don Giovanni* at Glyndebourne behind him and several hundred performances in other houses John Pritchard made only rare appearances at the early rehearsals. He was at Covent Garden also in early May for *L'elisir d'amore*, where the principals in the revival of Donizetti's opera were suffering from a variety of ailments. The cast ended by bearing virtually no resemblance to the one originally announced, but Pritchard at Glyndebourne appeared little worried that the Royal Opera House was still searching for an Adina for the following night's performance. While Peter Hall was finding a path through the problems presented by Mozart and Da Ponte, John Pritchard would patter gently into the rehearsal stage, listen for a quarter of an hour, make a few suggestions, take up the baton for a time. Sometimes a beckoning forefinger would pull one or two of the singers away for some individual practice, rather in the way a don might suggest an extra tutorial before Finals are too close. More often Pritchard would retire just as softly as he had arrived.

He agreed that he was an old hand at pacing his involvement with rehearsals. 'Perhaps Peter would like me to spend more time with him, but I hardly think that would be right. In the old days conductors would often not appear until the opera was actually on stage, although Fritz Busch who taught me so much about Mozart here was an exception—he would rehearse and rehearse at the piano.

'My rôle when the production is still trying to find its shape is to apply a little touch of the rein, to stop singers being pushed too far, to weed out anything which goes against the score. I have to parcel out my time to go along with Peter's method of working. With Rennert, for example, the plan would have been absolutely clear and devised well in advance, so I would know exactly when to come in. With this *Don Giovanni* it is different. Peter has an eye for the end result and then applies himself to the mechanics of the scene. Of course I want to look at Plan C or D rather than go through Plan A. The best performances are made when there are strong ties between producer, designer and conductor—I think of the Visconti–Giulini *Don Carlo* at Covent Garden or the Busch–Ebert–Messel *Idomeneo* here. I've tried to establish similar links at Glyndebourne with Rennert and later with John Cox and Peter Hall, but to do that you must not interfere too much or too early.

'I admire the way Peter tackles problems other people ignore and becomes positively stimulated by them. Busch would never have puzzled over apparent anomalies in the libretto. He simply reacted as the music directed. Yet by worrying away at something Peter often comes up with an answer. The Act I finale is an example. He fretted for a long time because he did not know how to stage it. Then he arrived at a solution and I am sure he would not have got there any faster had I been on hand with suggestions.'

The London Philharmonic Orchestra, which replaced the Royal Philharmonic at Glyndebourne in 1964 primarily at John Pritchard's instigation, arrived ten days before the first night of *Don Giovanni*. The house was now fully active: queues formed at the Courtyard Café in the rehearsal breaks, the pub near Glynde station which is famed for its locally brewed beer started putting on hot and cold buffets in the evening. The orchestra spent the first day without the singers, looking at *Don Giovanni*, which they had not played for a decade, at Poulenc's *La Voix humaine* and at *The Cunning Little Vixen*, which Simon Rattle had taken over from its 1975 conductor, Raymond Leppard. The LPO obviously enjoy their Glyndebourne stint and the level of the musical accompaniment in a house where the acoustics are not easy has risen mightily over the past few years. John Pritchard must take a good deal of credit for this, although he is fond of quoting Vittorio Gui who once said that it took ten years to make an opera orchestra.

The first *Giovanni* stage rehearsal with orchestra sounded rushed. A few of the singers over-reacted to the new voice which had joined their own after four weeks of a single piano. The instrumentalists in several cases were trying too hard. John Pritchard as ever was unperturbed:

'The LPO have always had a habit of charging in on the first run-through and when they do I know it will all calm down the next time round. My job as a conductor is to channel an orchestra's interest and this is never achieved by harassing them and certainly not by lecturing. If something goes wrong I say nothing—a tap of the baton on the desk is sufficient and we start again. Ten days of preparation for the opening of the season is sufficient. Sometimes I wish we could call the singers for a short and more intensive rehearsal period, and I've suggested it, but it simply does not give the technical staff enough time.

'The main musical problem in *Don Giovanni* is to respond to the changes of mood which are swifter than in any other Mozart opera. Fritz Busch said that the life blood of a conductor came from the choice of tempi. At the beginning of my career I used to worry about it—was I being too brilliant, was I plodding? Now I can't analyse the speeds I choose because they are as instinctive as the overall musical balance. All I can say is that I am not erratic: I timed a recent run of ten performances at Covent Garden and overall variation was only a shade over ten seconds.

'I agree that at Glyndebourne we've been searching none too successfully for the right man to sing Giovanni during my years

Fritz Busch at rehearsal

here, although Raimondi was certainly most impressive. There is always something wrong—a good voice coupled with a negative presence on stage, a handsome figure but no colour in the singing, dash spoiled by vulgarity. I'm not even impressed by the general admiration for Siepi who struck me as being far too mannered. Perhaps like Carmen it is an impossible rôle, or perhaps in Ben Luxon we have found the right answer. But in this production I am convinced of our rightness in two respects: attention has been paid at all times to the original stage instructions of Da Ponte and we have concentrated on the recitatives. They may be difficult to accompany and to convey to an audience with imperfect Italian, but in them are found the roots of each character in the opera.'

11 The Run In

The low point, Peter Hall admitted, usually came about three weeks into rehearsals. The design had been mapped out and yet the opening night was still too far away to provide real inspiration. 'There's a moment in every production when my own juices are not running strongly. You've made your discoveries and then you have to put them into operation, which is less exciting. You know the strength of your various components and you fit them together like the pieces of a jigsaw. Sometimes at this stage in the past I've got positively bored and have appeared to do nothing; then suddenly a crisis occurs and I do the Lazarus bit, arising from the dead and solving a problem or two.

'What are my doubts now? Not the Act I finale, I think we have that one right. Not the graveyard scene, although it's a bugger to stage. I'm a little worried about the Empire setting. I'm sure we took the right decision to nudge the opera forward in that direction. Have we gone too far? I don't know—I'll tell you after the second dress rehearsal, but my instinct is that we're on line. I'm still not sure about the Epilogue. Who are these six people who ask the audience to repeat the old refrain, "*L'antichissima canzon*"? The three low-life characters— Leporello, Zerlina and Masetto—start it off and then the aristos join in. Should the artists resume their own offstage personae? Probably they are six performers at the end, not six characters.'

Were they like Prospero at the close of *The Tempest*? 'In a way, but the mood here is quite different. It's brief, ironic,

Mozart's and Da Ponte's cynical epilogue:
Masetto (John Rawnsley), Zerlina (Elizabeth
Gale), Leporello (Stafford Dean), Don Ottavio
(Leo Goeke), Donna Elvira (Rosario Andrade),
Donna Anna (Joan Carden)

humorous, resolved and it utterly contradicts any idea of
heaven, hell or the sublime, which we may have been considering
over the past three hours or so.'

Glyndebourne and the *Don Giovanni* were waiting for Hall to
make last-minute adjustments to a production which had gone
almost suspiciously smoothly. After the first dress rehearsal he
congratulated the singers on not over-reacting but warned them
that the next ten days would not be a holiday. 'We've a very good
idea of where we are going and I know that some opera
producers like to slacken off at this point so that you can all relax
until the final Dress. I don't much care for that approach. I
reckon that some of our most intensive work is going to occur
over the next week and I want to rehearse with each of you
individually.' He started with the two-hour session with Rosario
Andrade already described.

The short speech was very much that of a theatre director
working in the opera, as Peter Hall well knew. 'Opera-singers

behave in quite a different way to actors in the straight theatre. Actors tend to worry more, they stick around after rehearsals talking to one another about the progress they are making or not making; singers usually disperse at once. If I were to say to the *Giovanni* cast, "Take the three days before the dress rehearsal off," they would be more than happy; if I made the same proposal to a group of actors they would go berserk with anxiety and believe that the première was going to be a disaster. It is important to keep everyone on a high during the last few days and dispel the feeling that all is now permanently fixed. It isn't. Yet if you nibble at the opera, making irritating, tiny alterations here or there, then there is the danger that some of the artists will start to retire into their shells.'

It is possible that for these very reasons Peter Hall makes late switches which can provoke grumbling all the way from the workshops to the Lewes restaurants favoured by the singers. When you are suddenly called for an evening rehearsal the *tagliatelle* grows cold on the plate. 'I find last-minute thoughts generally inspiring and at the same time realise that I run the risk of antagonising others. But it's a risk I'm prepared to take because it is fundamental to my approach to opera production. Does the director arrive from on high with every move mapped out in advance? If he does, then I missed that particular boat long ago. Sometimes I've been accused of making these changes just to keep my own adrenalin flowing and subconsciously perhaps I do. My excuse is that I push myself hard during the last few days, making the work more intense, so it's reasonable to expect the same of others.'

In the final week of rehearsals Peter Hall's visits back to London became more frequent. The cast were anticipating that the run-through on the Friday before the final dress rehearsal, which is traditionally open to Glyndebourne's friends and helpers, would be a lengthy one. Peter Hall asked the cast to invite their own relatives into the theatre that day to give the feel of an audience. He was still stressing the need for each singer to seize the attention during the moments of Suspended Time, which were growing in number and emphasis during the final days. 'When we come to the final Dress on Sunday the most important thing of all is to establish that relationship with the audience. Each of you has got to believe that you, and you alone, are understood when you start to confide in those out front.'

The changes were not to come.

The penultimate dress rehearsal of *Don Giovanni* was scheduled for 2.30 on 27 May with no time fixed for the close because it was expected that there would be a lengthy session of production notes, the process by which the director comments on every performance front-stage and back-stage after the orchestra has gone home. Nobody expected the Staff Restaurant to be full of the cast that lunchtime: singers tend to eat and drink little, if anything, before a performance. The production team on the other hand usually fills up in anticipation of a long afternoon, evening and possibly night ahead. And Peter Hall was not there eating.

Word got round that he had been detained in London. Stewart Trotter began the rehearsal on time saying that Peter hoped to be joining them just as soon as he could. The first act went through without Hall's arrival, then it was announced on the late afternoon news that there would be no performances at the National Theatre that evening: one of the plumbers there had been dismissed for failing on a number of occasions to do what was required of him and the back-stage staff had walked out in sympathy with him. The reason for Hall's frequent trips to London was now clear. Midway through the second act a call came through to Moran Caplat from Peter Hall saying that there was no chance of being in Glyndebourne that evening, but that he would be there for the public dress rehearsal on Sunday.

Stewart Trotter gathered the cast on stage at the end of the dress rehearsal and explained the situation. The note-giving was brief and everyone retired into the night much earlier than they expected. Despite Trotter's enthusiasm the feeling was rather flat. Those last-minute swerves in course which everyone had been anticipating could not possibly come now. In a way it was almost disappointing.

The disruption at the National had been brewing for some time and there was speculation that it had been timed deliberately to coincide with the approach of the *Giovanni* première. Nothing was proved, but the situation grew worse. Pickets were placed outside the National Theatre and attempts were made, unsuccessfully, to draw the actors into the dispute. Peter Hall tried to divorce his London problems as much as he could from his Glyndebourne work in exactly the way he had given no reason for his evening trips back to London. When he arrived for the public Dress on Sunday, 29 May, he did however hint that he might not be present at the first night two days later.

At the end of that final rehearsal he called the cast and the stage crew together in the Green Room. There was a pause while pints of lager were brought up from the Staff Bar. At 11.00 p.m. Hall started to talk.

'Thank you all for meeting tonight so late. I won't keep you long—one of the reasons is that I have my first strike meeting at the National tomorrow at 8.30 a.m. First let me say that this is the best *Don Giovanni* I've ever seen. Fuck it, we've got that far.

'The only general criticism is that apart from Stafford you're all a bit shy on stage. The key to the whole performance is that immediate contact with the audience, particularly when we pass into Suspended Time. You've got to move into it from the word go, you've got to connect and not only with the middle stalls. Work the whole house when you're addressing them—You lot up there—have you got it? And what about you over there—are you paying attention? Don't hold back, after all the audience obviously liked you.'

Then he went straight on to individual points: the pub sign was invisible, the arrival of the peasants on their way to church was clumsy, the cut of Ottavio's recitative after '*Non mi dir*' was wrong ... Then the praise returned.

'The opera balanced beautifully and each scene told its story. It isn't as good as it should be. Nor ought it to be at this point. But we're almost there.'

Peter Hall's optimism was justified by the reception of the first performance which was as warm as for any Glyndebourne première since *Calisto*. Peter Hall was not there to hear it and Moran Caplat explained briefly to the audience why not. Indeed Peter Hall was not to see *Don Giovanni* at Glyndebourne until 4 June, the third performance.

Epilogue

That *Don Giovanni* on 4 June was the only public performance Peter Hall saw of the cast he had coached for five weeks. After giving the production notes on the dress rehearsal he went straight back to London and was dealing with the National Theatre's labour problems at eight o'clock the next morning. Stewart Trotter reported back from Glyndebourne after every performance, discussing slight changes of emphasis here and there and adjustments in the lighting. But Trotter was well aware that the HQ in London was considerably more beleaguered than the front line at Glyndebourne. There was no chance for Hall to come back to Sussex that month.

He eventually returned at the beginning of July just before the Series II cast was to take over. With the exception of Philip Langridge, who had stood in as Ottavio while Leo Goeke was away, they had been coached entirely by Stewart Trotter and Glyndebourne's Musical Director elect, Bernard Haitink. They were physically and vocally different. Tom Allen in the title rôle looked younger than Ben Luxon, a dapper twenty-three-year-old in place of Luxon's much fiercer figure. The new Elvira, Rachel Yakar, substituted a fevered tension for Rosario Andrade's outbursts of emotion. Anna, Horiana Branisteanu, brought out the self-obsession of that secretive lady, demonstrating that Ottavio is no match for her, in all senses of that phrase.

Some minor alterations had been made. In the opening scene Ottavio and Anna now spotted the corpse of the Commendatore simultaneously. Giovanni was more openly sexual in his wooing of Zerlina in '*Là ci darem*' and, as if to mirror this, Leporello

(Richard Van Allan) in disguise was more insistent in his mock flattery of Elvira. Hall approved virtually all the Trotter glosses on his original text.

'Certain movements were much tighter. That "seduction" of Elvira by Leporello became much more real and terrible. Earlier we had underplayed the total cynicism of his action. I think we now have "*Non mi dir*" right: Ottavio comes in a moment after Anna at the beginning, with the implication that he has just been to the police to report Giovanni's crimes—that was Stewart's idea—and his recitative at the end of the number has now been restored. Those couple of lines provoked the only real dispute I had with John Pritchard during the whole rehearsal period. I gave way, but Bernard Haitink agrees that they round off the scene. So back they have gone and that is where they will stay.

'I admit that when I did get back to Glyndebourne at the beginning of July I couldn't resist throwing my weight around a little. Probably it was the sheer joy of being back. But I found when I arrived that Anna, Elvira and Ottavio were refusing to wear their masks in "*Protegga il giusto cielo*". Some of the music staff were mildly sympathetic, but I wasn't. I told them that if those masks were not reinstated at once I would call a rehearsal the next day, which was their Saturday off. The threat had the desired effect.'

Would Peter Hall have made last-minute changes at the end of May had he been allowed to? 'I expect so, but only minor ones. Opera is not like the theatre: there is a limit on what you can do. Singers have to be rested; actors can be worked right up to the very last moment and probably benefit from sudden swerves in direction. In normal circumstances I would spend those last few days in clarification.

'After the dress rehearsal I would have concentrated on detail, trying to elucidate here and explain there. But during that nightmare at the National there was no possibility of my dealing in changes. In the week preceding the Dress I had scarcely no sleep and this had to be concealed from the cast. Then it became clear that there was no possibility of attending the first night; I had the feeling of being wrenched away from the bedside at the very moment the birth was happening.

'In happier circumstances I would have liked to do more work on Ottavio. I don't think that we fully established him as the pillar of morality and that of course was mainly because of Leo's absence in Canada in the middle of rehearsals. I think we were on to something by showing Ottavio as the equable, calm, rational man who is finally made a monkey of by Anna. She by contrast is the over-sexed woman who will go searching for a husband to torment and a substitute for the father she has lost. That relationship needed more investigation.

'On a totally different plane I still regret losing that leap from the balcony in the opening scene. It is basically a moment of invaluable comedy: there is the lover sliding down the drainpipe, or whatever support he can find, and coming face to face with the outraged woman he thought he had just escaped from.' The effect was achieved later in the Glyndebourne run and, when *Don Giovanni* came to the National, more comedy came unintentionally. John Bury had put a hidden block on his set midway between the balcony and stage level as a toe-hold for Giovanni, who was back at balcony level. Ben Luxon, who had returned to the title rôle, missed his footing and fell flat on his back. An undignified entrance, which ironically looked back to the very first day of rehearsal in Glyndebourne.

After being temporarily winded, Luxon survived the second drop and that performance at the National, like the other five there, played to a house which had been sold out several weeks in advance. *Don Giovanni* had already been filmed by Southern Television after the end of the Glyndebourne run and the cast for the five-city tour in the autumn was well into rehearsal. Peter Hall had by now turned his attention to Wycherley's *The Country Wife*, scheduled to open on the South Bank in November. At the Salzburg Festival Jean-Pierre Ponnelle had opened another *Giovanni*, which was as controversial as Hall's. Oddly, both productions had one thing in common: Ponnelle, like Hall, cleared the stage of everyone apart from the principals at the end of Act I.

Did Hall regret anything about his staging? Had he learned anything from the reviews?

'The criticisms were the ones I expected. We knew that those who were against us would attack us for being unglamorous, too dark, pessimistic, nihilistic, too black. Someone was bound to ask where sunny Mozart was. But I believe it is dangerous to involve oneself too deeply with notices. They are often of course right in their praise or their blame, but they are not part of your own work process. They can, either way, be terribly confusing. So I speed-read them. Try to keep them at arm's length, and get on with my job. During my early days at Stratford, I was often told by the press that I knew nothing about Shakespeare. I hoped that I did. So I had to dismiss the general criticism, so that I did not go into the theatre each day with a nasty bubble of fretfulness floating around in my head. So now, after *Don Giovanni*, which has provoked a very great deal of praise, it would be equally crass of me to go around thinking that I have found all the solutions.

'When you are at work you are as naked as a peeled prawn and you have to protect yourself from outside influences by every possible means. So I look at notices in much the same way that I draw the curtains to see the weather in the morning. "Good," you say, "everyone's favourable, sun's shining! Lovely!" Then when the reverse happens you mutter, "Raining . . . horrible," and get on with the work you are doing. I appreciate the difficulty facing the critic with an opera like *Don Giovanni*: he has to write on how it compares with other *Giovannis* he has seen and in making this comparison he probably has to go to extremes in order to put his point across. And perhaps in the same way I sometimes go to extremes in order to put my point across. I think I can learn from the notices that my next *Don Giovanni* must have, on the few occasions where it is possible, more extreme splashes of sunlight. But that would be to make the darkness more intense.

'For a long time during the preparation of *Giovanni* I simply saw a journey and I had no idea where I would end up. As a producer I can only make a voyage of discovery and that is probably why I am more skilful in the theatre and the opera house than in the cinema. I've only made two films of which I am proud, *Akenfield* and *The Homecoming*. Why? In that particular medium the journey has to be made in the cutting-room, which is not the most congenial place in the world. I need to do a scene badly several times in order to end up doing it well. And that is not possible behind the camera.

'In opera my instinct is triggered by the music and what it says about character. I had the idea of emphasising the romanticism in *Don Giovanni* from the beginning, but I tried to arrive with very few other preconceived notions. If they are there when you start then you have to spend time eradicating them instead of discovering what you want to say through work and instinct— no apologies for re-employing that word.

'I think we've come close to solving some of the problems Mozart and Da Ponte posed. I've always felt before that the supper scene is too long after the arrival of the Commendatore. It isn't. I think we got near to releasing the extreme emotion in the trio. The graveyard, I'm convinced now, has to be staged by placing the absurd and the sublime side by side—in complete extremes. There is one of the grandest moments in the opera when the trombone sounds off stage and the Commendatore sings out of the darkness followed by an immediate switch into the comedy of the nodding of heads. I'm satisfied with the way both *"Finch'han dal vino"* and the Serenade are performed: it is all too easy to let them become separate numbers unrelated to Giovanni's character and I hope we've avoided that particular pitfall. Other difficulties remain—Zerlina's exit at the end of the first act and her return is still not right; nor is Elvira's first entrance.

'Ideally I would have liked more opportunity to experiment with light. I'm intrigued by the possibility of flooding the stage with all the brilliance available so that the characters could move from night to blazing sunlight so making the contrasts crueller. At one time I had slight worries about the period we chose, but I would not now alter that. My concern would be to find ways of bringing out the fierceness of the work even more emphatically.'

In the autumn of 1977 Peter Hall looked back on his summer's work and conceded that *Giovanni* had given him more satisfaction than any of his other Mozart productions, including *Figaro* which was perhaps a shade too comfortable. *Così* was to come. And perhaps in the future the cycle would be started again.

'I couldn't contemplate a world in which I could not return to *Giovanni* and *Così*, but I need enough time to elapse for each to be totally different the next time round.'

Don Giovanni's descent into hell

Don Giovanni or The Libertine's Punishment

Opera in Two Acts

Music by Wolfgang Amadeus Mozart
Libretto by Lorenzo Da Ponte
(English translation by Ellen H. Bleiler)

Cast

DON GIOVANNI, a libertine   *Bass or baritone*

LEPORELLO, servant to Don Giovanni   *Bass*

DONNA ANNA, a noblewoman whom Don
    Giovanni unsuccessfully assaults   *Soprano*

DON OTTAVIO, betrothed of Donna Anna   *Tenor*

THE COMMENDATORE, an elderly nobleman,
    father of Donna Anna   *Bass*

DONNA ELVIRA, a lady whom Don Giovanni
    loved and left in Burgos   *Soprano*

ZERLINA, a peasant girl   *Soprano*

MASETTO, bridegroom of Zerlina   *Bass*

Servants, peasants, musicians, chorus.

Act I

SCENE I. Seville in the seventeenth century. Late evening, outside the palace of the Commendatore. At the foot of the stairs which lead from the palace, Leporello, dressed in a cloak, paces back and forth.

LEPORELLO: Notte e giorno faticar, per chi nulla sa gradir; piova e vento sopportar, mangiar male e mal dormir! Voglio far il gentiluomo, e non voglio più servir, no, non voglio più servir.

LEPORELLO: Toiling night and day, for someone whom nothing can please; withstanding rain and wind, eating poorly and sleeping badly! I want to be a gentleman, and I don't want to serve any longer, no, I don't want to serve any longer.

He turns towards the palace with an impatient gesture.

Oh che caro galantuomo! Voi star dentro colla bella, ed io far la sentinella! Voglio far il gentiluomo, e non voglio più servir, no, non voglio più servir.

Oh that dear gentleman! It's for you to stay inside with the pretty lady, and for me to play the sentinel! I want to be a gentleman, and I don't want to serve any longer, no, I don't want to serve any longer.

He listens attentively.

Ma mi par, che venga gente; no, non mi voglio far sentir.

But I think that someone is coming; no, I don't want to be seen.

Leporello hides to one side, as Donna Anna and Don Giovanni come down the palace stairs struggling. She attempts to discover the Don's identity, he to hide it.

DONNA ANNA: Non sperar, se non m'uccidi, ch'io ti lasci fuggir mai.

DONNA ANNA: Do not expect me ever to let you escape, unless you kill me.

DON GIOVANNI: Donna folle! indarno gridi, chi son io, tu non saprai.

DON GIOVANNI: Foolish woman! you scream in vain, you shall not know who I am.

LEPORELLO: Che tumulto! o ciel! che gridi! Il padron in nuovi guai.

LEPORELLO: What a racket! o heavens! what screams! My master in a fresh scrape.

Donna Anna calls for help.

DONNA ANNA: Gente! Servi! al traditore!

DONNA ANNA: Help! Servants! get the traitor!

Don Giovanni tries to stifle Donna Anna's cries.

DON GIOVANNI: Taci, e trema al mio furore!

DON GIOVANNI: Be quiet, and tremble at my rage!

DONNA ANNA: Scellerato!

DONNA ANNA: Villain!

DON GIOVANNI: Sconsigliata!

DON GIOVANNI: Foolish woman!

LEPORELLO: Sta a veder che il libertino mi farà precipitar.

LEPORELLO: I can see that the libertine will be my undoing.

DONNA ANNA: Come furia disperata ti saprò perseguitar.

DONNA ANNA: I shall persecute you like a maddened fury.

DON GIOVANNI: Questa furia disperata mi vuol far precipitar.

DON GIOVANNI: This desperate fury will by my undoing.

The Commendatore approaches, carrying a light in one hand, a sword in the other. Donna Anna flees into the palace, leaving Don Giovanni and the Commendatore to face one another.

COMMENDATORE: Lasciala, indegno, battiti meco!

COMMENDATORE: Leave her be, wretch, and duel with me!

DON GIOVANNI: Va, non mi degno di pugnar teco.

DON GIOVANNI: *Haughtily.* Go, I will not stoop to fight with you.

COMMENDATORE: Così pretendi da me fuggir?

COMMENDATORE: Do you imagine you'll escape me thus?

LEPORELLO: (Potessi almeno di quà partir!)

LEPORELLO: *Aside.* If at least I could get away from here!

COMMENDATORE: Battiti!

COMMENDATORE: Fight!

Don Giovanni draws his sword.

DON GIOVANNI: Misero! attendi se vuoi morir!

DON GIOVANNI: Wretched man! Look out, if you wish to die!

He knocks the torch from the Commendatore's hand, and they duel. After several passes, Don Giovanni fatally wounds the Commendatore, who falls to the ground.

COMMENDATORE: Ah! soccorso!

COMMENDATORE: Ah! help!

LEPORELLO: Qual misfatto! Qual ecceso! Entro il sen dallo spavento palpitar il cor mi sento! Io non sò che far, che dir.

LEPORELLO: What a tragedy! What a crime! I feel my heart pounding with fear in my breast! I don't know what to do, what to say.

DON GIOVANNI: Ah! già cade il sciagurato, affannoso e agonizzante già dal seno palpitante veggo l'anima partir.

DON GIOVANNI: Ah! already the villain is fallen, gasping and breathing his last, already I see his soul parting from his heaving breast.

COMMENDATORE:—son tradito! l'assassino m'ha ferito, e dal seno palpitante sento l'anima partir.

COMMENDATORE:—I am betrayed! the assassin has run me through, and I feel my soul parting from my heaving breast.

Meanwhile, the palace windows are lighted up; servants run to and fro in great agitation. Some servants go to the street and return with Don Ottavio, who enters the palace in the background. Don Giovanni replaces his sword at his side.

DON GIOVANNI: Leporello, ove sei?

DON GIOVANNI: Leporello, where are you?

LEPORELLO: Son quì, per mia disgrazia; e voi?

LEPORELLO: I'm here, by my bad luck; and you?

DON GIOVANNI: Son quì.

DON GIOVANNI: I am here.

LEPORELLO: Chi è morto, voi o il vecchio?

LEPORELLO: Who's dead, you or the old man?

DON GIOVANNI: Che domanda da bestia! il vecchio.

DON GIOVANNI: What a stupid question! the old man.

LEPORELLO: Bravo! due imprese leggiadre! Sforzar la figlia, ed ammazzar il padre!

LEPORELLO: Hurray, two charming undertakings! Forcing the daughter and murdering the father.

DON GIOVANNI: L'ha voluto, suo danno.

DON GIOVANNI: He asked for it, it's his loss.

LEPORELLO: Ma Donn'Anna, cosa ha voluto?

LEPORELLO: But Donna Anna, what did she ask for?

Don Giovanni lashes out at Leporello.

DON GIOVANNI: Taci, non mi seccar! Vien meco, se no vuoi qualche cosa ancor tu.

DON GIOVANNI: Be quiet, don't anger me! Come with me, if you don't want something too.

LEPORELLO: Non vo' nulla, Signor, non parlo più.

LEPORELLO: I don't want anything, Sir, I won't say another word.

Don Giovanni and Leporello exit together. Donna Anna and Don Ottavio emerge from the palace, accompanied by servants who light the scene with torches.

DONNA ANNA: Ah! Del padre in periglio in soccorso voliam!

DONNA ANNA: Ah! Let us fly to the relief of my father in his danger!

Don Ottavio draws his sword.

DON OTTAVIO: Tutto il mio sangue verserò, se bisogna: ma dov'è il scellerato?

DON OTTAVIO: If need be, I shall shed all my blood: but where is the villain?

DONNA ANNA: In questo loco.

DONNA ANNA: Right here.

Donna Anna sees the Commendatore's body. She does not yet recognize it, and kneels to examine it.

DONNA ANNA: Ma qual mai s'offre, oh Dei, spettacolo funesto agli occhi miei!

DONNA ANNA: But oh Gods, what distressing sight presents itself to my eyes!

She embraces the body.

Padre, padre mio! mio caro padre!

Father, my father! my dear father!

DON OTTAVIO: Signore!

DON OTTAVIO: Sir!

DONNA ANNA: Ah, l'assassino mel trucidò. Quel sangue—quella piaga—quel volto—tinto e coperto del color di morte.

DONNA ANNA: Ah, the assassin has slain him. That blood—that wound—that face—stained and covered with the hue of death.

Don Ottavio tries to raise her, but she refuses.

Ei non respira più! Fredde le membra!

He breathes no more! His limbs are icy!

She gets up and nearly swoons. Don Ottavio helps her to a seat.

Padre mio! caro padre! padre amato! io manco! io moro!

My father! dear father! beloved father! I falter! I shall die!

Don Ottavio assists her and addresses the servants.

DON OTTAVIO: Ah! soccorrete, amici, il mio tesoro! Cercatemi, recatemi qualche odor, qualche spirito! ah non tardate! Donn'Anna!

DON OTTAVIO: Ah! friends, help my loved one! Find for me, bring to me some smelling salts, some spirits! ah do not delay! Donna Anna!

A servant runs into the palace and returns with some smelling salts, which are offered to Donna Anna.

sposa! amica! il duolo estremo la meschinella uccide! Ahi! già rinviene! datele nuovi aiuti.

bride! friend! her extreme grief is killing the poor creature! Ah! she is reviving! give her more help.

DONNA ANNA: Padre mio!

DONNA ANNA: *Weakly.* My father!

Don Ottavio addresses the servants again.

DON OTTAVIO: Celate, allontanate agli occhi suoi quell'oggetto d'orrore!

DON OTTAVIO: Hurry, remove that object of horror from her sight!

Servants carry the Commendatore's body into the palace.

Anima mia, consolati! fa core!

My soul, console yourself! take heart!

Donna Anna leaps to her feet and turns wildly from Don Ottavio.

DONNA ANNA: Fuggi, crudele, fuggi! lascia che mora anch'io! Ora ch'è morto, o Dio! chi a me la vita diè.

DONNA ANNA: Get away, cruel one, get away! let me die too! Now he is dead, o God, he who gave life to me.

DON OTTAVIO: Senti, cor mio, deh senti, guardami un solo istante, ti parla il caro amante, che vive sol per te.

DON OTTAVIO: Listen, my heart, come listen, attend me only a moment, your dear lover, who lives only for you, speaks to you.

Donna Anna, relenting, reaches out to Don Ottavio.

DONNA ANNA: Tu sei! Perdon, mio bene, l'affanno mio, le pene ...

DONNA ANNA: It is you! Forgive me, my love—my suffering, my sorrows ...

She looks at the place where the Commendatore lay.

ah! il padre mio dov'è?

ah! where is my father?

DON OTTAVIO: Il padre? Lascia, o cara, la rimembranza amara! hai sposo e padre in me.

DON OTTAVIO: Your father? Let the bitter memory be, o dearest! You have a husband and a father in me.

Donna Anna turns proudly and faces Don Ottavio.

DONNA ANNA: Ah! vendicar, se il puoi, giura quel sangue ognor!

DONNA ANNA: Ah! swear ever to avenge that blood, if you are able!

DON OTTAVIO: Lo giuro agli occhi tuoi, lo giuro al nostro amor!

DON OTTAVIO: I swear it by your eyes, I swear it by our love!

DONNA ANNA AND DON OTTAVIO: Che giuramento, o Dei! che barbaro momento! tra cento affetti e cento vammi ondeggiando il cor.

DONNA ANNA AND DON OTTAVIO: What an oath, oh Gods! what a cruel moment! My heart is wavering midst a hundred, hundred sorrows.

Together they slowly enter the palace.

SCENE II. A morning or two later, on a street in Seville. Don Giovanni and Leporello enter, conversing.

DON GIOVANNI: Orsù, spicciati presto— cosa vuoi?

DON GIOVANNI: Come, speak up quickly—what do you want?

LEPORELLO: L'affar, di cui si tratta, è importante!

LEPORELLO: The matter in question is important!

DON GIOVANNI: Lo credo.

DON GIOVANNI: I believe it.

LEPORELLO: È importantissimo!

LEPORELLO: It is very, *very* important!

DON GIOVANNI: Meglio, ancora, finiscila!

DON GIOVANNI: All the better then, come out with it!

LEPORELLO: Giurate di non andar in collera!

LEPORELLO: Promise you won't get angry!

DON GIOVANNI: Lo giuro sul mio onore, purchè non parli del Commendatore.

DON GIOVANNI: On my honour I promise, just don't speak about the Commendatore.

LEPORELLO: Siamo soli?

LEPORELLO: Are we alone?

DON GIOVANNI: Lo vedo!

DON GIOVANNI: Yes indeed!

LEPORELLO: Nessun ci sente?

LEPORELLO: Nobody is listening to us?

DON GIOVANNI: Via!

DON GIOVANNI: Come!

LEPORELLO: Vi posso dire tutto liberamente?

LEPORELLO: I can speak to you in complete freedom?

DON GIOVANNI: Sì!

DON GIOVANNI: Yes!

Leporello begins confidentially and ends almost shouting.

LEPORELLO: Dunque quand'è così—
Caro Signor padrone, la vita che menate
è da briccone!

LEPORELLO: Now then, if it is so—my
dear master, you're leading a rogue's
life!

DON GIOVANNI: Temerario, in tal guisa?

DON GIOVANNI: Foolhardy one! Do you
speak to me in this manner?

LEPORELLO: E il giuramento?

LEPORELLO: And your promise?

DON GIOVANNI: Non sò di giuramenti;
taci, o ch'io—

DON GIOVANNI: I know of no promises;
be quiet, or I—

LEPORELLO: Non parlo più, non fiato, o
padron mio!

LEPORELLO: I won't speak any more, I
won't breathe, o my master!

DON GIOVANNI: Così saremo amici, or
odi un poco! sai tu perchè son qui?

DON GIOVANNI: That way we shall be
friends, now listen a bit! do you know
why I am here?

LEPORELLO: Non ne sò nulla! ma es-
sendo l'alba chiara, non sarebbe qualche
nuova conquista? io lo devo saper, per
porla in lista!

LEPORELLO: No, I know nothing about
it! but since it's clearly daybreak,
mightn't it be some new conquest? I
ought to know, in order to put it on the
list!

DON GIOVANNI: Va là, che sei il
grand'uom! Sappi ch'io sono in-
namorato d'una bella dama, e son certo
che m'ama; la vidi, le parlai, meco al
casino questa notte verrà: Zitto! mi pare
sentir odor di femmina!

DON GIOVANNI: Go on, what a fine
specimen you are! Know that I am in
love with a beautiful lady, and I am
certain she loves me; I saw her, I spoke to
her, she will come with me to the casino
tonight: Hush! I seem to smell fem-
ininity!

LEPORELLO: (Cospetto, che odorato per-
fetto!)

LEPORELLO: *Aside.* Lord, what a perfect
sense of smell!

DON GIOVANNI: All'aria, mi par bella.

DON GIOVANNI: At first glance, she
seems pretty.

LEPORELLO: (E che occhio! dico!)

LEPORELLO: *Aside.* And what an eye! I
must say!

DON GIOVANNI: Ritiriamoci un poco, e
scopriamo terren.

DON GIOVANNI: Let's withdraw here a
little and look over the terrain.

LEPORELLO: (Già prese foco!)

LEPORELLO: *Aside.* Already he's caught
fire!

Don Giovanni and Leporello step into a doorway as Donna Elvira enters.

DONNA ELVIRA: Ah! chi mi dice mai, quel barbaro dov'è? che per mio scorno amai, che mi mancò di fè?

DONNA ELVIRA: Ah! who will ever tell me where the cruel man is? he whom I loved to my disgrace, who broke faith with me?

Meanwhile, Leporello brushes and tidies Don Giovanni.

Ah! se ritrovo l'empio, e a me non torna ancor, vo' farne orrendo scempio, gli vo' cavar il cor!

Ah! if I find the wicked man again, and he still does not come back to me, I will devise a dreadful torture for him, I will tear out his heart!

Don Giovanni prods Leporello.

DON GIOVANNI: Udisti? qualche bella, dal vago abbandonata?

DON GIOVANNI: *To Leporello.* Did you hear? Some pretty lady, abandoned by her lover?

Poverina! Poverina! Cerchiam di consolare il suo tormento.

Poor little thing! Poor little thing! Let's try to console her sorrow.

LEPORELLO: (Così ne consolò mille e otto cento.)

LEPORELLO: *Aside.* That's how he's consoled eighteen hundred of them.

Don Giovanni grows more and more interested. He tries to attract Donna Elvira's attention but, failing to do so, finally approaches her with a sweeping bow.

DON GIOVANNI: Signorina! Signorina!

DON GIOVANNI: Signorina! Signorina!

DONNA ELVIRA: Chi è là?

DONNA ELVIRA: Who is there?

Don Giovanni is startled.

DON GIOVANNI: Stelle! che vedo!

DON GIOVANNI: *To himself.* Ye Gods! whom do I see!

LEPORELLO: O bella! Donna Elvira!

LEPORELLO: *To himself.* O lovely! Donna Elvira!

DONNA ELVIRA: Don Giovanni! sei qui? mostro! fellon! nido d'inganni!

DONNA ELVIRA: *Furiously.* Don Giovanni! are you here? monster! criminal! bundle of deceit!

LEPORELLO: Che titoli cruscanti! manco male che lo conosce bene.

LEPORELLO: *Aside.* What refined titles! she obviously knows him well.

DON GIOVANNI: Via, cara Donna Elvira, calmate questa collera! sentite, lasciatemi parlar!

DONNA ELVIRA: Cosa puoi dire, dopo azion si nera? In casa mia entri furtivamente, a forza d'arte, di giuramenti, e lusinghe arrivi a sedurre il cor mio; m'innamori, o crudele! mi dichiari tua sposa, e poi, mancando della terra e del ciel al santo dritto, con enorme delitto dopo tre dì da Burgos t'allontani, m'abbandoni, mi fuggi, e lasci in preda al rimorso ed al pianto per pena forse che t'amai cotanto.

LEPORELLO: (Pare un libro stampato!)

DON GIOVANNI: Oh in quanto a questo ebbi le mie ragioni! è vero?

LEPORELLO: È vero! e che ragioni forti!

DONNA ELVIRA: E quali sono, se non la tua perfidia, la leggerezza tua? Ma il giusto cielo volle ch'io ti trovassi, per far le sue, le mie vendette.

DON GIOVANNI: Eh via, siate più ragionevole: (mi pone a cimento, costei) se non credete al labbro mio, credete a questo galantuomo.

LEPORELLO: (Salvo il vero.)

DON GIOVANNI: Via, dille un poco.

LEPORELLO: (E cosa devo dirle?)

DON GIOVANNI: Sì, sì, dille pur tutto.

DON GIOVANNI: Come now, dear Donna Elvira, calm this rage! Listen, let me speak!

DONNA ELVIRA: What can you say after such a black deed? You entered my house furtively, you managed to seduce my heart with the strength of your artfulness, with promises and flatteries; you won my love, o cruel man! you declared me your wife, and then, breaking the sacred law of heaven and earth, in an enormous misdeed, you left Burgos after three days, you abandoned me, you ran away from me, and perhaps as punishment for loving you so much, you left me the prey to remorse and weeping.

LEPORELLO: *Aside.* Just like a printed book!

DON GIOVANNI: Oh, as for this I had my good reasons! *To Leporello.* Isn't that so?

LEPORELLO: That's so! and what powerful reasons!

DONNA ELVIRA: And what are such reasons, if not your deceitfulness and inconstancy? But a just heaven willed that I would find you, in order to accomplish its own revenge and mine.

DON GIOVANNI: Oh come now, be more reasonable: (she puts me to the test, this one) if you don't believe it from my lips, believe this gentleman.

LEPORELLO: *Aside.* Except for the truth.

DON GIOVANNI: *To Leporello.* Go on, tell her a little.

LEPORELLO: *To Don Giovanni.* And what should I tell her?

DON GIOVANNI: Yes, yes, tell her everything.

Leporello addresses Donna Elvira as Don Giovanni slyly slips away.

DONNA ELVIRA: Ebben, fa presto!

DONNA ELVIRA: *To Leporello.* Well, be quick!

LEPORELLO: Madama, veramente, in questo mondo conciossiacosa quando fosse che il quadro non è tondo!

LEPORELLO: Madam, truly seeing that however it might be in this world, a square is not round!

DONNA ELVIRA: Sciagurato! Così del mio dolor gioco ti prendi?

DONNA ELVIRA: Villain! Are you making fun of my sorrow in this way?

She turns to find Don Giovanni gone.

Ah voi! stelle! l'iniquo fuggì! misera me! dove? in qual parte?

Ah you! ye gods! the scoundrel has escaped! unhappy me! where? where did he go?

LEPORELLO: Eh, lasciate che vada; egli non merta che di lui ci pensiate.

LEPORELLO: Oh, let him go; he isn't worth thinking about.

DONNA ELVIRA: Il scellerato m'ingannò, mi tradì!

DONNA ELVIRA: The villain deceived me, he betrayed me!

She sadly turns to a bench and sits down.

LEPORELLO: Eh, consolatevi! non siete voi, non foste, e non sarete nè la prima, nè l'ultima;

LEPORELLO: Oh, console yourself! you are not, you were not, and you will not be the first one or the last one;

Leporello produces a long quarto or scroll, which he opens so that it extends from his hands to the floor. He shows this to Donna Elvira.

guardate, questo non picciol libro è tutto pieno dei nomi di sue belle; ogni villa, ogni borgo, ogni paese, è testimon di sue donnesche imprese.

look, this not-so-small book is completely filled with the names of his beauties; every home, every village, every town has witnessed his enterprises with womankind.

Madamina: il catalogo è questo delle belle che amò il padron mio; un catalogo egli è, che ho fatto io; osservate, leggete con me! osservate, leggete con me! In Italia sei cento e quaranta; in Almagna due cento e trent'una, cento in Francia, in Turchia novant'una; ma in Ispagna, ma in Ispagna son già mille e tre!

Dear lady: this is a catalogue of the beauties my master has loved; it is a catalogue which I have made; look at it, read it with me! look at it, read it with me! In Italy, six hundred and forty; in Germany, two hundred and thirty-one, one hundred in France, ninety-one in Turkey; but in Spain, but in Spain there are already a thousand and three!

V'han fra queste contadine, cameriere, cittadine, v'han contesse, baronesse, marchesane, principesse, e v'han donne d'ogni grado, d'ogni forma, d'ogni età.

Nella bionda egli ha l'usanza di lodar la gentilezza, nella bruna la costanza, nella bianca la dolcezza. Vuol d'inverno la grassotta, vuol d'estate la magrotta. È la grande maestosa; la piccina è ognor vezzosa; delle vecchie fa conquista, pel piacer di porle in lista. Sua passion predominante è la giovin principiante; non si picca se sia ricca, se sia brutta, se sia bella, purchè porti la gonnella, voi sapete quel che fa.

Among these there are countrywomen, chambermaids, citywomen, there are countesses, baronesses, marchionesses, princesses, and there are women of every rank, of every shape, of every age.

With blondes it is his custom to praise their gentleness, with brunettes their constancy, with white-haired ones their sweetness. In winter he wants plumpness, in summer he wants leanness. The tall woman is stately; the little tiny girl is always charming, he makes conquests among old women for the pleasure of adding them to the list. His outstanding passion is the youthful beginner; he doesn't care if she's rich, if she's ugly, if she's beautiful, provided she wears a skirt, *you* know what he does.

Leporello bows himself hurriedly off the stage.

DONNA ELVIRA: In questa forma dunque mi tradì il scellerato! è questo il premio che quel barbaro rende all'amor mio! Ah, vendicar vogl'io l'ingannato mio cor! pria ch'ei mi fugga, si ricorra, si vada; io sento in petto sol vendetta parlar, rabbia e dispetto!

In this manner, then, the villain betrayed me! this is the reward which that cruel man offers for my love! Ah, I want to avenge my deceived heart! before he flies from me, let me after him, let me go; in my breast I only hear revenge speaking, rage and spite!

Exit Donna Elvira.

SCENE III. Zerlina and Masetto enter, surrounded by peasant youths and maidens who dance around them.

ZERLINA: Giovinette, che fate all'amore, non lasciate che passi l'età! Se nel seno vi bulica il core, il rimedio vedetelo quà! che piacer che sarà!

ZERLINA: *To the girls.* Young maids who play at love, don't let your youth pass by! If your heart leaps in your breast, you see the cure for it right here! what fun it will be!

GIRLS: Ah! che piacer che sarà, lalarelala, lalarelala!

GIRLS: Ah! what fun it will be, lalarelala, lalarelala!

MASETTO: Giovinetti, leggieri di testa, non andate girando di quà e là; poco dura de'matti la festa ma per me cominciato non ha!

MASETTO: *To the boys.* Young lads, be carefree, don't go moping about hither and yon; the fools' holiday will just last a short while, but for me it hasn't begun.

BOYS: Che piacer che sarà! Che piacer che sarà! lalarelala, lalarelala!

BOYS: What fun it will be! What fun it will be! lalarelala, lalarelala!

Both groups move towards centre stage; Zerlina and Masetto come forward as the others continue to dance around them.

ZERLINA AND MASETTO: Vieni, vieni { carino, carina, } godiamo, e cantiamo, e balliamo, e suoniamo, che piacer che sarà.

ZERLINA AND MASETTO: Come, come dear, let's be merry, and let's sing, and let's dance, and let's rejoice, what fun it will be.

CHORUS: Ah! che piacer che sarà! Lalarelala, relala, relala!

CHORUS: Ah! what fun it will be! Lalarelala, relala, relala!

Meanwhile Don Giovanni and Leporello have appeared and are watching.

DON GIOVANNI: (Manco male, è partita.) Oh guarda che bella gioventù! che belle donne!

DON GIOVANNI: *Aside.* Good enough, she's gone. *To Leporello.* Oh look, what attractive young people! what pretty girls!

LEPORELLO: (Fra tante, per mia fè, vi sarà qualche cosa anche per me.)

LEPORELLO: *To himself.* By my faith, among so many, there will be something for me too.

Leporello advances towards the girls as Don Giovanni accosts Zerlina and Masetto.

DON GIOVANNI: Cari amici, buon giorno! seguitate a stare allegramente, seguitate a suonar, o buona gente! C'è qualche sposalizio?

DON GIOVANNI: Good day, dear friends! go on being merry, go on rejoicing, o good people! Is there a wedding?

Zerlina curtsies to the Don.

ZERLINA: Sì, Signore, e la sposa son io.

ZERLINA: Yes, Sir, and I am the bride.

DON GIOVANNI: Me ne consolo—lo sposo?

DON GIOVANNI: I'm glad of it—and the bridegroom?

Masetto comes forward with an awkward bow.

MASETTO: Io, per servirla.

MASETTO: I, at your service.

DON GIOVANNI: Oh, bravo! per servirmi; questo è vero parlar da galantuomo.

DON GIOVANNI: Oh, good! at my service; this is spoken like a gallant.

LEPORELLO: (Basta, che sia marito!)

LEPORELLO: *Aside.* It's enough that he be a husband!

ZERLINA: Oh, il mio Masetto è un uom d'ottimo core.

ZERLINA: Oh, my Masetto is a man of the best heart.

DON GIOVANNI: Oh, anch'io, vedete! voglio che siamo amici; il vostro nome?

DON GIOVANNI: Oh, I too, do you see! I want us to be friends. *To Zerlina.* Your name?

ZERLINA: Zerlina.

ZERLINA: Zerlina.

DON GIOVANNI: E il tuo?

DON GIOVANNI: *To Masetto.* And yours?

MASETTO: Masetto.

MASETTO: Masetto.

Don Giovanni slips one arm around Zerlina's waist and the other around Masetto.

DON GIOVANNI: O caro il mio Masetto! cara la mia Zerlina! v'esibisco la mia protezione: Leporello! cosa fai lì, birbone?

DON GIOVANNI: O my dear Masetto! my dear Zerlina! I offer you my protection: Leporello! what are you doing over there, rascal?

Leporello answers from among the peasant girls.

LEPORELLO: Anch'io, caro padrone, esibisco la mia protezione.

LEPORELLO: I too, dear master, am offering my protection.

DON GIOVANNI: Presto va con costor; nel mio palazzo conducili sul fatto: ordina ch'abbiano cioccolate, caffè, vini, presciutti; cerca divertir tutti, mostra loro il giardino, la galleria, le camere; in effetto fa che resti contento il mio Masetto, hai capito?

DON GIOVANNI: Go quickly with these people; take them to my palace immediately: order chocolate, coffee, wines, hams for them; try to amuse everyone, show them the garden, the gallery, the rooms; in short, see to it that Masetto is happy, do you understand?

At the last phrase he gives Leporello an insinuating dig in the side.

LEPORELLO: Ho capito; andiam.

LEPORELLO: I understand. *To the peasants.* Let's go.

MASETTO: Signore!

MASETTO: Sir!

DON GIOVANNI: Cosa c'è?

DON GIOVANNI: What is it?

He holds back Zerlina as the other peasants leave.

MASETTO: La Zerlina senza me non può star.

MASETTO: Zerlina can't stay without me.

LEPORELLO: In vostro loco ci sarà sua Eccellenza, e saprà bene fare le vostri parti.

LEPORELLO: *To Masetto.* His Excellency will be here in your place, and he can well take your part.

DON GIOVANNI: Oh, la Zerlina è in man d'un Cavalier; va pur, fra poco ella meco verrà.

DON GIOVANNI: Oh, Zerlina is in the hands of a nobleman; you go now, she'll come with me in a little while.

ZERLINA: Va! non temere! nelle mani son io d'un Cavaliere.

ZERLINA: Go on! don't be afraid! I'm in the hands of a nobleman.

MASETTO: E per questo?

MASETTO: And so?

ZERLINA: E per questo non c'è da dubitar.

ZERLINA: And so there's nothing to worry about.

Masetto tries to pull Zerlina with him.

MASETTO: Ed io, sospetto—

MASETTO: And I, confound it—

Don Giovanni separates them cleverly.

DON GIOVANNI: Olà, finiam le dispute! Se subito senza altro replicar non te ne vai, Masetto, guarda ben, ti pentirai!

DON GIOVANNI: Well, let's put an end to the argument. If you don't leave immediately without another word, Masetto, look out, you'll be sorry!

Don Giovanni taps his sword significantly, and Masetto, somewhat abashed, begins to back away.

MASETTO: Ho capito, Signor, sì! Signor, sì! Chino il capo e me ne vo, giacchè piace a voi così, altre repliche non fo. Cavalier voi siete già, dubitar non posso affè, me lo dice la bontà che volete aver per me.

MASETTO: I understand, yes, Sir! yes, Sir! I'll bow my head and go away, since this is your pleasure, I have no further answers. You are indeed a nobleman, in faith, I cannot doubt it, the kindness which you have for me tells me so.

He turns to Zerlina.

Bricconaccia, malandrina, fosti ognor la mia ruina!

Little minx, evil girl, you were always my ruin!

He turns to Leporello who is waiting to take him away.

Vengo, vengo!
Resta, resta!

I'm coming, I'm coming!
To Zerlina: Stay here, stay here!

È una cosa molto onesta!
Faccia il nostro Cavaliere Cavaliera ancora te.

To himself. It's a very fine situation!
To Zerlina, with bitterness. Let our gentleman make a lady even of you.

Leporello finally succeeds in leading Masetto away.

DON GIOVANNI: Al fin siam liberati, Zerlinetta gentil, da quel scioccone, che ne dite, mio ben? sò far pulito?

DON GIOVANNI: At last we're free of that stupid oaf, pretty little Zerlina, what do you say to that, my dear? do I know how to get what I want?

He tries to put his arm around Zerlina, but she shrinks back.

ZERLINA: Signore, è mio marito!

ZERLINA: Sir, he's my fiancé!

DON GIOVANNI: Chi? colui? vi par che un onest'uomo, un nobil Cavalier, qual io mi vanto, possa soffrir che quel visetto d'oro, quel viso inzuccherato da un bifolcaccio vil sia strapazzato?

DON GIOVANNI: Who? He? do you think that an honest man, a noble gentleman such as I am proud of being, can suffer that little precious face, that sweet face, to be insulted by a low boor?

ZERLINA: Ma Signor, io gli diedi parola di sposarlo.

ZERLINA: But Sir, I gave him my word to marry him.

DON GIOVANNI: Tal parola non vale un zero: voi non siete fatta per esser paesana, un altra sorte vi procuran quegli occhi bricconcelli, quei labbretti sì belli, quelle dituccia candide e odorose; parmi toccar giuncata, e fiutar rose.

DON GIOVANNI: Such a word is not worth anything: you are not destined to be a peasant, those roguish little eyes will win you another lot, those lovely little lips, those white and fragrant little fingers; it's like touching reeds and smelling roses.

ZERLINA: Ah, non vorrei—

ZERLINA: Ah, I wouldn't—

DON GIOVANNI: Che non vorreste?

DON GIOVANNI: What wouldn't you?

ZERLINA: Alfine ingannata restar. Io sò che raro colle donne voi altri cavalieri siete onesti e sinceri.

ZERLINA: Be betrayed in the end. I know how seldom it is that you noblemen are honest and sincere with women.

DON GIOVANNI: Eh, un'impostura della gente plebea! la nobiltà ha dipinta negli occhi l'onestà. Orsù, non perdiam tempo; in questo istante io vi voglio sposar.

DON GIOVANNI: Oh, that's a slander among the common people! the aristocracy has honesty painted in its eyes. Now then, let's not lose any time; I want to marry you this instant.

ZERLINA: Voi?

ZERLINA: You?

Don Giovanni waves a hand in the direction of his castle.

DON GIOVANNI: Certo, io. Quel casinetto è mio, soli saremo. E là, giojello mio, ci sposeremo. Là ci darem la mano, là mi dirai di sì; vedi, non è lontano, partiam, ben mio, da qui.

DON GIOVANNI: Certainly, I. That little house is mine, we shall be alone. And there, my jewel, we shall wed one another. There we shall join our hands, there you shall say yes to me; you see, it isn't far away, let's go, my dear.

ZERLINA: Vorrei, e non vorrei, mi trema un poco il cor, felice, è ver, sarei ma può burlarmi ancor!

ZERLINA: I would, and I would not, my heart is trembling a little, I would be happy, it's true, but you may yet be making fun of me!

DON GIOVANNI: Vieni, mio bel diletto!

DON GIOVANNI: Come, my lovely delight!

ZERLINA: Mi fa pietà Masetto!

ZERLINA: I feel sorry for Masetto!

DON GIOVANNI: Io cangierò tua sorte!

DON GIOVANNI: I'll change your lot!

ZERLINA: Presto non son più forte!

ZERLINA: Soon I'll no longer resist!

Meanwhile, Donna Elvira appears on the sidelines and watches these goings-on.

DON GIOVANNI: Vieni, vieni! Là ci darem la mano—

DON GIOVANNI: Come, come! There we shall join hands—

ZERLINA: Vorrei, e non vorrei—

ZERLINA: I would, and I would not—

ZERLINA AND DON GIOVANNI: Andiam, andiam, mio bene, a ristorar le pene d'un innocente amor!

ZERLINA AND DON GIOVANNI: Let us go, let us go, my dear, to relieve the pangs of an innocent love!

Donna Elvira, who has been moving nearer and nearer to the pair during all this, catches up with them and stops them, just as they are about to leave with their arms around one another.

DONNA ELVIRA: Fermati, scellerato! il ciel mi fece udir le perfidie; io sono a tempo di salvar questa misera innocente dal tuo barbaro artiglio!

DONNA ELVIRA: Stop, villain! heaven made me overhear your lies; I am in time to save this unhappy innocent girl from your cruel clutches!

ZERLINA: Meschina! cosa sento!

ZERLINA: Poor me! what do I hear!

DON GIOVANNI: (Amor, consiglio!)

DON GIOVANNI: *To himself.* Cupid, help me!

Idol mio, non vedete ch'io voglio divertirmi?

Aside to Donna Elvira. My idol, don't you see that I want to amuse myself?

DONNA ELVIRA: Divertirti? È vero! divertirti: io sò, crudele, come tu ti diverti.

ZERLINA: Ma, Signor Cavaliere, è ver quel ch'ella dice?

DON GIOVANNI: La povera infelice è di me innamorata, e per pietà deggio fingere amore; ch'io son per mia disgrazia uom di buon core.

DONNA ELVIRA: Ah! fuggi il traditor! Non lo lasciar più dir; il labbro è mentitor, fallace il ciglio! Dai miei tormenti impara a creder a quel cor; e nasca il tuo timor dal mio periglio, ah fuggi, fuggi! Ah, fuggi il traditor!

DONNA ELVIRA: Amuse yourself? That's true! amuse yourself! Cruel man, I know how you amuse yourself.

ZERLINA: *To Don Giovanni.* But Sir Nobleman, is what she says true?

DON GIOVANNI: *To Zerlina.* The poor unhappy thing is in love with me, and out of pity I must pretend to love her; it's my undoing that I'm a kind-hearted man.

DONNA ELVIRA: Ah! fly from the betrayer! Do not let him say any more; his lips are lying, his brow is deceitful! Learn from my suffering to believe my heart; and may my danger give birth to your fear, ah fly, fly! Ah, fly from the betrayer!

Donna Elvira takes Zerlina by the hand and they exit together. Donna Anna, dressed in deep mourning, enters with Don Ottavio.

DON GIOVANNI: Mi par ch'oggi il demonio si diverta d'opporsi a miei piacevoli progressi; vanno mal tutti quanti.

DON OTTAVIO: Ah ch'ora, idolo mio, son vani i pianti, di vendetta si parli! Oh, Don Giovanni!

DON GIOVANNI: (Mancava questo, in ver!)

DONNA ANNA: Signore, a tempo vi ritroviam: avete core? avete anima generosa?

DON GIOVANNI: (Sta a vedere che il diavolo le ha detto qualche cosa.) Che domanda! perchè?

DONNA ANNA: Bisogno abbiamo della vostra amicizia.

DON GIOVANNI: I think today the devil is amusing himself by opposing the progress of my pleasure; everything is going wrong.

DON OTTAVIO: Ah, my idol, now tears are in vain, one must speak of revenge! Oh, Don Giovanni!

DON GIOVANNI: *To himself.* Just what I needed, in truth!

DONNA ANNA: *To Don Giovanni.* Sir, we meet you at the right time: have you a heart? have you a noble spirit?

DON GIOVANNI: *To himself.* I can see that the devil has told her something.
To Donna Anna. What a question! why?

DONNA ANNA: We have need of your friendship.

DON GIOVANNI: (Mi torna il fiato in corpo.)
Comandate; i congiunti, i parenti, questa man, questo ferro, i beni, il sangue spenderò per servirvi: ma voi, bella Donn'Anna, perchè così piangete? Il crudele chi fu che osò la calma turbar del viver vostro?

DON GIOVANNI: *To himself.* I can breathe again.
To Donna Anna. Command it: my friends, my relatives, this hand, this sword, my wealth, my life—I would sacrifice them all to serve you: but you, beautiful Donna Anna, why are you weeping like this? What cruel person dared trouble your tranquil life?

Donna Elvira returns.

DONNA ELVIRA: Ah, ti ritrovo ancor, perfido mostro?
Non ti fidar, o misera, di quel ribaldo cor! me già tradì quel barbaro, te vuol tradir ancor.

DONNA ELVIRA: Ah, do I meet you again, lying monster?
To Donna Anna. O unhappy woman, do not place your trust in that evil heart! that cruel man has already betrayed me, he wants to betray you, too.

DONNA ANNA AND DON OTTAVIO: Cieli! che aspetto nobile! che dolce maestà! il suo dolor, le lagrime m'empiono di pietà, m'empiono di pietà!

DONNA ANNA AND DON OTTAVIO: Heavens! what a noble aspect! what sweet dignity! her sorrow, her tears fill me with pity, fill me with pity!

Don Giovanni attempts to pull Donna Elvira away, but she refuses to leave. Presently he takes her hand and draws her beside him.

DON GIOVANNI: La povera ragazza è pazza, amici miei! lasciatemi con lei, forse si calmerà!

DON GIOVANNI: *In a stage whisper.* The poor girl is mad, my friends! leave me with her, perhaps she'll pull herself together!

DONNA ELVIRA: Ah! non credete al perfido!

DONNA ELVIRA: Ah! don't believe the liar!

DON GIOVANNI: È pazza, non badate!

DON GIOVANNI: She's mad, don't pay any attention!

DONNA ELVIRA: Restate, o Dei, restate!

DONNA ELVIRA: Stay here, ye Gods, stay here!

DONNA ANNA AND DON OTTAVIO: A chi si crederà?

DONNA ANNA AND DON OTTAVIO: *Aside.* Whom should one believe?

DONNA ANNA, DON OTTAVIO AND DON GIOVANNI: Certo moto d'ignoto tormento—

DONNA ANNA, DON OTTAVIO AND DON GIOVANNI: I feel an impulse of unknown anguish—

DONNA ELVIRA: Sdegno, rabbia, dispetto, pavento—

DONNA ELVIRA: Anger, fury, spite, fear—

DONNA ANNA, DON OTTAVIO AND DON GIOVANNI: —dentro l'alma girare mi sento—

DONNA ANNA, DON OTTAVIO AND DON GIOVANNI: —turning within my mind—

DONNA ELVIRA: —dentro, l'alma girare mi sento—

DONNA ELVIRA: —turning within my mind—

DONNA ANNA, DON OTTAVIO AND DON GIOVANNI: —che mi dice per quella infelice cento cose, che intender, non sa!

DONNA ANNA, DON OTTAVIO AND DON GIOVANNI: —something that tells me a hundred things in favour of that unhappy girl, which it cannot speak, no!

DONNA ELVIRA: —che mi dice di quel traditore cento cose che intender non sa, no—

DONNA ELVIRA: —something that tells me a hundred things about that betrayer, which it cannot speak, no—

DON OTTAVIO: Io di quà non vado via, se non sò com'è l'affar!

DON OTTAVIO: *Aside.* I shall not leave here if I don't know how this matter goes!

DONNA ANNA: Non ha l'aria di pazzia il suo tratto, il suo parlar.

DONNA ANNA: *Aside.* She does not have the appearance of madness in her bearing, in her speech.

DON GIOVANNI: (Se men vado, si potria qualche cosa sospettar.)

DON GIOVANNI: *Aside.* If I go away, somebody may suspect something.

Donna Elvira angrily turns to Don Giovanni.

DONNA ELVIRA: Da quel ceffo si dovria la ner'alma giudicar.

DONNA ELVIRA: One ought to recognize your black soul by your ugly face.

DON OTTAVIO: Dunque quella—?

DON OTTAVIO: *To Don Giovanni.* Then she—?

DON GIOVANNI: È pazzarella!

DON GIOVANNI: She's a little crazy!

DONNA ANNA: Dunque quegli—?

DONNA ANNA: *To Donna Elvira.* Then he—?

DONNA ELVIRA: È un traditore—

DONNA ELVIRA: He's a betrayer—

DON GIOVANNI: Infelice!

DON GIOVANNI: Unhappy girl!

DONNA ELVIRA: —mentitore!

DONNA ELVIRA: *To Don Giovanni.* —liar!

DONNA ANNA AND DON OTTAVIO: Incomincio a dubitar.

DONNA ANNA AND DON OTTAVIO: I am beginning to have doubts.

DON GIOVANNI: Zitta, zitta, che la gente si raduna a noi d'intorno. Siate un poco più prudente, vi farete criticar.

DON GIOVANNI: *Aside to Donna Elvira.* Hush, hush, for a crowd is gathering around us. Be a little more prudent, you'll make yourself ridiculous.

DONNA ELVIRA: Non sperarlo, o scellerato, ho perduta la prudenza, le tue colpe ed il mio stato voglio a tutti palesar!

DONNA ELVIRA: *To Don Giovanni.* Don't hope it, o villain, I have lost my prudence, I want to show everyone your guilt and my condition!

Donna Anna and Don Ottavio look at Don Giovanni curiously.

DONNA ANNA AND DON OTTAVIO: Quegli accenti sì sommessi, quel cangiarsi di colore, son indizi troppo espressi che mi fan determinar!

DONNA ANNA AND DON OTTAVIO: Those very subdued tones, that change of colouring are expressive enough signs to make me resolve!

Don Giovanni finally manages to draw Donna Elvira away from the scene, and then returns to the others.

DON GIOVANNI: Povera sventurata! i passi suoi voglio seguir; non voglio che faccia un precipizio: Perdonate, bellissima Donn'Anna! se servirvi poss'io, in mia casa v'aspetto. Amici, addio!

DON GIOVANNI: Poor wretched girl! I will follow her; I don't want her to do anything rash: Pardon me, most beautiful Donna Anna! if I can serve you, I shall await you in my house. Friends, goodbye!

He leaves hastily, pretending to follow Donna Elvira. Donna Anna becomes very upset.

DONNA ANNA: Don Ottavio! son morta!

DONNA ANNA: Don Ottavio! I am dead!

DON OTTAVIO: Cosa è stato?

DON OTTAVIO: What is the matter?

DONNA ANNA: Per pietà, soccorretemi!

DONNA ANNA: For pity's sake, help me!

DON OTTAVIO: Mio bene, fate coraggio!

DON OTTAVIO: Have courage, my dear!

Donna Anna makes a sweeping gesture in the direction of Don Giovanni's exit.

DONNA ANNA: O Dei! Quegli è il carnefice del padre mio!

DONNA ANNA: Ye Gods! That man is my father's murderer!

DON OTTAVIO: Che dite?

DON OTTAVIO: What are you saying?

DONNA ANNA: Non dubitate più; gli ultimi accenti che l'empio proferì, tutta la voce, richiamar nel cor mio di quell'indegno, che nel mio appartamento—

DON OTTAVIO: Oh ciel! possibile, che sotto il sacro manto d'amicizia—ma come fu, narratemi lo strano avvenimento.

DONNA ANNA: Era già alquanto avanzata la notte, quando nelle mie stanze, ove soletta mi trovai per sventura, entrar io vidi in un mantello avvolto un uom che al primo istante avea preso per voi; ma riconobbi poi, che un'inganno era il mio!

DON OTTAVIO: Stelle! seguite!

DONNA ANNA: Tacito a me s'appressa, e mi vuole abbracciar; scogliermi cerco, ei più mi stringe, io grido! non viene alcun; con una mano cerca d'impedire la voce, e coll'altra m'afferra stretta così, che già mi credo vinta.

DON OTTAVIO: Perfido! e alfin?

DONNA ANNA: Alfine il duol, l'orrore dell'infame attentato accrebbe sì la lena mia, che a forza di svincolarmi, torcermi, e piegarmi da lui mi sciolsi!

DON OTTAVIO: Ohimè! respiro.

DONNA ANNA: Allora rinforzo i stridi miei, chiamo soccorso, fugge il fellon, arditamente il seguo fin nella strada per fermarlo, e sono assalitrice d'assalita; il

DONNA ANNA: Do not doubt it any longer; the last words which that wicked man spoke, his whole voice, made me think of that wretch within my rooms—

DON OTTAVIO: Oh heavens! is it possible that under the sacred cloak of friendship—but how did it happen, tell me about those strange events.

DONNA ANNA: It was already quite late at night, I was alone in my rooms, to my misfortune, when I saw someone enter, wrapped in a cloak, whom I at first took to be you; but then I perceived my mistake!

DON OTTAVIO: O God! go on!

DONNA ANNA: Stealthily he approached me and would embrace me; I tried to free myself, he held me more tightly; I shouted! no one came; with one hand he tried to stifle my cries, and with the other he caught hold of me so tightly that I thought myself surely overcome.

DON OTTAVIO: *Excitedly.* Villain! and finally?

DONNA ANNA: Finally, the pain, the horror of the attempted outrage gave me enough breath that I had strength to struggle, twist, and I wrenched myself free from him!

DON OTTAVIO: *Relieved.* Oh! I can breathe again.

DONNA ANNA: Then I renewed my cries, I shouted for help, the criminal fled, boldly I followed him down to the street to stop him, and I became the assailer of

padre v'accorre, vuol conoscerlo, e l'indegno, che del povero vecchio era più forte, compie il misfatto suo, col dargli morte.

Or sai chi l'onore rapire a me volse, che fu il traditore, che il padre mi tolse. Vendetta ti chieggio, la chiede il tuo cor. Rammenta la piaga del misero seno, rimira di sangue coperto il terreno, se l'ira in te langue d'un giusto furor!

the assailant; my father came running, demanded his identity, and the criminal who was stronger than the poor old man, crowned his misdeeds by killing him.

Now you know who tried to rob me of my honour, who the traitor was that stole my father from me. I demand revenge of you, your heart demands it. Remember the wounds in that poor breast, recall the ground covered with blood, should the fury of a just anger wane in you!

Donna Anna leaves, and Don Ottavio remains alone on the stage.

DON OTTAVIO: Come mai creder deggio di sì nero delitto capace un cavaliere! Ah, di scoprire il vero ogni mezzo si cerchi; io sento in petto e di sposo e d'amico il dover che mi parla; disingannar la voglio, o vendicarla!

Dalla sua pace, la mia dipende, quel che a lei piace, vita mi rende, quel che le incresce, morte mi dà. S'ella sospira, sospiro anch'io, è mia quell'ira, quel pianto è mio; e non ho bene s'ella non l'ha!

DON OTTAVIO: How can I ever believe a nobleman to be capable of such a black crime! Ah, every means must be sought to discover the truth; in my heart I hear speaking to me the duty of both a husband and a friend; I will undeceive her, or avenge her!

My peace depends on hers, that which pleases her is life to me, that which grieves her is death to me. If she sighs, I sigh also, her wrath is mine, her tears are mine; and I have no pleasure if she has none!

Exit Don Ottavio.

In the score, the following action takes place without a pause or change of scene. In production, however, there is sometimes a break, and this scene is set in Don Giovanni's castle, an introduction, as it were, to the "Party Scene" (Scene V) which ends Act I. When the action is continuous, Don Giovanni and Leporello re-enter from opposite sides; the Don is in fine fettle, his servant is grumbling.

LEPORELLO: Io deggio ad ogni patto per sempre abbandonar questo bel matto! eccolo qui; guardate, con qual indifferenza se ne viene!

DON GIOVANNI: Oh, Leporello mio! va tutto bene?

LEPORELLO: I ought to leave this madman forever, on any condition! there he is; look how nonchalantly he comes along!

DON GIOVANNI: *Cheerfully.* Oh, my Leporello! is everything going all right?

LEPORELLO: Don Giovannino mio, va tutto male!

DON GIOVANNI: Come va tutto male?

LEPORELLO: Vado a casa, come m'ordinaste, con tutta quella gente.

DON GIOVANNI: Bravo!

LEPORELLO: A forza di chiacchere, di vezzi e di bugie, ch'ho imparto sì bene a star con voi, cerco d'intrattenerli.

DON GIOVANNI: Bravo!

LEPORELLO: Dico mille cose a Masetto per placarlo, per trargli dal pensier la gelosia—

DON GIOVANNI: Bravo! in coscienza mia!

LEPORELLO: Faccio che bevano, e gli uomini e le donne son già mezzi ubbriacchi: altri canta, altri scherza, altri seguita a ber; in sul più bello, chi credete che capiti?

DON GIOVANNI: Zerlina!

LEPORELLO: Bravo! e con lei chi viene?

DON GIOVANNI: Donna Elvira!

LEPORELLO: Bravo! e disse di voi—

DON GIOVANNI: Tutto quel mal che in bocca le venia!

LEPORELLO: Bravo! in coscienza mia!

DON GIOVANNI: E tu, cosa facesti?

LEPORELLO: *Angrily.* My little Don Giovanni, everything is going all wrong!

DON GIOVANNI: How is everything going wrong?

LEPORELLO: I went to the house with all those people, as you ordered me to.

DON GIOVANNI: Splendid!

LEPORELLO: I tried to entertain them with chit-chat, flatteries, and lies, all of which I have learned so well from being with you.

DON GIOVANNI: Splendid!

LEPORELLO: I told Masetto thousands of things to calm him, to distract him from his jealous thoughts—

DON GIOVANNI: Splendid! by my faith!

LEPORELLO: I made them drink, and soon the men and women were half-drunk; some sang, some joked, some went on drinking; on top of it all, who do you think came along?

DON GIOVANNI: *Carelessly.* Zerlina!

LEPORELLO: Splendid! and who came with her?

DON GIOVANNI: *Carelessly.* Donna Elvira!

LEPORELLO: Splendid! and she said of you—

DON GIOVANNI: *Cheerfully.* Everything nasty that came into her mouth!

LEPORELLO: Splendid! by my faith!

DON GIOVANNI: And you, what did you do?

LEPORELLO: Tacqui.

DON GIOVANNI: Ed ella?

LEPORELLO: Seguì a gridar.

DON GIOVANNI: E tu?

LEPORELLO: Quando mi parve che già fosse sfogata, dolcemente fuor dell'orto la trassi, e con bell'arte, chiusa la porta a chiave io mi cavai, e sulla via soletta la lasciai.

DON GIOVANNI: Bravo! bravo! arcibravo! l'affar non può andar meglio; incominciasti, io saprò terminar. Troppo mi premono queste contadinotte; le voglio divertir finchè vien notte.
Finch'han dal vino calda la testa, una gran festa fa preparar! Se trovi in piazza qualche ragazza, teco ancor quella cerca menar. Senza alcun ordine la danza sia, chi'l menuetto, chi la follia, chi l'alemana farai ballar!

Ed io frattanto dall'altro canto con questa e quella vo' amoreggiar. Ah, la mia lista doman mattina d'una decina devi aumentar.

LEPORELLO: I kept still.

DON GIOVANNI: And she?

LEPORELLO: She went right on screaming.

DON GIOVANNI: And you?

LEPORELLO: When I thought she had run dry, I gently led her out of the garden, and with fine skill locked the gate and took off, and left her alone in the street.

DON GIOVANNI: Splendid! Splendid! Absolutely splendid! the thing couldn't have gone better; you began it, I can end it. These country girls are very dear to me; I will amuse them until nightfall.

Have a grand party prepared so that their heads will be hot with the wine! If you find some girl in the square, try to bring her with you too. Let there be dancing without any order, have some dance the minuet, some the follia, the allemande!

And meanwhile, on the other hand, I'll make love to this one and that one. Ah, tomorrow morning my list should be increased by half a score.

Don Giovanni usually laughs boisterously at the end of this, the "Champagne Aria".
When the scene takes place in the Don's castle, it is often the custom, at the end of the
song, for the Don to shatter a champagne glass he has been holding.

SCENE IV. Evening of the same day, in the garden outside Don Giovanni's castle.
A balcony of the castle overlooks arbors and shrubbery. Masetto enters, striding
huffily; he tries to shake off Zerlina, who follows him, tugging at his sleeve or his hand,
and doing her best to gain his attention.

ZERLINA: Masetto, senti un po'! Masetto, dico!

ZERLINA: Masetto, listen a bit! Masetto, I say!

MASETTO: Non mi toccar!

ZERLINA: Perchè?

MASETTO: Perchè mi chiedi? perfida! il tatto sopportar dovrei d'una man infedele?

ZERLINA: Ah no, taci, crudele, io non merto da te tal trattamento.

MASETTO: Come? ed hai l'ardimento di scusarti? star sola con un uom: abbandonarmi il dì delle mie nozze! porre in fronte a un villano d'onore questa marca d'infamia! Ah, se non fosse lo scandalo, vorrei—

Zerlina ducks out of Masetto's reach.

ZERLINA: Ma se colpa io non ho, ma se da lui ingannata rimasi, e poi che temi? tranquillati, mia vita: non mi toccò la punta delle dita: non me lo credi? Ingrato! vien qui: sfogati, ammazzami, fa tutto di me quel che ti piace; ma poi, Masetto mio, ma poi fa pace.

Batti, batti, o bel Masetto, la tua povera Zerlina: starò qui come agnellina le tue botte ad aspettar.

Masetto looks at Zerlina crossly.

Lascierò straziarmi il crine, lascierò cavarmi gli occhi, e le care tue manine lieta poi saprò baciar.

Masetto visibly begins to give in.

Ah, lo vedo, non hai core. Pace, pace, o vita mia! in contento ed allegria notte e dì vogliam passar.

Masetto relents and they fly into one another's arms.

MASETTO: Don't touch me!

ZERLINA: Why?

MASETTO: You ask me why? faithless girl! am I supposed to put up with the touch of an unfaithful hand?

ZERLINA: Ah no, cruel fellow, be quiet, I don't deserve such treatment from you.

MASETTO: What! and you have the insolence to make excuses? to remain alone with a man: to desert me on my wedding day! to put this mark of shame on the forehead of an honourable villager! Ah, if there wouldn't be a scandal, I'd like to—

ZERLINA: But if I'm blameless, even if I was misled by him, then what are you afraid of? calm yourself, my life: he didn't touch my fingertips: don't you believe me? Thankless fellow! come here: give vent to your anger, murder me, do anything you like to me; but then, my Masetto, but then make peace. O handsome Masetto, beat, beat your poor Zerlina: I'll stand here like a little lamb and wait for your blows.

I'll let you tear my hair, I'll let you gouge out my eyes, and then I shall kiss your dear hands happily.

Ah, I see, you haven't the heart. Peace, peace, oh my life! we'll spend our days and nights in contentment and happiness.

MASETTO: Guarda un po', come seppe questa strega sedurmi! siamo pure i deboli di testa!

MASETTO: Just see how that witch was able to win me over! Ah, but we men are a weak-headed lot!

Don Giovanni's voice comes from off-stage.

DON GIOVANNI: Sia preparato tutto a una gran festa.

DON GIOVANNI: Let everything be made ready for a grand ball.

Zerlina draws nearer to Masetto.

ZERLINA: Ah, Masetto, Masetto, odi la voce del Monsù Cavaliero!

ZERLINA: Ah, Masetto, Masetto, do you hear the voice of his Lordship the Cavalier!

MASETTO: Ebben, che c'è?

MASETTO: Well, what of it?

ZERLINA: Verrà!

ZERLINA: He's coming!

MASETTO: Lascia che venga.

MASETTO: Let him come.

ZERLINA: Ah, se vi fosse un buco da fuggir!

ZERLINA: Ah, if there were a hiding place to run to!

MASETTO: Di cosa temi, perchè diventi pallida? Ah, capisco! capisco, bricconcella: Hai timor ch'io comprenda com'è tra voi passata la faccenda.

MASETTO: What are you afraid of, why are you turning pale? Ah, I understand! I understand, little minx: you're afraid I might see what has been going on between you.

He indicates some shrubbery to one side.

Presto, presto, pria ch'ei venga, por mi vo' da qualche lato; c'è una nicchia—qui celato, cheto, cheto mi vo' star.

Quick, quick, before he comes, I'll step off to the side; there's a corner—here I'll stay hidden, quietly, quietly.

ZERLINA: Senti, senti! dove vai? ah, non t'asconder, o Masetto! se ti trova, poveretto! tu non sai quel che può far.

ZERLINA: Listen, listen! where are you going? Ah, don't hide yourself, oh Masetto! if he finds you, poor you! you don't know what he might do.

Zerlina tries to hold Masetto back, but he is insistent.

MASETTO: Faccia, dica quel che vuole.

MASETTO: Let him do and say whatever he wants.

ZERLINA: (Ah, non giovan le parole!)

ZERLINA: *To herself.* Ah, words aren't of any use!

MASETTO: Parla forte e qui t'arresta!

MASETTO: Speak loudly and stay right here!

ZERLINA: Che capriccio ha nella testa!

ZERLINA: What mischief has he got in his head!

MASETTO: Capirò se m'è fedele, e in qual modo andò l'affar!

MASETTO: I'll find out if she's faithful to me, and how the affair went!

He hides in some shrubbery to one side.

ZERLINA: Quell'ingrato, quel crudele, oggi vuol precipitar.

ZERLINA: That thankless fellow, that cruel man wants to be rash today.

Peasants and villagers begin to come on stage. Don Giovanni, in full finery, enters with his servants.

DON GIOVANNI: Sù! svegliatevi da bravi! Sù! coraggio, o buona gente! vogliam stare allegramente, vogliam ridere e scherzar.
Alla stanza della danza conducete tutti quanti, ed a tutti in abbondanza, gran rinfreschi fate dar!

DON GIOVANNI: *To the crowd.* Come! rouse yourselves like good folk! Come! be of good heart, o good people! we will be happy, we will laugh and joke.
To the servants. Take everyone to the ballroom and have them all given many refreshments in abundance!

SERVANTS: Sù, svegliatevi da bravi! Sù, coraggio, o buona gente! vogliam stare allegramente, vogliam ridere e scherzar.

SERVANTS: Come, rouse yourselves like good folk! Come, be of good heart, o good people! We will be happy, we will laugh and joke.

The servants lead the peasants and villagers into the castle, and Don Giovanni begins to look about for Zerlina. She, seeing that the Don is looking for her, tries to hide.

ZERLINA: Tra quest' arbori celata, si può dar che non mi veda.

ZERLINA: If I'm hidden among those trees, maybe he won't see me.

Don Giovanni sees her and tries to hold her.

DON GIOVANNI: Zerlinetta, mia garbata, t'ho già visto, non scappar.

DON GIOVANNI: Little Zerlina, my pleasure, I've already seen you, don't break away.

Zerlina tries to wrench loose.

ZERLINA: Ah, lasciatemi andar via!

ZERLINA: Ah, let me go away!

DON GIOVANNI: No, no, resta, gioia mia!

DON GIOVANNI: No, no, stay, my joy!

ZERLINA: Se pietade avete in core—

ZERLINA: If you have pity in your heart—

DON GIOVANNI: Sì, ben mio, son tutto amore; vieni un poco in questo loco!

DON GIOVANNI: Yes, my dear, I am all love; come into this place a while!

He tries to pull Zerlina into the shrubbery with him.

fortunata io ti vo' far!

I want to make you rich!

ZERLINA: Ah! s'ei vede il sposo mio, sò ben io quel che può far.

ZERLINA: Ah! if he sees my husband, I well know what he might do.

Don Giovanni drags Zerlina into the shrubbery and stops in amazement as he sees Masetto.

DON GIOVANNI: Masetto?!

DON GIOVANNI: Masetto?!

MASETTO: Sì, Masetto!

MASETTO: Yes, Masetto!

Momentarily taken aback, the Don quickly regains his poise.

DON GIOVANNI: E chiuso là, perchè? La bella tua Zerlina non può, la poverina, più star senza di te.

DON GIOVANNI: And why hidden there? Your pretty Zerlina, the poor thing, couldn't stand it any more without you.

MASETTO: Capisco, sì, Signore.

MASETTO: *With heavy sarcasm.* I understand, yes, Sir.

DON GIOVANNI: Adesso fate core.

DON GIOVANNI: Now take heart.

He offers an arm to each of them.

I suonatori udite, venite omai con me!

Listen to the musicians, now come with me!

ZERLINA AND MASETTO: Sì, sì, facciamo core, ed a ballar cogli altri andiamo tutti tre.

ZERLINA AND MASETTO: Yes, yes, let's take heart, and all three go dance with the others.

These three enter the castle together as Don Ottavio, Donna Anna, and Donna Elvira approach, dressed in cloaks and dominoes.

DONNA ELVIRA: Bisogna aver coraggio, o cari amici miei! e i suoi misfatti rei scoprir, scoprir potremo allor.

DONNA ELVIRA: We must have courage, o my dear friends! and then we can expose, expose his base misdeeds.

DON OTTAVIO: L'amica dice bene! coraggio aver conviene; discaccia, o vita mia, l'affanno ed il timor!

DON OTTAVIO: Our friend speaks truly! it's necessary to have courage; dispel, o my life, your uneasiness and your fear!

DONNA ANNA: Il passo è periglioso, può nascer qualche imbroglio. Io temo pel caro sposo, e per noi temo ancor!

DONNA ANNA: It is a dangerous way, some complication may arise. I am afraid for my dear fiancé, and I am afraid for us as well!

Leporello opens the door, leans over the balcony, and sees the masked trio. The famous minuet can be heard from inside.

LEPORELLO: Signor, guardate un poco che maschere galanti!

LEPORELLO: *Calling.* Sir, look a bit, what elegant masqueraders!

Don Giovanni comes to the balcony to see.

DON GIOVANNI: Falle passar avanti, di' che ci fanno onor!

DON GIOVANNI: Have them come near, request them to honour us.

DON OTTAVIO, DONNA ANNA AND DONNA ELVIRA: Al volto ed alla voce si scopre il traditore!

DON OTTAVIO, DONNA ANNA AND DONNA ELVIRA: We recognize the betrayer by his face and by his voice!

LEPORELLO: Zì! zì! Signore maschere! Zì! zì!

LEPORELLO: St! st! Masked gentlefolk! st! st!

DONNA ANNA AND DONNA ELVIRA: Via rispondete.

DONNA ANNA AND DONNA ELVIRA: *To Don Ottavio.* Come, answer.

LEPORELLO: Zì! zì! Signore maschere!

LEPORELLO: St! st! Masked gentlefolk!

DON OTTAVIO: Cosa chiedete?

DON OTTAVIO: *To Leporello.* What do you ask?

LEPORELLO: Al ballo, se vi piace, v'invita il mio Signor.

LEPORELLO: If it please you, my Lord invites you to the ball.

DON OTTAVIO: Grazie di tanto onore!

Andiam, compagne belle!

DON OTTAVIO: *To Leporello.* Thank you for such an honour!
To his ladies. Let us go, lovely companions!

LEPORELLO: L'amico anche su quelle prova farà d'amor!

LEPORELLO: *To himself.* My friend will try to make love to those ladies too!

The trio remove their dominoes and prepare to enter the castle.

DONNA ANNA AND DON OTTAVIO: Protegga il giusto cielo il zelo del mio cor!

DONNA ANNA AND DON OTTAVIO: May the just heaven protect the fervour of my heart!

DONNA ELVIRA: Vendichi il giusto cielo il mio tradito amor!

DONNA ELVIRA: May the just heaven avenge my betrayed love!

They resume their dominoes and solemnly enter the castle.

SCENE V. The brilliantly lighted and decorated ballroom of Don Giovanni's castle. Three separate orchestras on the stage provide three different kinds of dance music. The dancing is in progress; Don Giovanni escorts various girls, and Leporello busies himself among other guests.

DON GIOVANNI: Riposate, vezzose ragazze!

DON GIOVANNI: Rest, charming girls!

LEPORELLO: Rinfrescatevi, bei giovinetti!

LEPORELLO: Refresh yourselves, handsome youths!

DON GIOVANNI AND LEPORELLO: Tornerete a far presto le pazze, tornerete a scherzar e ballar!

DON GIOVANNI AND LEPORELLO: You'll soon be wildly celebrating again, joking and dancing.

LEPORELLO: Ehi, caffè! Cioccolatte!

LEPORELLO: *To servants.* Hey, coffee! chocolate!

MASETTO: Ah, Zerlina! giudizio!

MASETTO: *Worriedly.* Ah, Zerlina! be sensible!

DON GIOVANNI: Sorbetti!

DON GIOVANNI: Ices!

LEPORELLO: Confetti!

LEPORELLO: Sweets!

MASETTO: Ah, Zerlina, giudizio!

MASETTO: Ah, Zerlina, be sensible!

ZERLINA AND MASETTO: Troppo dolce comincia la scena, in amaro potria terminar!

ZERLINA AND MASETTO: *Both to themselves.* This scene is beginning too sweetly, it could end bitterly!

DON GIOVANNI: Sei pur vaga, brillante Zerlina!

DON GIOVANNI: *Insinuatingly.* You're so delightful, sparkling Zerlina!

ZERLINA: Sua bontà!

ZERLINA: You are kind!

MASETTO: La briccona fa festa!

MASETTO: *Aside, furiously.* The minx is having fun!

LEPORELLO: Sei pur cara, Giannotta, Sandrina!

LEPORELLO: *Mimicking Don Giovanni to other girls.* You're so sweet, Giannotta, Sandrina!

MASETTO: Tocca pur, che ti cada la testa.

MASETTO: *To himself.* Touch her, and I'll take your head off.

Zerlina gives an anxious side-glance at Masetto.

ZERLINA: Quel Masetto mi par stralunato, brutto, brutto si fa quest'affar!

DON GIOVANNI AND LEPORELLO: Quel Masetto mi par stralunato, qui bisogna cervello adoprar.

MASETTO: La briccona mi fa disperar!

Don Ottavio, Donna Anna and Donna Elvira enter, masked.

LEPORELLO: Venite pur avanti, vezzose mascherette!

Don Giovanni greets the masked trio.

DON GIOVANNI: È aperto a tutti quanti, viva la libertà.

DONNA ANNA, DONNA ELVIRA AND DON OTTAVIO: Siam grati a tanti segni di generosità.

DON GIOVANNI: Ricominciate il suono! tu accoppia i ballerini! Meco tu dei ballare; Zerlina, vien pur quà!

Don Giovanni and Zerlina dance.

LEPORELLO: Da bravi via ballate!

DONNA ELVIRA: Quella è la contadina.

DONNA ANNA: Io moro!

DON OTTAVIO: Simulate.

DON GIOVANNI AND LEPORELLO: Va bene, in verità!

MASETTO: Va bene in verità!

ZERLINA: I think that Masetto is in a frenzy, this affair is going nastily, nastily!

DON GIOVANNI AND LEPORELLO: I think that Masetto is in a frenzy, here one needs to use one's brains.

MASETTO: The minx is driving me to despair!

LEPORELLO: *To the newcomers.* Now come forward, charming masqueraders!

DON GIOVANNI: Everyone is free to come in, long live freedom.

DONNA ANNA, DONNA ELVIRA AND DON OTTAVIO: We are grateful for so many signs of generosity.

DON GIOVANNI: *To the stage orchestras.* Start playing again! *To Leporello.* You pair off the dancers! *To Zerlina.* You must dance with me; come here now, Zerlina!

LEPORELLO: *To other guests.* Dance on like good folk!

DONNA ELVIRA: *To Donna Anna.* That one is the country girl.

DONNA ANNA: *To Don Ottavio.* I am dying!

DON OTTAVIO: *To Donna Anna.* Dissemble.

DON GIOVANNI AND LEPORELLO: In truth, it goes well!

MASETTO: *With heavy sarcasm.* In truth, it goes well!

DON GIOVANNI: A bada tien Masetto.

DON GIOVANNI: *To Leporello.* Keep Masetto at bay.

Leporello approaches Masetto with deep mock concern.

LEPORELLO: Non balli, poveretto!

LEPORELLO: You poor man, you're not dancing!

DON GIOVANNI: Il tuo compagno io sono, Zerlina, vien pur quà!

DON GIOVANNI: *To Zerlina.* I'm your partner, Zerlina, now come here!

LEPORELLO: Vien quà, Masetto caro! facciam quel ch'altri fa.

LEPORELLO: *To Masetto.* Come here, dear Masetto! Let's do what the others are doing.

MASETTO: No, no, ballar non voglio!

MASETTO: *Angrily.* No, no, I don't want to dance.

LEPORELLO: Eh, balla, amico mio!

LEPORELLO: Ah, dance, my friend!

MASETTO: No!

MASETTO: No!

Leporello tries to force Masetto to dance.

LEPORELLO: Sì! caro Masetto! Eh, balla, amico mio! facciam quel ch'altri fa.

LEPORELLO: Yes! dear Masetto! Ah, dance, my friend! let's do what the others are doing.

Awkwardly, Leporello forces an extremely unwilling Masetto to dance with him.

DONNA ANNA: Resister non poss'io!

DONNA ANNA: *To Don Ottavio and Donna Elvira.* I cannot endure it!

DONNA ELVIRA AND DON OTTAVIO: Fingete, per pietà!

DONNA ELVIRA AND DON OTTAVIO: *To Donna Anna.* Pretend, for pity's sake!

Don Giovanni, dancing with Zerlina, has slyly manoeuvred her towards a door on one side; now he tries to pull her through it.

DON GIOVANNI: Vieni con me, mia vita!

DON GIOVANNI: *To Zerlina.* Come with me, my life!

MASETTO: Lasciami! Ah no! Zerlina!

MASETTO: Let me go! Ah no! Zerlina!

ZERLINA: O numi! son tradita!

ZERLINA: Ye gods! I'm betrayed!

Don Giovanni pulls Zerlina with him off to the side.

LEPORELLO: Qui nasce una ruina.

LEPORELLO: A disaster is hatching here.

He hurriedly follows the Don and Zerlina.

DONNA ANNA, DONNA ELVIRA AND DON OTTAVIO: L'iniquo da se stesso nel laccio se ne va!

DONNA ANNA, DONNA ELVIRA AND DON OTTAVIO: The wicked man is throwing himself into the trap!

Zerlina screams from off-stage, causing a great commotion. The musicians stop playing, etc.

ZERLINA: Gente, aiuto! aiuto! gente!

ZERLINA: Somebody, help! help! somebody!

Donna Anna, Donna Elvira and Don Ottavio start towards the sound of Zerlina's screams.

DONNA ANNA, DONNA ELVIRA AND DON OTTAVIO: Soccorriamo l'innocente!

DONNA ANNA, DONNA ELVIRA AND DON OTTAVIO: Let us help the innocent girl!

MASETTO: Ah, Zerlina!

MASETTO: Ah, Zerlina!

ZERLINA: Scellerato!

ZERLINA: *From off-stage.* Villain!

DONNA ANNA, DONNA ELVIRA AND DON OTTAVIO: Ora grida da quel lato!

DONNA ANNA, DONNA ELVIRA AND DON OTTAVIO: Now she is calling from that side!

ZERLINA: Scellerato!

ZERLINA: Villain!

DONNA ANNA, DONNA ELVIRA AND DON OTTAVIO: Ah, gittiamo giù la porta!

DONNA ANNA, DONNA ELVIRA AND DON OTTAVIO: Ah, let us knock the door down!

ZERLINA: Soccorretemi! son morta!

ZERLINA: Help me! I am dead!

DONNA ANNA, DONNA ELVIRA, DON OTTAVIO AND MASETTO: Siam qui noi per tua difesa!

DONNA ANNA, DONNA ELVIRA, DON OTTAVIO AND MASETTO: We are here in your defence!

Just as they manage to batter down the door, Don Giovanni re-enters, holding Leporello at arm's length, and pretending with simulated fury that the servant is the culprit.

DON GIOVANNI: Ecco il birbo che t'ha offesa! ma da me la pena avrà, la pena avrà! Mori, iniquo!

DON GIOVANNI: Here's the rogue who has offended you! but he'll get his punishment, he'll get his punishment from me! Die, wretch!

Don Giovanni touches the sword at his side, and Leporello falls to his knees.

LEPORELLO: Ah, cosa fate!

LEPORELLO: Ah, what are you doing!

DON GIOVANNI: Mori, dico!

DON GIOVANNI: Die, I say!

LEPORELLO: Ah, cosa fate!

LEPORELLO: Ah, what are you doing!

Don Ottavio produces a pistol and points it at Don Giovanni.

DON OTTAVIO: Nol sperate! nol sperate!

DON OTTAVIO: Don't try that! don't try that!

Donna Anna, Donna Elvira and Don Ottavio remove their dominoes.

DONNA ANNA, DONNA ELVIRA AND DON OTTAVIO: L'empio crede con tal frode di nasconder l'empietà!

DONNA ANNA, DONNA ELVIRA AND DON OTTAVIO: With such fraud, the wicked man thinks he will disguise his wickedness!

Don Giovanni releases Leporello and starts back in surprise.

DON GIOVANNI: Donna Elvira!

DON GIOVANNI: Donna Elvira!

DONNA ELVIRA: Sì, malvagio!

DONNA ELVIRA: Yes, evil one!

DON GIOVANNI: Don Ottavio?!

DON GIOVANNI: Don Ottavio?!

DON OTTAVIO: Sì, Signore!

DON OTTAVIO: Yes, sir!

DON GIOVANNI: Ah credete—

DON GIOVANNI: Ah believe—

DONNA ANNA: Traditore—

DONNA ANNA: Betrayer—

DONNA ANNA, DONNA ELVIRA, ZERLINA, DON OTTAVIO AND MASETTO: Traditore, traditore! Tutto, tutto già si sa!

DONNA ANNA, DONNA ELVIRA, ZERLINA, DON OTTAVIO AND MASETTO: Betrayer, betrayer! We already know everything, everything!

Don Ottavio, Masetto and several of the men guests begin closing in on Don Giovanni, who stands quite coolly, hand on sword, and looks at them.

DONNA ANNA, DONNA ELVIRA, ZERLINA, DON OTTAVIO AND MASETTO: Trema, trema, scellerato! Saprà tosto il mondo intero il misfatto orrendo e nero, la tua fiera crudeltà!

DONNA ANNA, DONNA ELVIRA, ZERLINA, DON OTTAVIO AND MASETTO: Tremble, tremble, villain! Soon the whole world will know your black and dreadful crime, your cruelty!

DON GIOVANNI: È confusa la mia testa, non sò più quel ch'io mi faccia, e un orribile tempesta minacciando, o Dio, mi va.

DON GIOVANNI: My mind is confused, I no longer know what to do with myself, and a horrible storm is threatening me, oh God!

LEPORELLO: È confusa la sua testa, non sa più quel ch'ei si faccia, e un orribile tempesta minacciando, o Dio, lo va.

LEPORELLO: His mind is confused, he no longer knows what to do with himself, and a horrible storm is threatening him, oh God!

Leporello ducks behind Don Giovanni who now brandishes his sword and tries to clear a path for himself through the crowd.

DONNA ANNA, DONNA ELVIRA, ZERLINA, DON OTTAVIO AND MASETTO: Odi il tuon della vendetta, che ti fischia intorno, intorno, sul tuo capo in questo giorno il suo fulmine cadrà!

DONNA ANNA, DONNA ELVIRA, ZERLINA, DON OTTAVIO AND MASETTO: Hear the thunder of revenge clattering around and around you, on this day its bolt will fall on your head.

DON GIOVANNI: Ma non manca in me coraggio—

DON GIOVANNI: But I do not lack courage—

LEPORELLO: Ma non manca in lui coraggio—

LEPORELLO: But he does not lack courage—

DON GIOVANNI: —non mi perdo, o mi confondo.

DON GIOVANNI: —I'll not lose heart or go to pieces.

LEPORELLO: —non si perde, o si confonde.

LEPORELLO: —he'll not lose heart or go to pieces.

DON GIOVANNI: Se cadesse ancora il mondo nulla mai temer mi fa!

DON GIOVANNI: Even if the world should fall apart, nothing will ever make me be afraid!

Don Giovanni seizes Leporello, and pushing the servant before himself, forces his way through the crowd which surrounds him and escapes.

End of Act I

Act II

SCENE I. Evening in a square by the house of Donna Elvira. Don Giovanni and Leporello appear, arguing.

DON GIOVANNI: Eh via, buffone, non mi seccar.

DON GIOVANNI: Oh, come now, clown, don't bother me.

LEPORELLO: No, no, padrone, non vo' restar!

LEPORELLO: No, no, master, I don't want to stay!

DON GIOVANNI: Sentimi, amico—

DON GIOVANNI: Listen to me, friend—

LEPORELLO: Vo' andar, vi dico!

LEPORELLO: I want to go, I tell you!

DON GIOVANNI: Ma che ti ho fatto, che vuoi lasciarmi?

DON GIOVANNI: What have I done to you, that you want to leave me?

LEPORELLO: O niente affatto, quasi ammazzarmi.

LEPORELLO: Oh nothing at all, you almost murdered me.

DON GIOVANNI: Va che sei matto, fu per burlar.

DON GIOVANNI: Don't be crazy, it was in fun.

LEPORELLO: Ed io non burlo, ma voglio andar!

LEPORELLO: And I'm not joking, but I want to go!

Half-heartedly, Leporello tries to sneak away. Don Giovanni pulls him back and tosses him a purse of money.

DON GIOVANNI: Leporello!

DON GIOVANNI: Leporello!

LEPORELLO: Signore!

LEPORELLO: Sir!

DON GIOVANNI: Vien qui, facciamo pace, prendi!

DON GIOVANNI: Come here, let's make peace, take this!

LEPORELLO: Cosa?

DON GIOVANNI: Quattro doppie.

Leporello eagerly counts his money.

LEPORELLO: Oh, sentite, per questa volta la cerimonia accetto; ma non vi ci avvezzate; non credete di sedurre i miei pari come le donne, a forza di danari.

DON GIOVANNI: Non parliam più di ciò! ti basta l'animo di far quel ch'io ti dico?

LEPORELLO: Purchè lasciam le donne.

DON GIOVANNI: Lasciar le donne? pazzo! lasciar le donne! Sai ch'elle per me son necessarie più del pan che mangio, più dell'aria che spiro!

LEPORELLO: E avete core d'ingannarle poi tutte?

DON GIOVANNI: È tutto amore; chi a una sola è fedele, verso l'altre è crudele; io che in me sento sì esteso sentimento, vo' bene a tutte quante; le donne poi chè calcolar non sanno, il mio buon natural chiamano inganno.

LEPORELLO: Non ho veduto mai naturale più vasto, e più benigno! Orsù, cosa vorreste?

DON GIOVANNI: Odi! vedesti tu la cameriera di Donn'Elvira?

LEPORELLO: Io, no.

DON GIOVANNI: Non hai veduto qualche cosa di bello, caro il mio Leporello; ora io con lei vo' tentar la mia sorte, ed ho pensato, giacchè siam verso sera, per

LEPORELLO: What?

DON GIOVANNI: Four doubloons.

LEPORELLO: Oh, listen, for this time I'll accept your compliments; but don't accustom yourself to it; don't think of buying someone like *me* in the same way as women, with your money.

DON GIOVANNI: Let's not talk about it any more. Have you enough spirit to do what I tell you?

LEPORELLO: Provided that we leave women alone.

DON GIOVANNI: Leave women alone? madman! leave women alone! You know that they're more necessary to me than the bread I eat, more than the air I breathe!

LEPORELLO: And you have the heart then to deceive them all?

DON GIOVANNI: It's all love; whoever is faithful only to one is cruel to the others; I, who feel such ample sentiment in myself, love all of them; and since women don't comprehend these things, they call my natural goodness deceit.

LEPORELLO: Never have I seen a nature more ample and more kind! Now then, what would you like?

DON GIOVANNI: Listen! have you seen Donna Elvira's chambermaid?

LEPORELLO: Not I.

DON GIOVANNI: Then you have not seen a thing of beauty, my dear Leporello; I now want to try my luck with her, and since it's toward evening, I have thought

aguzzarle meglio l'appetito, di present-
armi a lei col tuo vestito.

that I will better arouse her desire by
presenting myself to her in your clothes.

LEPORELLO: E perchè non potreste pre-
sentarvi col vostro?

LEPORELLO: And why couldn't you present yourself in yours?

DON GIOVANNI: Han poco credito con
gente di tal rango, gli abiti signorili.
Sbrigati, via!

DON GIOVANNI: Noble garments have
little prestige with people of such station. Come on, hurry!

LEPORELLO: Signor, per più ragioni—

LEPORELLO: Sir, for many reasons—

DON GIOVANNI: Finiscila! Non soffro
opposizione!

DON GIOVANNI: *Impatiently.* Have done
with it! I won't stand any opposition!

*Leporello gives up in disgust and exchanges hat and cloak with his master. The scene
darkens as evening advances. Don Giovanni and Leporello stand in the shadows of
Donna Elvira's house as Donna Elvira steps out onto a balcony.*

DONNA ELVIRA: Ah, taci, ingiusto core!
Non palpitarmi in seno! è un empio, è un
traditore, è colpa aver pietà.

DONNA ELVIRA: Ah, be still, unreasonable heart! Do not pound in my breast!
he is a wicked man, he is a betrayer, it is
wrong to have pity.

LEPORELLO: Zitto! di Donna Elvira,
Signor, la voce io sento!

LEPORELLO: *Whispering to Don Giovanni.*
Hush! Sir, I hear Donna Elvira's voice!

DON GIOVANNI: Cogliere io vo' il momento, tu fermati un po' là!

DON GIOVANNI: *Whispering to Leporello.* I
want to make use of this moment, you
stand there a while!

*Don Giovanni pushes Leporello under the balcony, just within Donna Elvira's view,
gets behind him, and manipulates his arms in the fashion of a serenader.*

Elvira, idolo mio!

Elvira, my idol!

Donna Elvira looks down, sees Leporello, and believes him to be Don Giovanni.

DONNA ELVIRA: Non è costui, l'ingrato?

DONNA ELVIRA: Isn't it he, the ingrate?

DON GIOVANNI: Sì, vita mia, son' io, e
chiedo carità!

DON GIOVANNI: Yes, my life, it's I, and I
plead for your mercy!

DONNA ELVIRA: Numi, che strano effeto
mi si risveglia in petto!

DONNA ELVIRA: Gods, what a strange
sensation is awakening in my breast!

LEPORELLO: State a veder la pazza, che
ancor gli crederà.

LEPORELLO: *Aside.* You'll see that the
madwoman is going to believe him.

Don Giovanni nudges Leporello into more excited motions.

DON GIOVANNI: Discendi, o gioia bella! vedrai che tu sei quella, che adora l'alma mia, pentito io sono già!

DONNA ELVIRA: No, non ti credo, o barbaro!

DON GIOVANNI: Ah, credimi! o m'uccido! Idolo mio, vien quà!

DONNA ELVIRA: Dei, che cimento è questo! non sò s'io vado, o resto? ah, proteggete voi la mia credulità!

DON GIOVANNI: Spero che cada presto! che bel colpetto è questo? più fertile talento del mio, no, non si dà!

LEPORELLO: Già quel mendace labbro torna a sedur costei, deh proteggete, o Dei! la sua credulità!

Donna Elvira leaves the balcony and re-enters the house.

DON GIOVANNI: Amico, che ti par?

LEPORELLO: Mi par che abbiate un'anima di bronzo.

DON GIOVANNI: Va la, che sei'l gran gonzo! Ascolta bene: quando costei qui viene, tu corri ad abbracciarla, falle quattro carezze, fingi la voce mia; poi con bell'arte cerca teco condurla in altra parte.

LEPORELLO: Ma, Signore—

DON GIOVANNI: Non più repliche.

LEPORELLO: E se poi mi conosce?

DON GIOVANNI: Non ti conoscerà, se tu non vuoi; zitto: ell'apre, ehi, giudizio!

DON GIOVANNI: Come down, o beautiful joy! You will see that you're the one whom my soul adores, oh yes, I am repentant!

DONNA ELVIRA: No, I do not believe you, o cruel man!

DON GIOVANNI: Ah, believe me! or I'll kill myself! My idol, come here!

DONNA ELVIRA: Gods, what a trial this is! I don't know whether to go or to stay? ah, protect ye my trust!

DON GIOVANNI: I hope she will break down soon! what a pretty little trick this is? there is no talent more versatile than mine!

LEPORELLO: Already those lying lips begin to seduce her again, come, protect, o Gods! her trust!

DON GIOVANNI: Friend, what do you think?

LEPORELLO: I think you have a lot of nerve.

DON GIOVANNI: Go on, you're a big blockhead! listen closely: when she comes here, you run to embrace her, give her a couple of caresses, imitate my voice; then, with nice artfulness, try to lead her elsewhere.

LEPORELLO: But Sir—

DON GIOVANNI: Don't talk back.

LEPORELLO: And then if she recognizes me?

DON GIOVANNI: She won't recognize you if you don't want her to; hush, she's unlocking the door, careful!

Don Giovanni takes cover and watches. Donna Elvira comes out of the house and meets Leporello, who goes to her, keeping his face averted.

DONNA ELVIRA: Eccomi a voi.

DONNA ELVIRA: *To Leporello.* I've come to you.

DON GIOVANNI: (Veggiamo che farà.)

DON GIOVANNI: *To himself.* Let's see what she will do.

LEPORELLO: (Che imbroglio!)

LEPORELLO: *To himself.* What a mess!

DONNA ELVIRA: Dunque creder potrò che i pianti miei abbian vinto quel cor? dunque pentito, l'amato Don Giovanni, al suo dovere, e all'amor mio ritorna?

DONNA ELVIRA: Can I believe that my tears have conquered that heart? so repentant, my beloved Don Giovanni returns to his obligation and to my love?

Leporello manages a muffled approximation of Don Giovanni's voice.

LEPORELLO: Sì, carina!

LEPORELLO: Yes, dear!

DONNA ELVIRA: Crudele! se sapeste quante lagrime e quanti sospir voi mi costate!

DONNA ELVIRA: Cruel man! if you knew how many tears and how many sighs you cost me!

LEPORELLO: Io, vita mia?

LEPORELLO: I, my life?

DONNA ELVIRA: Voi.

DONNA ELVIRA: You.

LEPORELLO: Poverina! quanto mi dispiace!

LEPORELLO: Poor little girl! how sorry I am!

DONNA ELVIRA: Mi fuggirete più?

DONNA ELVIRA: Will you run away from me again?

LEPORELLO: No, muso bello!

LEPORELLO: No, pretty little face!

DONNA ELVIRA: Sarete sempre mio?

DONNA ELVIRA: Will you always be mine?

LEPORELLO: Sempre!

LEPORELLO: *Most amorously.* Always!

DONNA ELVIRA: Carissimo!

DONNA ELVIRA: Dearest!

LEPORELLO: Carissima! (La burla mi dà gusto.)

LEPORELLO: Dearest!
To himself. This joke suits me.

DONNA ELVIRA: Mio tesoro!

DONNA ELVIRA: My treasure!

LEPORELLO: Mia Venere!

LEPORELLO: My Venus!

Donna Elvira flings her arms about Leporello.

DONNA ELVIRA: Son per voi tutta foco.

DONNA ELVIRA: I'm all aflame for you.

LEPORELLO: Io tutto cenere.

LEPORELLO: I'm all ashes.

DON GIOVANNI: (Il birbo si riscalda.)

DON GIOVANNI: *To himself.* The rascal is becoming passionate.

DONNA ELVIRA: E non m'ingannerete?

DONNA ELVIRA: And you won't deceive me?

LEPORELLO: No, sicuro.

LEPORELLO: Certainly not.

DONNA ELVIRA: Giuratemi.

DONNA ELVIRA: Swear it to me.

LEPORELLO: Lo giuro a questa mano, che bacio con trasporto, e a quei bei lumi.

LEPORELLO: I swear it by this hand, which I kiss with rapture, and by those beautiful eyes.

Don Giovanni leaps out in front of them and pretends to be a robber assaulting them.

DON GIOVANNI: Ih, eh, ah, ah; sei morto!

DON GIOVANNI: Hee, heh, hah, hah; you're dead!

DONNA ELVIRA AND LEPORELLO: O Numi!

DONNA ELVIRA AND LEPORELLO: O Gods!

Donna Elvira and Leporello flee hastily. Don Giovanni recovers the mandolin which Leporello had pretended to use earlier.

DON GIOVANNI: Ih, eh, ih, eh, ah, ah! Par che la sorte mi secondi; veggiamo. Le finestre son queste; ora cantiamo.

DON GIOVANNI: Hee, heh, hee, heh, hah, hah! It seems luck is with me; let's see. These are the windows; now let's sing.

He strums the mandolin beneath the balcony and sings a serenade.

Deh vieni alla finestra, o mio tesoro, deh vieni a consolar il pianto mio. Se neghi a me di dar qualche ristoro, davanti agli occhi tuoi morir vogl'io! Tu ch'hai la bocca dolce, più che il miele, tu che il zucchero porti in mezzo al core! Non esser, gioia mia, con me crudele! lasciati almen veder, mio bell'amore!

Come, come to the window, oh my treasure, come, come to console my tears. If you refuse to give me some relief, I will die before your eyes! You have a mouth sweeter than honey, you who bring sweetness to the depths of my heart! Do not be cruel with me, my joy! At least let yourself be seen, my beautiful love!

As Don Giovanni finishes his serenade, Masetto appears, carrying weapons. With him are peasants and village men, also armed with guns and clubs.

DON GIOVANNI: V'è gente alla finestra; sarà dessa! Zi, zi!

DON GIOVANNI: There's somebody at the window; it must be she! Psst, psst!

MASETTO: Non ci stanchiamo; il cor mi dice che trovarlo dobbiam.

MASETTO: *To his companions.* Let's not give up; my heart tells me that we shall find him.

DON GIOVANNI: (Qualcuno parla!)

DON GIOVANNI: *To himself.* Someone is speaking!

MASETTO: Fermatevi; mi pare che alcuno qui si muova.

MASETTO: Stand still; I think someone is moving around here.

Don Giovanni wraps Leporello's cloak about himself and pulls his servant's hat over his face.

DON GIOVANNI: (Se non fallo, è Masetto!)

DON GIOVANNI: *To himself.* If I'm not mistaken, it's Masetto!

MASETTO: Chi va là? non risponde; animo, schioppo al muso! Chi va là?

MASETTO: Who goes there? He doesn't answer; courage, guns up! Who goes there?

DON GIOVANNI: (Non è solo; ci vuol giudizio.)

DON GIOVANNI: *To himself.* He's not alone; this needs prudence.

Don Giovanni feigns Leporello's voice.

Amici! (Non mi voglio scoprir.) Sei tu, Masetto?

Friends! (I don't want to be found out.) Is it you, Masetto?

MASETTO: Appunto quello: e tu?

MASETTO: *With surprise.* Just so: and you?

DON GIOVANNI: Non mi conosci? il servo son io di Don Giovanni.

DON GIOVANNI: Don't you know me? I'm Don Giovanni's servant.

MASETTO: Leporello! servo di quell'indegno cavaliere!

MASETTO: Leporello! servant of that unworthy nobleman!

DON GIOVANNI: Certo, di quel briccone!

DON GIOVANNI: Certainly, of that rogue!

MASETTO: Di quell'uom senza onore: ah, dimmi un poco, dove possiam trovarlo; lo cerco con costor per trucidarlo.

MASETTO: Of that man without honour: ah, tell me a bit where we can find him; I'm looking for him with these men in order to kill him.

DON GIOVANNI: (Bagatelle!) Bravissimo, Masetto! anch'io con voi m'unisco, per fargliela a quel birbo di padrone; or senti un po' qual è la mia

DON GIOVANNI: *Aside.* Rubbish! *Aloud.* Very good, Masetto! I'll join you, too, in order to do in that rogue of a master; now listen a bit to what my plan is. Half

intenzione. Metà di voi quà vadano, e gli altri vadan là! e pian pianin lo cerchino, lontan non sia di quà, no! lontan non sia di quà! Se un uom e una ragazza passeggian per la piazza, se sotto a una finestra fare all'amor sentite, ferite, pur, ferite, il mio padron sarà! In testa egli ha un cappello con candidi pennacchi, addosso un gran mantello, e spada al fianco egli ha.

of you go that way, and the others go there! and look for him quietly, quietly, he may not be far from here, no! he may not be far from here! If a man and a maid are walking through the square, if you hear someone making love under a window, strike, then, strike, it will be my master! He has a hat with white plumes on his head, a big cloak around him, and he has a sword at his side.

He waves the men off in all directions.

Andate, fate presto.

Go, be quick.

He turns to Masetto.

Tu sol verrai con me.

You alone will come with me.

He pretends great friendship for Masetto.

Noi far dobbiam il resto, e già vedrai cos'è.

We must do what's left, and you'll soon see what it is.

The peasants scatter in all directions. Don Giovanni manoeuvres Masetto into the shadows.

Zitto, lascia ch'io senta! Ottimamente! Dunque dobbiam ucciderlo?

Hush, let me listen! Excellent! Should we kill him, then?

MASETTO: Sicuro!

MASETTO: Surely!

DON GIOVANNI: E non ti basteria rompergli l'ossa, fracassargli le spalle?

DON GIOVANNI: And it won't satisfy you to break his bones, to fracture his back?

MASETTO: No, no, voglio ammazzarlo, vo' farlo in cento brani.

MASETTO: *Angrily and with determination.* No, no, I want to kill him, I want to chop him into a hundred pieces.

DON GIOVANNI: Hai buone armi?

DON GIOVANNI: Have you got good weapons?

MASETTO: Cospetto! ho pria questo moschetto, e poi, questa pistola.

MASETTO: Yes, by God! I've got first this musket, and then this pistol.

Masetto proudly hands his weapons to the supposed Leporello for inspection.

DON GIOVANNI: E poi?

DON GIOVANNI: And then?

MASETTO: Non basta?

MASETTO: Isn't that enough?

Don Giovanni knocks Masetto down with his own weapons and beats him.

DON GIOVANNI: Oh, basta, certo: or prendi, questa per la pistola, questa per il moschetto!

DON GIOVANNI: Oh, it's enough, certainly: now take this for the pistol, this for the musket!

MASETTO: Ahi, ahi! la testa mia!

MASETTO: Oh, oh! my head!

DON GIOVANNI: Taci, o sei morto! Questa per ammazzarlo, questa per farlo in brani! Villano, mascalzon! ceffo da cani!

DON GIOVANNI: Be quiet, or you're dead! This is for killing him, this for chopping him into bits! Villain, scoundrel! Dirty dog!

Tossing the gun and pistol down beside Masetto, Don Giovanni beats a hasty retreat.

MASETTO: Ahi, ahi! la testa mia! ahi, ahi! le spalle, e il petto—

MASETTO: Oh, oh! my head! oh, oh! my shoulders and my chest—

Zerlina enters, carrying a light.

ZERLINA: Di sentire mi parve la voce di Masetto!

ZERLINA: I think I hear Masetto's voice!

MASETTO: O Dio, Zerlina, Zerlina mia, soccorso!

MASETTO: O God, Zerlina, my Zerlina, help!

ZERLINA: Cosa è stato?

ZERLINA: What's happened?

MASETTO: L'iniquo, il scellerato mi ruppe l'ossa e i nervi.

MASETTO: The wicked man, the villain broke my bones and sinews.

ZERLINA: Oh poveretta me! chi?

ZERLINA: Oh poor me! who?

MASETTO: Leporello! o qualche diavol che somiglia a lui!

MASETTO: Leporello! or some devil that looks like him!

Zerlina helps Masetto stagger to his feet.

ZERLINA: Crudel! non tel diss'io che con questa tua pazza gelosia ti ridurresti a qualche brutto passo? dove ti duole?

ZERLINA: Cruel man! didn't I tell you that your crazy jealousy would bring you to grief? where does it hurt you?

MASETTO: Qui.

MASETTO: *Whining*. Here.

ZERLINA: E poi?

ZERLINA: Where else?

MASETTO: Qui, ancora qui.

MASETTO: Here, here too.

ZERLINA: E poi non ti duol altro?

ZERLINA: And it doesn't hurt you anywhere else?

MASETTO: Duolmi un poco questo piè, questo braccio, e questo mano.

ZERLINA: Via, via, non è gran mal, se il resto è sano. Vientene meco a casa; purchè tu mi prometta d'essere men geloso, io, io ti guarirò, caro il mio sposo.
Vedrai, carino, se sei buonino, che bel rimedio ti voglio dar. È naturale, non dà disgusto, e lo speziale non lo sa far, no. È un certo balsamo che porto addosso, dare tel posso, se il vuoi provar. Saper vorresti dove mi sta?

MASETTO: This foot hurts me a little, this arm, and this hand.

ZERLINA: Come, come, it's not very bad if the rest is all right. Come home with me; provided you promise me to be less jealous, I, I'll heal you, my dear husband.

You'll see, dearest, if you're very good, what a lovely medicine I'll give you. It's natural, it won't make you sick, and the apothecary doesn't know how to make it.
It's a certain balm that I carry with me, I can give it to you if you want to try it. Would you like to know where I keep it?

Zerlina takes Masetto's hand and holds it to her heart.

Sentilo battere, toccami quà!

Feel it beating, touch me here!

Exit Zerlina and Masetto, their arms about one another.

SCENE II. Later the same night, in a dark courtyard or garden outside the house of Donna Anna. Leporello enters, escorting Donna Elvira. He is still dressed in the Don's hat and cloak, and still tries to keep his face averted from Donna Elvira's direct sight.

LEPORELLO: Di molte faci il lume s'avvicina, o mio ben; stiamo qui ascosi, finchè da noi si scosta.

DONNA ELVIRA: Ma che temi, adorato mio sposo?

LEPORELLO: Nulla, nulla, certi riguardi, io vo' veder se il lume è già lontano. (Ah, come da costei liberarmi?) Rimanti, anima bella.

DONNA ELVIRA: Ah! non lasciarmi! Sola, sola in buio loco palpitar il cor mi sento, e m'assale un tal spavento, che mi sembra di morir.

LEPORELLO: Lights are coming toward us from all around, o my dear; let's stay hidden here until they go away from us.

DONNA ELVIRA: But what are you afraid of, my adored husband?

LEPORELLO: Nothing, nothing, certain considerations, I want to see whether the lights are gone away yet. *To himself.* Ah, how to get rid of her? *Aloud.* Stay here, beautiful spirit.

DONNA ELVIRA: Ah! don't leave me! Alone, alone in a dark place, I feel my heart pounding, and such fear overwhelms me that I think I'm dying.

Leporello fumbles about in the dark.

LEPORELLO: Più che cerco, men ritrovo questa porta, questa porta sciagurata;

LEPORELLO: The more I look, the less I find this door, this confounded door;

He gropes his way to the door and loses it again in the dark.

piano, piano, l'ho trovata! ecco il tempo di fuggir!

softly, softly, I've found it! now's the time to get away!

Don Ottavio and Donna Anna enter. She is still dressed in mourning.

DON OTTAVIO: Tergi il ciglio, o vita mia, e dà calma al tuo dolore! l'ombra omai del genitore pena avrà de' tuoi martir.

DON OTTAVIO: Dry your eyes, o my life, and calm your sorrow! you will grieve your parent's shade with your torment.

DONNA ANNA: Lascia almen alla mia pena questo piccolo ristoro; sol la morte, o mio tesoro, il mio pianto può finir.

DONNA ANNA: Leave at least this small relief to my suffering; only death, o my treasure, can end my weeping.

Meanwhile, Donna Elvira and Leporello remain unnoticed.

DONNA ELVIRA: Ah, dov'è lo sposo mio?

DONNA ELVIRA: Ah, where is my husband?

LEPORELLO: Se mi trova, son perduto!

LEPORELLO: If I'm found, I'm lost!

DONNA ELVIRA AND LEPORELLO: Una porta là vegg'io, cheta, cheta io vo' partir.

DONNA ELVIRA AND LEPORELLO: I see a door over there, I want to depart quietly, quietly.

As Leporello tries to sneak through the door, he is seized by Masetto and Zerlina, who enter.

ZERLINA AND MASETTO: Ferma, briccone, dove ten vai?

ZERLINA AND MASETTO: Stop, rogue, where are you going?

They push Leporello before Don Ottavio and Donna Anna. Leporello falls to his knees and buries his face in his (i.e. Don Giovanni's) cloak.

DONNA ANNA AND DON OTTAVIO: Ecco il fellone, com'era quà?

DONNA ANNA AND DON OTTAVIO: Here is the criminal, how came he here?

DONNA ANNA, ZERLINA, DON OTTAVIO AND MASETTO: Ah, mora il perfido! che m'ha tradito!

DONNA ANNA, ZERLINA, DON OTTAVIO AND MASETTO: Ah, death to the wicked man! he that has betrayed me!

Donna Elvira steps forth and reveals her presence to the others.

DONNA ELVIRA: O mio marito! pietà, pietà!

DONNA ELVIRA: O my husband! have pity, have pity!

DONNA ANNA, ZERLINA, DON OTTAVIO AND MASETTO: È Donna Elvira quella ch'io vedo? appena il credo! No, morrà!

DONNA ANNA, ZERLINA, DON OTTAVIO AND MASETTO: Is it Donna Elvira that I see? I can hardly believe it! No, he shall die!

As they seize the supposed Don Giovanni, Leporello grovels before them and reveals his identity. All the others are appalled, especially Donna Elvira, who runs to Donna Anna, as if for comfort.

LEPORELLO: Perdon, perdono! Signori miei! quello io non sono, sbaglia costei, viver lasciatemi, per carità!

LEPORELLO: Forgive me, forgive me! my lords and ladies! I'm not him, she's mistaken, let me live, for pity's sake!

DONNA ANNA, DONNA ELVIRA, ZERLINA, DON OTTAVIO AND MASETTO: Dei! Leporello? Che inganno è questo! Stupida resto! Che mai sarà!

DONNA ANNA, DONNA ELVIRA, ZERLINA, DON OTTAVIO AND MASETTO: Gods! Leporello? what deceit is this! I am stunned! Whatever can it mean!

LEPORELLO: Mille torbidi pensieri mi s'aggiran per la testa; se mi salvo in tal tempesta è un prodigio in verità.

LEPORELLO: A thousand confused thoughts are churning through my head; if I save myself in this storm, it will truly be a marvel.

DONNA ANNA, DONNA ELVIRA, ZERLINA, DON OTTAVIO AND MASETTO: Mille torbidi pensieri mi s'aggiran per la testa. Che giornata, o stelle, è questa! Che impensata novità!

DONNA ANNA, DONNA ELVIRA, ZERLINA, DON OTTAVIO AND MASETTO: A thousand confused thoughts are churning through my head. What a day, o my stars, is this! What an unexpected development!

LEPORELLO: Ah, pietà! Signori miei! ah, pietà di me! Dò ragioni a voi, a lei. Ma, ma il delitto mio non è. Il padron con prepotenza l'innocenza mi rubò.

Donna Elvira! compatite! Voi capite come andò!
Di Masetto non sò nulla, vel dirà questa fanciulla. È un'oretta circumcirca, che con lei girando vo.

A voi, Signore! non dico niente, certo timore—certo accidente—di fuori chiaro—di dentro oscuro—non c'è riparo—la porta, il muro—io me ne vo

LEPORELLO: Ah, have mercy! My lords and ladies! ah, have mercy for me! I'll explain to you, to her. But, but the fault isn't mine. My master haughtily robbed me of my innocence.
To Donna Elvira. Donna Elvira! have sympathy! You know how it went!
To Masetto. About Masetto I know nothing, this girl, will tell you so. It's more or less a short hour that I've been strolling with her.
To Don Ottavio. To you, Sir! I'll say nothing—a certain fear—certain events—light outside—dark inside—there wasn't any shelter—the door, the

da quel lato, poi qui celato, l'affar si sa! ma s'io sapeva, fuggia per quà.

wall—I want to get away this way, then hidden here—the matter is plain! But if I had known, I'd have left this way.

As he sings, Leporello edges toward the garden door and escapes.

DONNA ELVIRA: Ferma, perfido, ferma!

DONNA ELVIRA: Stop, deceiver, stop!

MASETTO: Il birbo ha l'ali ai piedi!

MASETTO: The rogue has wings on his feet!

ZERLINA: Con qual arte si sottrasse l'iniquo.

ZERLINA: How artfully the wicked man got away.

DON OTTAVIO: Amici miei, dopo eccessi sì enormi, dubitar non possiam che Don Giovanni non sia l'empio uccisore del padre di Donn'Anna; in questa casa poche ore fermatevi, un ricorso vo' far a chi si deve, e in poch'istanti vendicarvi prometto. Così vuole dover, pietade, affetto.
Il mio tesoro intanto andate, andate a consolar! e del bel ciglio il pianto cercate di asciugar. Ditele che i suoi torti a vendicar io vado; che sol di stragi e morti nunzio vogl'io tornar!

DON OTTAVIO: My friends, after his enormous excesses, we cannot doubt that Don Giovanni is the wicked murderer of Donna Anna's father; wait a few hours in this house, I want to make an appeal to those whose business it is, and in a little while I promise you vengeance. Thus duty, pity and affection will it.
Meanwhile, go, go to console my treasure! and try to dry the tears from her lovely lashes. Tell her that I am going to avenge her wrongs; that I will return only as news-bearer of destruction and death!

The aria "Il mio tesoro" originally marked the end of Scene II, Act II. Mozart added the following scene and Donna Elvira's aria "Mi tradì" for the Vienna première of Don Giovanni. *Because the scene itself is hardly ever performed, Donna Elvira generally sings her aria immediately after Don Ottavio makes his exit, above.*

SCENE III. A sparsely furnished room with a window on one side. Zerlina, flourishing a razor, half chases, half drags Leporello onto the stage.

ZERLINA: Restati quà! Restati quà!

ZERLINA: Stay right there! Stay right there!

LEPORELLO: Per carità!

LEPORELLO: For pity's sake!

Leporello struggles.

ZERLINA: Eh! non c'è carità per pari tuoi.

ZERLINA: Eh! there is no pity for the likes of you.

LEPORELLO: Dunque cavarmi vuoi ...?

LEPORELLO: So you want to tear out ...?

ZERLINA: I cappelli, la testa, il core, e gli occhi.

ZERLINA: Your hair, your head, your heart, and your eyes.

LEPORELLO: Senti, carina mia!

LEPORELLO: *Pleadingly.* Listen, my little dear!

ZERLINA: Guai, se mi tocchi! Vedrai, schiuma de' birbi, qual premio n'ha chi le ragazze ingiuria.

ZERLINA: Look out if you touch me! You'll see, rascally scum, what reward there is for someone who wrongs girls.

LEPORELLO: (Liberatemi, o Dei, da questa furia!)

LEPORELLO: *Aside.* Deliver me, o Gods, from this fury!

Zerlina continues to harass Leporello.

ZERLINA: Masetto! Olà! Masetto! dove diavolo è ito? Servi! gente! nessun vien, nessun sente—

ZERLINA: Masetto! Hey there! Masetto! where the devil has he gone? Servants! people! nobody comes, nobody hears—

A peasant wanders in.

LEPORELLO: Fa piano, per pietà! non strascinarmi a coda di cavallo!

LEPORELLO: Be careful, for pity's sake! don't drag me along tied to a horse's tail!

ZERLINA: Vedrai, vedrai come finisce il ballo! Presto quà quella sedia!

ZERLINA: You'll see, you'll see how the party ends! Quick, that chair here!

LEPORELLO: Eccola!

LEPORELLO: Here it is!

ZERLINA: Siedi!

ZERLINA: Sit down!

LEPORELLO: Stanco non son!

LEPORELLO: I'm not tired!

ZERLINA: Siedi, o con queste mani ti strappo il cor, e poi lo getto a'cani.

ZERLINA: Sit down or with these hands I'll tear out your heart, and then I'll throw it to the dogs.

Leporello seats himself with a sigh.

LEPORELLO: Siedo, ma tu, di grazia, metti giù quel rasoio! mi vuoi forse sbarbar?

LEPORELLO: I'll sit, but would you kindly put down that razor! possibly you want to shave me?

ZERLINA: Si, mascalzone, io sbarbare ti vo' senza sapone.

ZERLINA: Yes, scoundrel, I'll shave you without soap.

LEPORELLO: Eterni Dei!

LEPORELLO: Almighty Gods!

ZERLINA: Dammi la man.

ZERLINA: Give me your hand.

Leporello nervously extends his hand.

LEPORELLO: La mano.

LEPORELLO: My hand.

ZERLINA: L'altra!

ZERLINA: The other one!

Leporello complies.

LEPORELLO: Ma che vuoi farmi?

LEPORELLO: But what will you do to me?

ZERLINA: Voglio far, voglio far quello che parmi.

ZERLINA: I'll do, I'll do what I please.

The peasant wanders over and helps Zerlina tie Leporello's hands.

LEPORELLO: Per queste tue manine, candide e tenerelle, per questa fresca pelle, abbi pietà di me!

LEPORELLO: By these white and young little hands of yours, by that fresh complexion, have pity on me!

ZERLINA: Non v'è pietà, briccone, son una tigre irata, un'aspide, un leone!

ZERLINA: There is no pity for you, rascal, I'm a furious tigress, an asp, a lioness!

LEPORELLO: Ah, di fuggir si provi!

LEPORELLO: Ah, let me try to flee!

ZERLINA: Sei morto se ti movi!

ZERLINA: You're dead if you move!

LEPORELLO: Barbari, ingiusti Dei!

LEPORELLO: Cruel, unfair Gods!

ZERLINA: Barbaro traditore, del tuo padrone il core avessi qui con te!

ZERLINA: Cruel betrayer, if I only had your master's heart here with you!

LEPORELLO: In mano di costei, chi capitar mi fe'? Deh non mi stringer tanto! l'anima sen va!

LEPORELLO: Who made me fall into her hands? Come, don't squeeze me so hard! my breath is leaving me!

ZERLINA: Sen vada, o resti, intanto non partirai di quà!

ZERLINA: Let it leave, or let it stay, meanwhile you won't get away from here!

LEPORELLO: Che strette, oh Dei, che botte! è giorno ovver è notte?

LEPORELLO: What squeezes, oh Gods, what beatings! is it day or is it night?

ZERLINA: Di gioia e di diletto sento brillarmi il petto! così cogl'uomini si fa!

ZERLINA: I feel my breast burning with joy and delight! thus one acts with men!

LEPORELLO: È notte o giorno? che scosse di tremuoto, che buia oscurità!

LEPORELLO: Is it night or day? what earthquake tremblings, what gloomy darkness!

Zerlina leaves, and Leporello turns hopefully to the peasant.

Amico, per pietà un poco d'acqua fresca, o ch'io mi moro. Guarda un po' come stretto mi legò l'assassina.

Friend, for pity's sake, a little cold water, or else I'll die. Look a bit at how tightly the murderess tied me.

The peasant goes out.

Se potessi liberarmi coi denti? Oh venga il diavolo a disfar questi gruppi! io vo' vedere di rompere la corda—come è forte! paura della morte! E tu, Mercurio, protettor de' ladri, proteggi un galant'uom! coraggio—bravo! pria che costei ritorni, bisogna dar di sprone alle calcagna, e strascinar, se occorre, una montagna!

Could I free myself with my teeth? Oh, may the devil come untie these knots! I'll manage to break this rope—how strong it is! I'm scared of death! And you, Mercury, protector of thieves, protect a gallant! courage—hurray! before that woman returns, I'll have to give full speed to my heels, and if need be, drag along a mountain!

Wriggling violently, he manages to loosen his ropes, and jumps out of the window, chair, ropes and all. Zerlina returns, accompanied by Donna Elvira, Masetto and some peasants.

ZERLINA: Andiam, andiam, Signora! vedrete in qual maniera ho concio il scellerato.

ZERLINA: *To Donna Elvira.* Come, come, my lady! you'll see how I have fixed the villain.

DONNA ELVIRA: Ah, sopra lui si sfoghi il mio furor.

DONNA ELVIRA: Ah, let my rage break on him.

ZERLINA: Stelle! in qual modo si salvò quel briccone?

ZERLINA: Ye gods! how did that rogue get away?

DONNA ELVIRA: L'avrà sottratto l'empio suo padrone.

DONNA ELVIRA: His wicked master must have set him free.

ZERLINA: Fu desso senza fallo: anche di questo informiam Don Ottavio: a lui si spetta far per noi tutti, o domandar vendetta!

ZERLINA: It was undoubtedly he: let's tell Don Ottavio about this, too: he is supposed to act for all of us or to demand vengeance!

All leave except Donna Elvira.

DONNA ELVIRA: In quali eccessi, o Numi, in quai misfatti orribili, tremendi è avvolto il sciagurato! Ah no! non puote tardar l'ira del cielo, la giustizia tardar. Sentir già parmi la fatale saetta, che gli

DONNA ELVIRA: In what excesses, o Gods, in what horrible, tremendous misdeeds the villain is involved! Ah no! heaven's wrath, justice, cannot be delayed, cannot be delayed. I think I

piomba sul capo! aperto veggio il ba-
ratro mortal! Misera Elvira! che con-
trasto d'affetti in sen ti nasce! Perchè
questi sospiri? e quest'ambascie?

already sense the fatal thunderbolt that
will fall on his head! I see the deadly
chasm opening! Wretched Elvira! what
conflicting emotions arise in your
breast! why these sighs? and these
pangs?

Mi tradì quell'alma ingrata, quell'alma
ingrata, infelice, o Dio! mi fa! Ma tradita
e abbandonata provo ancor per lui pietà!
Quando sento il mio tormento, di vendetta il cor favella, ma se guardo il suo
cimento, palpitando il cor mi va.

That thankless spirit betrayed me, that
thankless spirit makes me miserable, o
God! But betrayed and abandoned, I
still feel pity for him! When I feel my
torment, my heart speaks of revenge,
but if I consider his peril, my heart goes
throbbing.

---

*SCENE IV. A graveyard in Seville, later that same night. The graveyard is
enclosed by a low wall. Grouped about are several monuments and statues, including one
of the Commendatore. (This is designated as an equestrian statue, but the horse is often
omitted in performance.) Don Giovanni, still attired in Leporello's cloak, leaps over
the wall, laughing. He does not notice Leporello, who is crouched in the shadow of the
wall, waiting for him.*

DON GIOVANNI: Ah, ah, ah, ah, questa è
buona, or lasciala cercar; che bella notte!
è più chiara del giorno, sembra fatta per
gir a zonzo a caccia di ragazze. È tardi?
Oh, ancor non sono due della notte;
avrei voglia un po' di saper come è finito
l'affar tra Leporello e Donn'Elvira:
s'egli ha avuto giudizio!

DON GIOVANNI: Ha, ha, ha, ha, that's
good, now let her search; what a lovely
night! it's lighter than day, it seems made
for strolling about on a girl-hunt. Is it
late? Oh, it's not yet two o'clock at
night: I'd like to know a little about how
the affair of Leporello and Donna Elvira
ended: whether he has been discreet!

LEPORELLO: (Alfin vuole ch'io faccia un
precipizio.)

LEPORELLO: *To himself.* To top it off, he
wants me to be ruined.

DON GIOVANNI: È desso; oh Leporello!

DON GIOVANNI: It's he; oh Leporello!

LEPORELLO: Chi mi chiama?

LEPORELLO: Who's calling me?

DON GIOVANNI: Non conosci il padron?

DON GIOVANNI: Don't you recognize
your master?

LEPORELLO: Così no conoscessi!

LEPORELLO: I wish I didn't recognize
him!

DON GIOVANNI: Come, birbo?

DON GIOVANNI: What, rogue?

Leporello, feigning great surprise, steps from the shadows.

LEPORELLO: Ah, siete voi? scusate!

LEPORELLO: Oh, is it you? pardon me!

DON GIOVANNI: Cosa è stato?

DON GIOVANNI: What's happened?

LEPORELLO: Per cagion vostra io fui quasi accoppato.

LEPORELLO: Because of you, I was practically beaten to death.

DON GIOVANNI: Ebben, non era questo un onore per te?

DON GIOVANNI: Well, wasn't that an honour for you?

LEPORELLO: Signor, vel dono.

LEPORELLO: Sir, I give it to you.

DON GIOVANNI: Via, via, vien quà! che belle cose ti deggio dir.

DON GIOVANNI: Now, now, come here! what fine things I must tell you.

LEPORELLO: Ma cosa fate qui?

LEPORELLO: But what are you doing here?

DON GIOVANNI: Vien dentro, e lo saprai: diverse istorielle che accadute mi son dacchè partisti, ti dirò un'altra volta: or la più bella ti vo' solo narrar.

DON GIOVANNI: Come inside, and you'll find out: another time I'll tell you various little tales about what happened to me since you left: now I just want to tell you the prettiest one.

LEPORELLO: Donnesca, al certo?

LEPORELLO: Concerning women, certainly?

DON GIOVANNI: C'è dubbio? una fanciulla, bella giovin galante, per la strada incontrai; le vado appresso, la prendo per la man, fuggir mi vuole; dico poche parole, ella mi piglia—sai per chi?

DON GIOVANNI: Why, of course! I met a beautiful, young, elegant girl on the street; I went up to her, I took her by the hand, she wanted to run away from me: I spoke a few words, she mistook me—for whom do you think?

LEPORELLO: Non lo sò.

LEPORELLO: I don't know.

DON GIOVANNI: Per Leporello.

DON GIOVANNI: For Leporello.

LEPORELLO: Per me?

LEPORELLO: For me?

DON GIOVANNI: Per te.

DON GIOVANNI: For you.

LEPORELLO: Va bene.

LEPORELLO: That's fine.

DON GIOVANNI: Per la mano essa allora mi prende—

DON GIOVANNI: So then she took me by the hand—

LEPORELLO: Ancora meglio.

DON GIOVANNI: M'accarezza, mi abbraccia: "Caro il mio Leporello! Leporello, mio caro!" allor m'accorsi ch'era qualche tua bella.

LEPORELLO: Oh, maledetto!

DON GIOVANNI: Dell' inganno approfitto; non sò come mi riconosce, grida: sento gente, a fuggire mi metto, e pronto, pronto per quel muretto in questo loco io monto.

LEPORELLO: E mi dite la cosa con tale indifferenza?

DON GIOVANNI: Perchè no?

LEPORELLO: Ma se fosse costei stata mia moglie?

Don Giovanni bursts out laughing.

DON GIOVANNI: Meglio ancora!

STATUE: Di rider finirai pria dell'aurora!

DON GIOVANNI: Chi ha parlato?

LEPORELLO: Ah, qualche anima sarà dell'altro mondo, che vi conosce a fondo.

Don Giovanni looks around and prepares to draw his sword.

DON GIOVANNI: Taci, sciocco! chi va là?

STATUE: Ribaldo audace! Lascia a'morti la pace!

LEPORELLO: Ve l'ho detto!

DON GIOVANNI: Sarà qualcun di fuori che si burla di noi! Ehi, del Commendatore

LEPORELLO: Better yet.

DON GIOVANNI: She caressed me, she embraced me: "My dear Leporello! Leporello, my dear!" so then it occurred to me that she was one of your pretty ladies.

LEPORELLO: Oh, damn!

DON GIOVANNI: I made the most of the deception; I don't know how she recognised me, she shouted: I heard people, I ran away, and quickly, quickly I climbed over that little wall here.

LEPORELLO: And you tell me the thing so casually?

DON GIOVANNI: Why not?

LEPORELLO: But what if she had been my wife?

DON GIOVANNI: Better yet!

STATUE: You will cease laughing before dawn!

DON GIOVANNI: *Surprised.* Who spoke?

LEPORELLO: Ah, it must be some spirit in the other world who knows you through and through.

DON GIOVANNI: Be quiet, stupid! who goes there?

STATUE: Brazen jester! Leave the dead in peace!

LEPORELLO: I told you so!

DON GIOVANNI: It must be someone outside who's making fun of us! Hey,

non è questa la statua? leggi un poco quella iscrizion.

isn't this the Commendatore's statue? read off that inscription.

LEPORELLO: Scusate, non ho imparato a leggere a' raggi della luna.

LEPORELLO: *Nervously.* Pardon me, I've not learned to read by moonlight.

DON GIOVANNI: Leggi, dico!

DON GIOVANNI: *Threateningly.* Read it, I say!

Leporello reads the inscription in a shaky voice.

LEPORELLO: "Dell'empio, che mi trasse al passo estremo, qui attendo la vendetta." Udiste? io tremo!

LEPORELLO: "Here I await vengeance on the wicked man who brought me to my death." Did you hear? I'm trembling!

DON GIOVANNI: O vecchio buffonissimo! digli che questa sera l'attendo a cenar meco!

DON GIOVANNI: O great old clown! tell him that I'll expect him to dine with me this evening!

LEPORELLO: Che pazzia! ma mi par, oh Dei, mirate, che terribili occhiate egli ci dà! par vivo! par che senta, e che voglia parlar!

LEPORELLO: What madness! but I think, oh Gods, look, that he is giving us a terrible stare! he seems alive! as if he were listening and wanted to speak!

DON GIOVANNI: Orsù, va là, o qui t'ammazzo, e poi ti seppellisco!

DON GIOVANNI: *More threateningly.* Hurry up, go over there, or I'll murder you right here and then bury you!

LEPORELLO: Piano, piano, Signore, ora ubbidisco.

LEPORELLO: *Quavering.* Softly, softly, Sir, I'll obey now.

Trembling, Leporello goes to the Commendatore's statue.

O statua gentilissima del gran Commendatore—Padron! mi trema il core, non posso terminar!

O most noble statue of the great Commendatore—Master! my very heart is trembling, I can't finish!

DON GIOVANNI: Finiscila, o nel petto ti metto questo acciar!

DON GIOVANNI: Stop that, or I'll stick this sword in your breast!

LEPORELLO: (Che impiccio, che capriccio! Io sentomi gelar!)

LEPORELLO: *To himself.* What a scrape, what a whim! I feel myself turning to ice!

DON GIOVANNI: (Che gusto! che spassetto! Lo voglio far tremar!)

DON GIOVANNI: *To himself.* What fun! what a joke! I'll make him tremble!

LEPORELLO: O statua gentilissima, benchè di marmo siate—Ah, padron mio! mirate! che seguita a guardar!

LEPORELLO: *To the statue.* O most noble statue, although you're made of marble—Ah, my master! look! how he seems to go on staring!

Don Giovanni makes a threatening movement towards Leporello.

DON GIOVANNI: Mori, mori!

DON GIOVANNI: Die, die!

LEPORELLO: No, attendete! Signor, il padron mio—badate ben, non io—vorria con voi cenar!

LEPORELLO: No, wait! *To the statue.* His Lordship, my master—mark you, not I—would like to dine with you!

To Leporello's horror, the statue nods its head.

Ah! ah! che scena è questa! o ciel! chinò la testa!

Oh! oh! what a scene this is! o heavens! he nodded his head!

DON GIOVANNI: Va là, che sei un buffone!

DON GIOVANNI: Go on, what a clown you are!

LEPORELLO: Guardate ancor, padrone!

LEPORELLO: Look again, master!

DON GIOVANNI: E che deggio guardar?

DON GIOVANNI: And what should I look at?

LEPORELLO: Colla marmorea testa ei fa così, così.

LEPORELLO: With his marble head he goes like this, like this.

Don Giovanni steps forward and addresses the statue.

DON GIOVANNI: Parlate! se potete. Verrete a cena?

DON GIOVANNI: Speak! if you are able. Will you come to dinner?

STATUE: Sì!

STATUE: Yes!

LEPORELLO: Mover mi posso appena, mi manca, o Dei, la lena! Per carità, partiamo, andiamo via di quà!

LEPORELLO: I can hardly stir, o Gods, my breath fails me! For pity's sake, let's leave, let's get away from here!

DON GIOVANNI: Bizarra è inver la scena, verrà il buon vecchio a cena. A prepararla andiamo, partiamo via di quà!

DON GIOVANNI: This scene is truly weird, the good old man will come to dinner. Let us go to prepare it, let's get away from here!

They leave—Don Giovanni swaggering, and Leporello cowering.

SCENE V. *The following day, in a sitting room of Donna Anna. She and Don Ottavio are present.*

DON OTTAVIO: Calmatevi, idol mio! di quel ribaldo vedrem puniti in breve i gravi eccessi, vendicati sàrem.

DON OTTAVIO: Calm yourself, my idol. In a short time we shall see that profligate's terrible crimes punished, we shall be avenged.

DONNA ANNA: Ma il padre, o Dio!

DONNA ANNA: But my father, o God!

DON OTTAVIO: Convien chinare il ciglio al volere del ciel. Respira, o cara! di tua perdita amara fia domani, se vuoi, dolce compenso questo cor, questa mano, che il mio tenero amor ...

DON OTTAVIO: One must bow one's head before the wish of heaven. Take heart, o dear! if you will it, your bitter loss can be sweetly recompensed tomorrow with this heart, this hand, which my tender love ...

DONNA ANNA: O Dei! che dite in sì tristi momenti.

DONNA ANNA: O Gods! how can you speak at such a sad time.

DON OTTAVIO: E che? vorresti con indugi novelli accrescer le mie pene? crudele!

DON OTTAVIO: And what? would you increase my sorrows with fresh delays? Cruel woman!

DONNA ANNA: Crudele? Ah no, mio bene! Troppo mi spiace allontanarti un ben che lungamente la nostr'alma desia. Ma il mondo, o Dio! non sedur la costanza del sensibil mio core; abbastanza per te mi parla amore!
Non mi dir, bell'idol mio, che son io crudel con te, tu ben sai quant'io t'amai, tu conosci la mia fè. Calma, calma il tuo tormento, se di duol non vuoi ch'io mora.
Forse un giorno il cielo ancora sentirà pietà di me!

DONNA ANNA: Cruel? Ah no, my dear! It makes me very unhappy to delay the reward that our soul has long desired. But the world, o God! do not tempt the constancy of my sensitive heart; love speaks sufficiently in your favour!
Do not tell me, my handsome idol, that I am cruel to you, you well know how much I did love you, you know my faithfulness. Calm, calm your torment, if you don't want me to die of sorrow. Perhaps one day heaven will yet feel pity for me!

Sadly Donna Anna sweeps out.

DON OTTAVIO: Ah, si segua il suo passo: io vo' con lei dividere i martiri; saran meco men gravi i suoi sospiri.

DON OTTAVIO: Ah, I must follow her steps: I wish to share her torments with her; with me, her sighs will be less heavy.

He follows Donna Anna.

SCENE VI. Don Giovanni's banquet-hall, on the following evening. Two doors to the rear of the stage, one on either side ; a table laden with wines and delicacies ; an alcove for musicians. Pretty girls flit about ; Don Giovanni enters and surveys the scene with pleasure.

DON GIOVANNI: Già la mensa è preparata. Voi suonate, amici cari! Giacchè spendo i miei danari, io mi voglio divertir. Leporello, presto in tavola.

DON GIOVANNI: The table is already prepared. *To musicians.* Play, dear friends! As long as I'm spending my money, I want to amuse myself. Leporello, serve quickly.

LEPORELLO: Son prontissimo a servir.

LEPORELLO: I'm very ready to serve.

The stage orchestra plays a selection from Vicente Martín y Solar's opera Un Cosa Rara, *a very popular work of Mozart's day. (Da Ponte wrote the libretto.)*

LEPORELLO: Bravi! "Cosa Rara."

LEPORELLO: Good men! "Cosa Rara."

DON GIOVANNI: Che ti par del bel concerto?

DON GIOVANNI: What do you think of the pretty concert?

LEPORELLO: È conforme al vostro merto.

LEPORELLO: It's fitting to your worth!

DON GIOVANNI: Ah che piatto saporito!

DON GIOVANNI: Ah, what a savoury dish!

LEPORELLO: Ah che barbaro appetito! che bocconi da gigante! mi par proprio di svenir.

LEPORELLO: *To himself.* Ah, what a monstrous appetite! what giant mouthfuls! I'll die if I don't get some.

DON GIOVANNI: Nel veder i miei bocconi, gli par proprio di svenir. Piatto!

DON GIOVANNI: *Chuckling to himself.* He's watching my mouthfuls, he'll die if he doesn't get some. Next course!

LEPORELLO: Servo!

LEPORELLO: Coming!

The stage orchestra plays a selection from Giuseppe Sarti's Fra i Due Litiganti il Terzo Gode, *another very popular opera of Mozart's time.*

LEPORELLO: Evvivano i litiganti!

LEPORELLO: Hurray for the *Litiganti!*

DON GIOVANNI: Versa il vino! Eccellente marsimino!

DON GIOVANNI: Now for the wine! Excellent marsimino!

LEPORELLO: Questo pezzo di fagiano, piano, piano vo' inghiottir.

LEPORELLO: *To himself.* I'll swallow this piece of pheasant quietly, quietly, quietly.

DON GIOVANNI: Sta mangiando quel marrano! fingerò di non capir.

DON GIOVANNI: *Mischievously to himself.* That boor is eating! I'll pretend not to catch on.

The stage orchestra plays the "Non più andrai" from Mozart's own Le nozze di Figaro, *another current favourite.*

LEPORELLO: Questa poi la conosco pur troppo.

LEPORELLO: This I also know too well.

Don Giovanni carefully averts his glance from Leporello.

DON GIOVANNI: Leporello!

DON GIOVANNI: Leporello!

LEPORELLO: Padron mio!

LEPORELLO: Master!

DON GIOVANNI: Parla schietto, mascalzone.

DON GIOVANNI: Speak up, scoundrel.

Leporello hastily gulps down the food.

LEPORELLO: Non mi lascia una flussione le parole proferir.

LEPORELLO: My catarrh doesn't permit me to enunciate the words.

DON GIOVANNI: Mentre io mangio, fischia un poco.

DON GIOVANNI: Whistle a bit while I eat.

LEPORELLO: Non sò far.

LEPORELLO: I can't do it.

Don Giovanni stares at him with great mock surprise.

DON GIOVANNI: Cos'è?

DON GIOVANNI: What's the matter?

LEPORELLO: Scusate! sì eccellente è'l vostro cuoco, che lo volli anch'io provar, che lo volli anch'io provar—

LEPORELLO: Pardon! your cook is so excellent, that I wanted to try some too, I wanted to try some too—

DON GIOVANNI: Sì eccellente è il cuoco mio, che lo volle anch'ei provar.

DON GIOVANNI: My cook is so excellent that he wanted to try some too.

The stage orchestra finishes playing. The girls depart, and Donna Elvira rushes in.

DONNA ELVIRA: L'ultima prova dell'amor mio ancor vogl'io fare con te. Più non rammento gl'inganni tuoi, pietade io sento!

DONNA ELVIRA: I want to prove my love for you one last time. I no longer remember your deceits, I feel pity!

Don Giovanni waves away the musicians.

DON GIOVANNI AND LEPORELLO: Cos'è? Cos'è?

DON GIOVANNI AND LEPORELLO: What's the matter? What's the matter?

Donna Elvira kneels pleadingly.

DONNA ELVIRA: Da te non chiede quest'alma oppressa della sua fede qualche mercè.

DONNA ELVIRA: This oppressed soul asks no thanks for its faithfulness to you.

DON GIOVANNI: Mi maraviglio! cosa volete? Se non sorgete, non resto in piè.

DON GIOVANNI: How wonderful! what do you want? If you don't get up, I won't stay on my feet.

He too kneels.

DONNA ELVIRA: Ah non deridere gli affanni miei!

DONNA ELVIRA: Ah, don't mock my sorrows!

LEPORELLO: Quasi di piangere mi fa costei!

LEPORELLO: She's almost making me cry!

Don Giovanni gets to his feet and pulls Donna Elvira up too.

DON GIOVANNI: Io te deridere! Cielo! perchè? Che vuoi, mio bene?

DON GIOVANNI: I, mock you! Heavens! why? What do you want, my dear?

DONNA ELVIRA: Che vita cangi!

DONNA ELVIRA: That you change your life!

DON GIOVANNI: Brava!

DON GIOVANNI: Good girl!

DONNA ELVIRA: Cor perfido!

DONNA ELVIRA: Faithless scoundrel!

Don Giovanni laughs and sits down at the table again.

DON GIOVANNI: Lascia ch'io mangi, e se ti piace, mangia con me!

DON GIOVANNI: Let me eat, and if you like, eat with me!

DONNA ELVIRA: Restati, barbaro! nel lezzo immondo esempio orribile d'iniquità!

DONNA ELVIRA: Remain, cruel man! a dreadful example of evil in your filthy stench!

LEPORELLO: Se non si muove del suo dolore, di sasso ha il core, o cor non ha!

LEPORELLO: If her sorrow doesn't move him, he has a heart of stone, or he hasn't got a heart!

Don Giovanni lifts his glass in a toast.

DON GIOVANNI: Vivan le femmine, viva il buon vino! sostegno e gloria d'umanità!

DON GIOVANNI: Long live women, long live good wine! sustenance and glory of humankind!

Donna Elvira rushes out one of the doors, starts back with a terrified scream, turns, and rushes out the other door.

DONNA ELVIRA: Ah!

DONNA ELVIRA: *Screaming.* Ah!

DON GIOVANNI: Che grido è questo mai? Va a veder che cosa è stato.

DON GIOVANNI: Whatever is that scream? Go to see what's happened.

Leporello goes to the first door, looks out, screams, and returns.

LEPORELLO: Ah!

LEPORELLO: *Screaming.* Ah!

DON GIOVANNI: Che grido indiavolato! Leporello, che cos'è?

DON GIOVANNI: What a devilish scream! Leporello, what is it?

LEPORELLO: Ah! Signor! per carità! non andate fuor di quà! l'uom di sasso, l'uomo bianco, ah! padrone! io gelo, io manco. Se vedeste che figura, se sentiste come fa ta, ta, ta, ta!

LEPORELLO: *Eyes bulging.* Ah! Sir! for pity's sake! don't go out of here! the man of stone, the white man, ah! master! I'm freezing, I'm faltering. If you had seen that form, if you had heard how it goes, ta, ta, ta, ta!

DON GIOVANNI: Non capisco niente affatto.

DON GIOVANNI: I don't understand anything at all.

LEPORELLO: Ta, ta, ta, ta!

LEPORELLO: *Imitating the statue.* Ta, ta, ta, ta!

DON GIOVANNI: Tu sei matto in verità!

DON GIOVANNI: In truth you're crazy!

A hollow knock sounds on the door.

LEPORELLO: Ah! sentite!

LEPORELLO: Ah! do you hear!

DON GIOVANNI: Qualcun batte! Apri!

DON GIOVANNI: *Impatiently.* Someone is knocking! Open!

LEPORELLO: Io tremo!

LEPORELLO: I'm trembling!

DON GIOVANNI: Apri, dico!

DON GIOVANNI: Open, I say!

LEPORELLO: Ah!

LEPORELLO: *Pleading, terrified.* Ah!

DON GIOVANNI: Apri!

DON GIOVANNI: Open!

LEPORELLO: Ah!

LEPORELLO: Ah!

DON GIOVANNI: Matto! Per togliermi d'intrico ad aprir io stesso andrò.

DON GIOVANNI: Madman! In order to clear up this mess, I'll go myself to open.

*Don Giovanni takes one of the candelabra from the table and goes to the door.
Leporello crawls underneath the table and cowers there.*

LEPORELLO: Non vo' più veder l'amico, pian, pianin m'asconderò!

LEPORELLO: I don't want to see my friend again, quietly, very quietly I'll hide myself!

With a rumbling of tympani, the marble statue of the Commendatore enters the room.

STATUE: Don Giovanni! a cenar teco m'invitasti! e son venuto!

STATUE: Don Giovanni! you invited me to dine with you! and I have arrived!

Don Giovanni is somewhat startled but conceals his surprise under an air of bravado.

DON GIOVANNI: Non l'avrei giammai creduto; ma farò quel che potrò. Leporello! un'altra cena! fa che subito si porti!

DON GIOVANNI: I should never have believed it; but I'll do what I can. Leporello! another dinner! have it brought immediately!

Leporello peers dazedly out from under the table.

LEPORELLO: Ah, padron, siam tutti morti!

LEPORELLO: Ah, master, we're all dead!

DON GIOVANNI: Vanne, dico!

DON GIOVANNI: Go to it, I say!

Leporello begins to crawl out.

STATUE: Ferma un po'! non si pasce di cibo mortale, chi si pasce di cibo celeste! Altre cure più gravi di queste, altra brama quaggiù mi guidò.

STATUE: Wait a bit! one who partakes of celestial food does not partake of mortal food. Other matters more serious than these, another desire brought me down here.

Leporello crawls back under the table.

LEPORELLO: La terzana d'avere mi sembra, e le membra fermar più non sò!

LEPORELLO: I seem to have the ague, and I can't stop shaking!

DON GIOVANNI: Parla dunque! che chiedi? che vuoi?

DON GIOVANNI: *To Statue.* Speak, then! what do you ask? what do you want?

STATUE: Parlo: ascolta! più tempo non ho.

STATUE: I speak: listen! I have not much time.

DON GIOVANNI: Parla, parla, ascoltando ti sto.

DON GIOVANNI: Speak, speak, I am listening to you.

STATUE: Tu m'invitasti a cena, il tuo dover or sai, rispondimi, rispondimi, verrai tu a cenar meco?

STATUE: You invited me to dinner, you know your obligation now, answer me, answer me, will you come to dine with me?

Leporello quavers from beneath the table.

LEPORELLO: Oibò, oibò; tempo non ha, scusate.

LEPORELLO: Oh, oh; he hasn't got time, sorry.

DON GIOVANNI: A torto di viltate tacciato mai sarò.

DON GIOVANNI: *Icily.* I shall never be accused of cowardice.

STATUE: Risolvi!

STATUE: Decide!

DON GIOVANNI: Ho già risolto!

DON GIOVANNI: I have already decided!

STATUE: Verrai?

STATUE: You will come?

LEPORELLO: Dite di no!

LEPORELLO: Say no!

DON GIOVANNI: Ho fermo il core in petto, non ho timor, verrò!

DON GIOVANNI: My heart is steady in my breast, I am not afraid, I shall come!

The Statue extends a hand toward Don Giovanni.

STATUE: Dammi la mano in pegno!

STATUE: Give me your hand as pledge!

Still defiant, Don Giovanni gives the Statue his hand.

DON GIOVANNI: Eccola! Ohimè!

DON GIOVANNI: Here it is! Ah!

STATUE: Cos'hai?

STATUE: What is the matter?

DON GIOVANNI: Che gelo è questo mai?

DON GIOVANNI: How freezing cold it is!

STATUE: Pentiti, cangia vita, è l'ultimo momento!

STATUE: Repent, change your life, it is your last moment!

Don Giovanni tries to withdraw his hand.

DON GIOVANNI: No, no, ch'io non mi pento, vanne lontan da me!

DON GIOVANNI: No, no, I do not repent, get you far away from me!

STATUE: Pentiti, scellerato!

STATUE: Repent, villain!

DON GIOVANNI: No, vecchio infatuato!

DON GIOVANNI: No, stupid old man!

STATUE: Pentiti!

STATUE: Repent!

DON GIOVANNI: No!

DON GIOVANNI: No!

With a desperate effort, he wrests his hand away from the Statue.

STATUE: Sì! Sì!

DON GIOVANNI: No! No!

STATUE: Yes! Yes!

DON GIOVANNI: No! No!

The Commendatore's Statue begins to move toward the door whence it entered. Roaring flames begin to surround Don Giovanni.

STATUE: Ah! tempo più non v'è!

STATUE: Ah! there is no more time!

DON GIOVANNI: Da qual tremore insolito sento assalir gli spiriti! dond'escono quei vortici di foco pien d'orror?

DON GIOVANNI: I feel my strength gripped by such unwonted trembling! whence come those horror-filled whirlpools of fire?

A chorus of ghostly demon voices sounds from below.

DEMON VOICES: Tutto a tue colpe è poco! vieni! c'è un mal peggior!

DEMON VOICES: All is as nothing compared to your crimes! come! worse is in store for you!

DON GIOVANNI: Chi l'anima mi lacera? Chi m'agita le viscere? Che strazio, ohimè, che smania! Che inferno, che terror!

DON GIOVANNI: Who tears my spirit? who shakes my innards? what twisting, alas, what frenzy! what hell, what terror!

LEPORELLO: Che ceffo disperato! Che gesti da dannato! che gridi! che lamenti! come mi fa terror!

LEPORELLO: What a despairing grimace! What gestures of a damned soul! what shouts! what wails! how terrified it makes me!

DEMON VOICES: Tutto a tue colpe è poco! Vieni! c'è un mal peggior!

DEMON VOICES: All is as nothing compared to your crimes! Come! worse is in store for you!

DON GIOVANNI: Ah!

DON GIOVANNI: *Screaming.* Ah!

Don Giovanni utters his final cry, is enveloped by flames and sinks to hell. Leporello echoes the Don's shout.

LEPORELLO: Ah!

LEPORELLO: *Screaming.* Ah!

EPILOGUE. The same setting as before, a few minutes later. Leporello is still crouched under the table. Donna Anna, Don Ottavio, Donna Elvira, Zerlina and Masetto enter, accompanied by minions of the law.

DONNA ELVIRA, ZERLINA, DON OTTAVIO AND MASETTO: Ah! dov'è il perfido? dov'è l'indegno? tutto il mio sdegno sfogar io vo'.

DONNA ELVIRA, ZERLINA, DON OTTAVIO AND MASETTO: Ah! where is the liar? where is the worthless man? I want to pour forth all my indignation.

DONNA ANNA: Solo mirandolo, stretto in catene, alle mie pene calma darò.

DONNA ANNA: Only seeing him bound in chains will ease my pain.

Leporello emerges from hiding, somewhat shaken.

LEPORELLO: Più non sperate di ritrovarlo, più non cercate—lontano andò.

LEPORELLO: Don't ever hope to see him again, don't look for him any more—he went far away.

DONNA ANNA, DONNA ELVIRA, ZERLINA, DON OTTAVIO AND MASETTO: Cos'è? favella! Via presto, sbrigati!

DONNA ANNA, DONNA ELVIRA, ZERLINA, DON OTTAVIO AND MASETTO: What is it? speak! Be quick, hurry up!

LEPORELLO: Venne un colosso—Ma se non posso—

LEPORELLO: Along came a colossus—but if I can't—

DONNA ANNA, DONNA ELVIRA, ZERLINA, DON OTTAVIO AND MASETTO: Presto favella, sbrigati!

DONNA ANNA, DONNA ELVIRA, ZERLINA, DON OTTAVIO AND MASETTO: Speak quickly, hurry up!

LEPORELLO: Tra fumo e fuoco—badate un poco—l'uomo di sasso—fermate il passo—giusto là sotto—diede il gran botto—giusto là il diavolo sel trangugiò.

LEPORELLO: Mid smoke and fire—wait a bit—the stone man—block the passage—right down there—gave the final blow—right over there the devil swallowed him up.

DONNA ANNA, DONNA ELVIRA, ZERLINA, DON OTTAVIO AND MASETTO: Stelle, che sento!

DONNA ANNA, DONNA ELVIRA, ZERLINA, DON OTTAVIO AND MASETTO: Ye gods! what do I hear!

LEPORELLO: Vero è l'evento.

LEPORELLO: It really happened.

DONNA ANNA, DONNA ELVIRA, ZERLINA, DON OTTAVIO AND MASETTO: Ah, certo è l'ombra, che m'incontrò.

DONNA ANNA, DONNA ELVIRA, ZERLINA, DON OTTAVIO AND MASETTO: Ah, it surely was the shade that met me.

Don Ottavio turns to Donna Anna.

DON OTTAVIO: Or che tutti, o mio tesoro! vendicati siam dal cielo, porgi a me un ristoro, non mi far languire ancor.

DONNA ANNA: Lascia, o caro! un anno ancora, allo sfogo del mio cor.

DONNA ANNA AND DON OTTAVIO: Al desio di chi { m'adora / t'adora ceder deve un fido amor.

DONNA ELVIRA: Io men vado in un ritiro a finir la vita mia!

ZERLINA: Noi, Masetto, a casa andiamo! a cenar in compagnia.

MASETTO: Noi, Zerlina, a casa andiamo! a cenar in compagnia.

LEPORELLO: Ed io vado all'osteria a trovar padron miglior.

ZERLINA, MASETTO AND LEPORELLO: Resti dunque quel birbon con Proserpina e Pluton. E noi tutti, o buona gente, ripetiam allegramente l'antichissima canzon:

ALL: Questo è il fin di chi fa mal. E de'perfidi la morte all vita è sempre ugual.

DON OTTAVIO: Now that we all have been avenged by heaven, o my treasure! offer to me some relief, do not make me suffer any longer.

DONNA ANNA: Let there be, o my dear! one year still for the relief of my heart.

DONNA ANNA AND DON OTTAVIO: To the wish of her who adores { me a faithful / you love must yield.

DONNA ELVIRA: *To the others.* I shall go away to end my days in a cloister!

ZERLINA: We, Masetto, are going home! to dine together.

MASETTO: We, Zerlina, are going home! to dine together.

LEPORELLO: And I'm going to the inn to find a better master.

ZERLINA, MASETTO AND LEPORELLO: May that rogue remain then with Proserpine and Pluto. And let us all, o good people, happily repeat the very ancient song:

ALL: This is the end of the evil-doer. And the death of wicked men is always just like their life.

Index

John Higgins

John Higgins was born in 1934 in Hong Kong. He was educated at King's College School, Wimbledon, and Worcester College, Oxford, as well as in the theatre galleries of Covent Garden and Sadler's Wells. Shortly after graduation he joined *The Financial Times* (London), where he became Features Editor and later Arts and Literary Editor.

In January 1970 he went to *The Times* (London) as Assistant Editor with responsibility for the coverage of the arts. On both newspapers he has travelled extensively, visiting theatres, and particularly opera houses, all over the world. Two European countries have honoured him for services to the arts: France made him a *Chevalier de l'Ordre des Arts et des Lettres* and Austria gave him the *Ehrenkreuz für Wissenschaft und Kunst* (First Class). He was the winner of the Salzburg Festival annual prize for criticism in 1977.

John Higgins is married to Linda Christmas, a fellow journalist.